AF531563

SANT NAMDEVA

GREAT SAINTS OF INDIA SERIES

SANT NAMDEVA

(The Facts of His Religious Ideology)

By

O.P. Ralhan

ANMOL PUBLICATIONS PVT. LTD.

NEW DELHI - 110 002 (INDIA)

ANMOL PUBLICATIONS PVT. LTD.
4374/4B, Ansari Road, Daryaganj
New Delhi - 110 002
Ph.: 23261597, 23278000
Visit us at: www.anmolpublications.com

Sant Namdeva

First Published, 2004

ISBN 81-261-1829-6

PRINTED IN INDIA

Published by J.L. Kumar for Anmol Publications Pvt. Ltd., New Delhi - 110 002 and Printed at Mehra Offset Press, Delhi.

Contents

Preface

The earliest biography, the Parcai of Anantadas, was written in 1588 A.D., more than 200 years after the death of Namadeva. He has briefly refers to a few miracles:

> The first devotee who lived in this Kali age was Namadeva he had God in his hands;
> he gave God milk, made the temple turn around
> and settled a quarrel with the Sultan.
>
> He surrendered mind and body to the ultimate Brahma
> reanimated a cow and scared an elephant.
> He retrieved a bed dry from a river;
> the king and all the people were witness.
>
> With his own hands Hari repaired the roof of his hut,
> He took the form of a dog to eat the bread offered by Namadev
> Namadeva also reanimated a bullock,
> So that the bullock cart could move again.
>
> Hari did everything for the sake of his devotee Namadeva,
> whose miraculous deeds cannot be counted.
> Bringing an image of stone to life,
> he even made Hari speak.

Similarly Mahipati (1715 A.D. - 1790 A.D.) who was born in 1715 A.D. at Taharabad, in the Rahruri sub-division about 35 miles from Ahmadnagar in the Bombay Presidency. He wrote the lives of saints in the Marathi language. His authorities were principally Nabhaji and Uddava Chidghan. He has himself given the Shaka year 1696 (A.D. 1774) as the date of the completion of his *Bhakta Lilamitra*. He died in A.D.

1790 (1715 A.D. - 1790 A.D.). He has referred the following miracles by Sant Shiromani Namadevaji Maharaj and details about his life :-

Namadeva - The incarnation of Uddhav; The image of god eats Namadeva's offering of Food; Conversation with god; God disguised as Keshavshet; Delhi king kills a cow which Namadeva restores to life; water comes in answer to Namadeva's prayer; Namadeva's kirtan at Nagnath; Brahmans angry with Namadeva; Namadeva's prayer; The temple facing east turns west; Penitent Brahmans; Krishna and Namadeva converse; Secret of the touchstone disclosed; Namadeva throws a touchstone into the river; Namadeva turns pebbles into touchstones; God tests Nama's belief that God is in all creatures; God invite Namadeva to eat; Namadeva's belief tested regarding the 11th of the month; Namadeva's resolve; People revile Namadeva; Krishna repairs Namadeva's hut; Krishna and Namadeva dine together; Krishna and Gyaneshwar go to Namadeva's house; Avtars of Namadeva and Janabai; Krishna leads in Namadeva's chorus etc.

Namdeva's life was the cream of Bhakti: His extraordinary love was for a time hidden in his heart, but his story has made it known worldwide. This story of Namdeva's is the height of hearing the highest contemplation for the mind, and the loved object of meditation. It is the summing up of thoughts, the centre of one's intelligence, the revelation of one's essence to the world. It is the marvellous doing of Bhakti, the soul of reverence, the glorification of honour manifested in the world. It is the life of all religious duties, it is the purifier of the pure or the store house of joy. It is the nectar of yoga accomplishment, the joy of bhaktas and the full life of desirelessness. It is the festival of God and his bhaktas. It is nectar brought to its perfection. He who will drink of it with foundness will without effort go to everlasting life. Those who listen to this story of the Tirthavali (Nama's wanderings to sacred bathing places will not have to be born again.

Sant Namadeva (1270 A.D. - 1350 A.D.) was one of the most outstanding saints from Maharashtra.

Sant Namadeva devoted his life for the emancipation of the downtrodden and stood for high ideals of universal brotherhood in the true tradition of Hindu thoughts.

In the constantly changing world of today, there is a great need for recalling the message and preachings of saints like Namadeva and practising some of their teachings in our daily lives. I am sure that this my effort will definitely hasten our march towards peace, progress, secularism, national integration and finally, universal brotherhood. I have no doubt that this biography of Namadevaji will help brought back the same period of brotherhood and exemplary Hindu-Muslim unity once again as it was during the glorious period of Baba Farid (1173 A.D. - 1265 A.D.) Hazrat Nizamudin Auliya (1238 A.D. - 1325 A.D.), Amir Khusru (1253 A.D. - 1325 A.D.), Acharya Ramanand (1299 A.D. - 1410 A.D.), Guru Nanak (1469 A.D. - 1539 A.D.) and Kabir Sahib (1398 A.D. - 1518 A.D.).

Sant Namadeva's authenticated period is 1270 A.D. - 1350 A.D. - Kabir Sahib 1398 A.D. - 1518 A.D. and Guru Nanak Dev's period was 1469 A.D. - 1539 A.D. Even the majority of the biographers of Sant Namadev have mentioned the meeting of Namadev with Kabir Sahib and Guru Nanak Dev. How they have reached to this conclusion rather difficult for me to comment because they are also author of great repute. As far as my study and research is concerned I think the idea of such meetings are hypothetical. I am of the firm opinion that meetings of Namadeva with Kabir Sahib and Guru Nanak never took place.

I have devoted near about 10 years to complete these biographies of Goswami Tulsidas Ji, Kabir Sahib, Surdas, Baba Sri Chand Ji Maharaj and Namadevaji.

Though in my personal life being a firm believer in the God Almighty and true 'Karamyogi", I have suffered a lot. My belief in hard working and devotion to duty have confirmed many folds after working on the biographies of these spiritual saints who were the incarnation of God . I am quite sure and of the firm opinion that whosoever will go through these biographies will definitely get rid of all the disappointments and miseries. I am also sure, that in this materialistic age when everything is going to dogs this biography of Namadevaji Maharaj will prove a great solace to the suffering mankind.

I do not agree with those authors who have rated Namadevaji Maharaj as low caste person. Profession of any one should not be treated and rated as caste. Those who have classified him as of a low origin, done a grave injustice to this great soul.

This book would not have seen the light of the day if the management of Namadeva Mission Trust, New Delhi, specifically Shri Chaman Lal Harsh, working President and Shri Somnath Vedi (President), Shri Sham Lal Mann, Vice-Chairman, Shri Inderjeet Sagar (Chairman) and Shri M.G. Harsh (General Secretary) have not co-operated with me whole heartedly. I am really thankful and obliged of all these honourable office bearers of Namadeva Mission Trust for their kind cooperation, help and guidance.

New Delhi

O.P. Ralhan

Brief History of Slave Dynasty and Personality of Balban

(A.D. 1266 - A.D.1286)

Saint Namadev Ji Maharaj was born in the year 1270 A.D. when one of the slave dynasty Sultan Balban was occupying the throne of Delhi. He ascended the throne in the year 1266 A.D. He reigned near about 20 years. He died in the year 1286 A.D.

Shams-ud-Din Iltutmish who ascended the throne in 1210 A.D. is the greatest of the slave Kings. He was the slave of a slave who rose to eminence by sheer dint of merit and it was solely by virtue of his fitness that he superseded the hereditary claimants to the throne.

Shams-ud-din Iltutmish was purchased by a certain merchant Jamal-ud-din, who brought him to Ghazni. From there he was taken to Delhi and was sold to Qutb-ud-din along with another slave named Bak. Sultan Mohammad Ghori is reported to have said to Qutb-ud-din: 'Treat Iltutmish well, for he will distinguish himself'. Shams-ud-din was first made Sarjanda to Qutb-ud-din and then promoted to the office of Amir-i-Shiljar and latter, when Gwalior was taken, he was appointed Amir of that place. Later he was entrusted with the change of Badaon.

Having overpowered all the Amirs and noblemen who opposed his succession to the throne, he brought the whole of the kingdom of Delhi together with its dependencies of

Badaon, Oudh, Banaras and the country of the Siwalik under his control. But his safety depended upon the suppression of his rivals and he at once turned his attention towards them. In the year 1221 A.D. Chingiz Khan invaded India. In the year 1235 Iltutmish expired.

Iltutmish is undoubtedly the real founder of the slave dynasty. It was he who consolidated the conquests that had been made by his master Qutb-ud-din. While he was young in years, he was cast off like Joseph by his envious brothers, but fortune smiled upon him, and he rose from poverty to Power. The Sultan was a great builder and the Qutb Minar which was originally 242 feet high, and which is unrivalled for its massive grandeur and beauty of design still stands as a worthy memorial of his greatness. As long as Iltutmish lived, he behaved like a great monarch, and his indefatigable labours came to an end only when ill health made him unfit for active work.

Iltutmish who was well aware of the incapacity of his sons had nominated his daughter Raziya as his heir. But the nobles who had a prejudice against the succession of a female, placed upon the throne Prince Rukn-ud-din, the eldest son of Iltutmish, a notorious debauchee, addicted to the most degrading sensual enjoyments. He was a handsome, open hearted, generous, pleasure loving fool, who took delight in the company of buffoons and fiddlers and squandered the riches of the state in ministering to his grosser appetites. So extravagant was he that, often, seated on an elephant he would drive through the bazar of Delhi in a state of intoxication and scatater tankas of red gold among the populace. While the young Prince was immersed in pleasures, the affairs of the state were managed by his mother, Shah Turkan, an ambitious lady who had an inordinate love of Power. But when mother and son brought about the cruel murder of Qutb-ud-din, another Prince of the blood royal, the Amirs assumed an attitude of hostality towards them. Shah Turkan was taken prisoner by the infuriated mob. Her fall prepared the way for Raziya. The Turkish Amirs and nobles rallied round her and saluted her as their sovereign. Rukn-ud-din was also seized and thrown into prison, where he died on November 9, 1236 A.D. after a brief reign of a little less than seven months.

After the death of Rukn-ud-din, Sultan Raziya accessioned to the throne. The first to raise the standard of revolt was Malik Ikhtiyar-ud-din Altunia in 1239 A.D. Raziya was put to death on October 15, 1240. Her brother Bahram Shah succeeded her. On 10 May 1242, Delhi capitulated; Bahram Shah was cast in prison where after a few days he was put to death. After the assasination of Bahram Shah the crown was offered to Ala-ud-din Masud Shah, a grandson of Iltutmish. Nizam-ud-din was put to death by the nobles and the office of minister was offered to Nizam-ud-din Abu Bakr and that of Amir-i-Hajib of the capital to ulug Khan-i-Muazzon,who was given the fief of Hansi. During the first two years of his rule, the Sultan obtained victorious in several parts of his kingdom, and carried on holy wars against the Hindus and hereties as enjoined by his creed. In December 1242, Tughril the governor of Bengal, advanced on the frontiers of Kara but he was persuaded by the historian Minhaj-us. Siraj to return to his country. In 1245 the Mongols again appeared in India and advanced upon Uchha but they were repelled with heavy losses. During the latter part of his reign, the Sultan began to behave like a tyrant, wantonly put to death several of his Maliks. Camp life and military society vitiated his morals; he become fond of pleasure, drinking and the chase, and paid no attention to the business of government. Disaffection grew apace; and the Amirs and Maliks invited Nasir-ud-din, another son of Iltutmish, to take charage of the kingdom. Masud was thrown into prison on June 10, 1246, where he was received into the Almight's mercy a few days afterwards.

The 'Corps of Forty' played an important part in the politics of Delhi. They made and unamde kings and as Sir

Welsley Haig rightly observes the throne itself would have been the prize of one of the Forty had not the jealousies of all prevented them from yielding precedence to one. They were obliged by their own differences to choose one of the sons of Iltutmish. The real authority, however belonged to them The Corps was finally destroyed by Balban when he became King (Cambridge History of India, Vol. III, p. 62).

Balban and His Successor

The throne of Delhi now fell to the lot of Nasir-ud-din Masad Shah, a younger son of Iltutmish in 1246 A.D. He was a pious, God fearing, compassionate ruler, who patronised the learned and sympathised with the poor and the distressed. He had the retired and obscure life of a darvesh, denied to himself the pleasures of royalty. By character and temperament he was unfitted to rule the kingdom of Delhi at a time when internal factions and Hindu revolts conspired to weaken the monarchy and the Mongals hammered upon the gates of India. But fortunately Nasir-ud-din had a very able and strong willed minister in Balban who guided the domestic as well as the foreign policy of the state throughout his master's reign.

During the year 1246-1252 various chieftains of North India was defeated and reduced to submission. In the year 1255 Qutlugh Khan revolted. In the year 1257 Mongols invaded India. In 1259 there was an expedition against Mewat.

For full two decades Balban exercised royal authority and preserved the satate from many a danger. It was a time of turmoil and anxiety, and only a man like Balban could put down with an iron hand the elements of disorder and strife. The frontier posts were strongly garrisoned, a large and effiant army was constanated and the Mongols were successfully repelled. The rebellions of the refractory Hindus of the Doab were suppressed, and sedition was thoroughly stamped out. The disaffected Amirs and Maliks, whose jealousies and mutual dissensions created disorder in the state, were effectively curbed. But for Balban's vigour and energy, the Kingdom of Delhi would have hardly survived the shocks of internal revolts and external invasions.

Balban becomes the King

After Nasir-ud-din's death on February 18, 1266 A.D. the mantle of sovereignty devolved upon Ghiyas-ud-dins Balban who was eminently fit for discharging the duties of the kingly office. The incompetence of the sons of Iltutmish and the over weening pride of Shamsi slaves had diminished the prestige of the crown, and Balban's first task was to reassert the authority of the state, to re-organise the administration and to take effective steps to prevent the recurring Mongol raids Barani writes : "Fear of the governing power, which is the basis of all good government, and the source of the glory and splendour of states, had departed from the hearts of all men, and the country had fallen into a wretched condition." By means of a drastic punishments and relentless measures the new Sultan, who was an adept in the art of government; suppressed the elements of disorder and taught people obedience and sub-missiveness.

Personality of Balban

Balban's career full of strenuous active extending over a period of forty years, is unique in the annuals of mediaeval India. The latter half of the thirteenth century was a period of unprecedented stress and storm, but Balban successfully managed him to grasp the prime need of the time the exaltation of the kingly office in the public eye and the recreation of order. He accomplished the first by maintaining a splendid court where he presented himself on Public occassions decked in the magnificent trappings of royalty. He always behaved like a well bred oriental monarch, his sense of Kingly dignity was so great that he never appeared but in full dress even before his private servants. He never laughed aloud nor joked in his darbar; nor did he permit any one to indulge in laughter or amusement in his presence. He despised the company of the low and the vulgar, and nothing could ever induce him into unnecessary dalliance or familiarity either with friends or strangers. So punctilious was he in maintaining the prestige of his office that on one occasion he refused a proffered gift of some lakhs from a rich upstart who had accumulated a vast fortune, but who could not claim a lofty pedigree. Low birth was the greatest disqualification for public office, and the nobles and officers never dared to recommend any but a well-born man for employment in the state. In his youth Balban had been addicted to wine and convivial feasts, where even the dice was looked upon as an innocent pastime, but when he became King, he laid himself under a self-denying ordinance and eschewed all such pleasures. He practised the observances of the faith like an orthodox Sunni and regularly attended the Friday prayers. He always dined in the company of learned and pious men and held converse with them on the subjects of law and religion. He paid visits to the houses of saints and went on pilgrimage to holy shrines. Like some other great mediaeval monarchs, he took delight in hunting excursions and often during the winter he went out on long expeditions in search of games in his own preserve which extended over 40 miles round about Delhi. In his private life the Sultan was affectionate and tender hearted. He was passionately fond of his sons, and when his eldest son Muhammad died, he was so overwhelmed with grief that he did not long survive the tragic catastrophe. He was kind to men in distress, and a large number of refugees from the countries of Central Asia found shelter at his court. When he crossed a bridge or a marshy place, he directed his nobles and Amirs to see that women, children and the aged and infirm were first allowed to cross in safety and given every kind of assistance. He attended the funerals of great men and expressed sympathy with their relatives and dependendents. But he could be terrible terribly cruel, when resistance was offered to his will, or the peace of the realm was disturbed.

When an officer or chief rebelled against the authority of the state, he acted with great rigour in dealing with him and did not deviate as much as a needless point from the ways of a tyrant. He extended favour only to those who loyally served him and carried out him behests with implicit obedience. His whole life was spent in a restless activity to maintain order and guard his dominious against the Mongol attacks. Still, he found time to appreciate the humanities of culture, and invited learned men to his court and extended his generous patronage to them. A great warrior, ruler and statesman, who saved the infant Muslim state from extinction at a critical time. Balban will ever remain a great figure in medieval Indian history. He was the precursor of Allauddin, but for the security and stability which he imparted to the struggling power of the Muslims in India. It would have been impossible for Alauddin to withstand successfully the Mongol attacks and to achieve conquests in distant lands, which have won for him an honoured place in the Walhalla of Muslim history.

Balban's death left a void that could not be filled. There was none among his survivors, who could wield the sceptre which he had swayed for 20 years with such ability and success.

After the death of Balban in the year 1286 A.D. the affairs of the state full into confusion, and the old confidence in the justice and strength of the administration was completely shaken.

Note: During Balban's regime in the year 1270 A.D. one of the greatest saints of the world Namadevaji Maharaj was born in Maharashtra.

(Ishwari Prasad--History of Mediaeval India)

The Khalji Dynasty

(A.D. 1290 - 1320 A.D.)

Jalal-ud-din Firoz Shah (A.D. 1290-96)

The accession of Malik Firoz on the throne of Delhi in June 1290 as Jalal-ud-din Firoz Shah caused so much resentment among the people of Delhi, that for about a year he thought it prudent to remain at Kilughari. The people had become accustomed to the rule of the Ilbari Turks for about eighty years and saw in Firoz Shah an Afghan usurper who had put an end to the Turkish rule. In reality, the Khaljis were not Afghansas they were erroneously believed to be, but Turks who had been settled for a long time in the region of Afghanistan called Khalji, lying on either side of the Helmand and had adopted Afghan manners and customs. They had migrated to Hindustan in the wake of Ghaznavis and the Ghurid invasions as well as the Mongol pressure in Central Asia and Afghanistan. Jalal-ud-din Firoz made Kilughari his capital completed the unfinished palace and gardens of Kaiqubad, and instructed his courtiers and followers to build their houses around the palace. Thus Kilughari soon became a beautiful suburb of Delhi humming with life.

The Khalji revolution put an end to the supermacy of the Ilbari Turks. Firoz, of course did not exclude them from office, but he appointed his own relations to positions of trust. Malik Chhajju, nephew of Balban and the only survivor of the late royal family was allowed to retain the fief of Kara Manikpur. The office of Chief Minister (Wazir) was conferred on Khwaja Khatir, who had held it under Balban and Kaiqubad. Fakhr-ud-din, the Kotwal of Delhi continued to hold his position. The kings eldest son obtained the title of Khan Khanan, the second, Arkali Khan, and the third, Qadr Khan. His younger brother was ennobled as Yaghrush Khan and appointed army minister (ariz-i-mumalik). His nephews Ala-ud-din and Almas Beg, obtained important posts in the royal household, while his relation, the witty but bluntly frank Malik Ahmad Chap, was appointed deputy master of the Ceremonies.

Never was a ruler a greater misfit in is time than the first Khalji King of Delhi. A pious and god-fearing Muslim Firoz was an old man of seventy when he came to the throne.

In the second year of the reign (1291) Malik Chhajju, a nephew of Balban raised the standard of revolt at Kara and caused Khutba to be read in his name. Rebellion of Chhajju was suppressed. Abdication of Nasir-ud-din Bughra and accession of Rukn-ud-din Kaikans in Bengal in 1291 and Mongol invasion took place in 1292 and Ala-ud-din Khalji invades Malwa and raids Bhilsa. In the year 1294 Ala-ud-din invades the Kingdom of Deogir, in the Deccan. In the year 1296 Jalal-ud-din Firoz Khalji was murdered and accession of Ala-ud-din Muhammad Khalji, took place.

Ala-ud-din Khalji (1296-1316)

The severed head of Jalal-ud-din Firoz Shah was yet dripping with blood, when the royal canopy was raised over the head of Ala-ud-din, and he was proclaimed King. The head of the murdered Sultan was placed on a spear and paraded through Kara and Manikpur and then through Awadh.

In the year 1297 Gujarat was conquered. In 1299 the Mongols invaded India and were defeated. In 1300 siege of Ranthambhor took place. Rebellion of Akat Khan was suppressed and rebellion of Haji Maula was also suppressed. In 1301 Ranthambhor was captured by Ala-ud-din. Accession of Shams-ud-din Firoz Shah in Bengal. Suhadeva sets up a government in

Kashmir. In 1302-1303 Chittor was captured. Failure of an expedition to Warangal-Mongol invasion and Ala-ud-din lays his new capital at Siri.

In 1306 Mongol invasion repelled by Ghiyas-ud-din Tughlaq. Death of Narasimha II of Orissa and accession of Bhanudeva II. In 1307 expedition of Kafur (Malik Naib) to Deogir. Ala-ud-din establishes his authority in Rajputana. In the year 1308 expedition to Warrangal. In the year 1310 Ghiyas-ud-din Bahadur assumes sovereignty in East Bengal. In the year 1316 death of Ala-ud-din and accession of Shihab-ud-din Umar. Death of Malik Naib. Deposition of Umar and accession of Qutb-ud-din Mubarak. In 1317 Mubarak's expedition to Deogir. Capture and death of Harapaladeva. In the year 1320 Mubarak was murderd and usurpation of Nasir-ud-din Khusrav. In the same year i.e. 1320 Khusrav was killed and Ghiyas-ud-din Tughluq took over.

(The History and culture of the Indian People - The Delhi Sultanate - Ed. R.C. Majumdar - and Ishwari Prasad - History of Mediaeval India).

Measures against the Hindus (During Ala-ud-din Khalji)

(A.D. 1296-1316)

After consolidating his powers Ala-ud-din next turned his attention to check the power and influence of the Hindu officials named *Khut, Chaudhri,* and *Muqaddam.* The first term, otherwise unknown, probably signified the class later known as Zamindar while the other two denoted, respectively, the headman of parganas and villages. These three classes of people were hereditary collector of revenue on behalf of the king, and it was alleged that they appropriated to themselves as much of the state revenue as they could evaded payment of taxes, and even ignored the Government. As the chronicler describes, they ride upon the horses, wear fine clothes, shoot with Persian bows, make war upon each other, and go out hunting... and hold drinking and convivial parties. Ala-ud-din sought to curb their powers by depriving them of all the special privileges which they enjoyed at the expense of the State. The standard of the revenue demand was raised to one half of the gross produce. The perquisites realized by the Chiefs were abolished and all concessions withdrawn; they were to pay land-revenue at the full rate and their land was to be brought under assessment; and all discriminations were done away with between the Chief and the humblest peasant (Khut-and balahar). The land revenue was to be assessed by the method of measurement on the basis of standard yields. Though the system did exist in India before the Muslim conquest. Ala-ud-din was the first Muslim ruler who introduced it; and it certainly marked an advance upon the sharing system, which was then prevalent. Besides, the king imposed two new taxes; a grazing tax on all milch cattle and a house tax. As a result of these legislations the objectives of the king were realized, though it may be questioned if the measures were economically sound. The motives of Ala-ud-din were decidedly political. The high revenue demand impoverished the peasants so much that the very source of the revenue collectors for extra profit was dried up which the assessment of their land reduced them to the condition of peasants; and besides the loss of perquisites they had now to pay additional taxes. In a sense the regulations were favourable to the peasants as the revenue collectors had also to bear the burden along with them. If the contemporary chronicler is to be believed these regulations were strictly enforced. The chiefs (Khuts) and the headmen of parganas as well as villages - they were all Hindus - were so much impoverished that no gold or silver was to be found in the houses of the Hindus; they could not afford to procure horses or weapons; and their wives had to serve for wages in the houses of the Muslims. "The people", we are told by Barani, were brought to such a state of obedience that one revenue officer would string twelve Khuts, muqaddams and chaudhris together by the neck and enforce payment by blows". Great credit was due to the deputy minister of finance, Sharaf Qaini, and his officials for the efficient operation of these regulations; but they become so unpopular that no one would offer the hand of his daughter to a revenue officer".

Two points should be noticed in connection with these regulations. They operated mainly in the central portion of the kingdom, and the victims of these measures were Hindus. It has been urged by some scholars that "when Ala-ud-din had not spared the Muslims or hesitated to deprive them of peculiar privileges, there was no reason why he should have shown any favour to the Hindu officials". There are, however, good grounds to believe that in dealing with the Hindus, Ala-ud-din was also actuated by communal considerations. This clearly follows from the prefatory remarks with which Barani introduces these regulations. The following is a liberal translation of the passage by Moreland: "Sultan Ala-ud-din demanded from learned men rules and regulations, so that the Hindu should be ground down, and property and possessions which are the causes of disaffection and rebellion, should not remain in his house.

Moreland adds that the Hindu in the above passage refers to the upper classes and not the peasants, but this interpretation is at least doubtful. But whatever it may mean Barani leaves no doubt that the measures were dictated as much by political considerations as by hatred against the Hindus. Even on general ground the attitude of the Sultan to the Hindus must be regarded as very different from that adopted towards the Muslim. Some privileges were taken away from the latter, but there was no question of deliberately reducing them, as a class to a state of grinding poverty and abject humiliation, which was the lot of the Hindus as described above on the authority of Barani.

This view is fully confirmed by the statement of Qazi Mughis-ud-din of Bayana whom the king consulted as to the legality of these measures and certain other questions. Mughis-ud-din whole heartedly justified Ala-ud-din's rigorous policy towards the Hindus and pointed out that Islamic law sanctioned sterner principle, so much so that, "if the revenue collector spits into a Hindu's mouth, the Hindu must open his mouth to receive it without hesitation." The Qazi however, declared mutilation, torture and other barbarous punishments prescribed by the king as un Islamic and illegal; which he condemned 'Ala-ud-din's appropriation of the wealth of Devagiri and his huge expenditure as unlawful, as the king had no unlimited rights upon the public treasury: "all the Krors of money and valuables which you take from the treasury and bestow upon your women, you will have to answer for in the day of account." Ala-ud-din, who got excited during the discussion, spoke not a word to the Qazi and retired. As the Qazi next day proceeded to the court from home, he was prepared for death, and bade his family farewell. He received a pleasant shock, however, when he was kindly received and presented with a robe and a thousand tankas by the king who appreciated his opinion. The king said that he did not know what was lawful, but followed what he thought to be for the good of the state or suitable for the emergency. Here we have Ala-ud-din's conception of sovereignty, in which the state was to be independent of the ulama. As Barani says: "When he became king, he came to the conclusion that policy and government are one thing, and the rules and decrees of law are another. Royal commands belong to the king, legal decrees rest upon the judgment of qazis and muftis.He was gratified to learn that his treatment of the Hindus was in full accordance with Islamic law and assured the Qazi that he had given order that the Hindus shall not be allowed to possess more than what is required for a bare subsistence. (Source: The History and Culture of the Indian People - The Delhi Sultanate Ed. by R.C. Majumdar. "The Khalji Dynasty - Jalal-ud-din's Firoz Shah (A.D. 1290-96) - Measures against the Hindus. (pp. 23-25)

Treatment of Hindus

(A.D. 1290 - 1320 A.D.)

The Hindus were treated with special severity. When the Sultan consulted the Qazi about the position of the Hindu in a Muslim state, the latter replied: They are called Khiraj-gazar (payers of tribute), and when the revenue officer demands silver from them, they should, without question and with all humility and respect, tender gold. If the muhassif (the tax collector) chooses to spit into the mouth of a Hindu, the latter must open his mouth without hesitation. The meaning of doing such a thing is that the Hindu by acting in this wise shows his meakness and humility and obedience and respect. The glorification of Islam is a duty, and contempt of the religion is vain. God himself has commanded their complete degradation, inasmuch as the Hindus are the deadliest foes of the prophet. The Prophet has said that they should either embrace Islam or they should be slain or enslaved, and their property should be confiscated to the state. No one except the great doctor Abu Hanifa allows the imposition of the jeziya upon the Hindus, while other schools are of opinion that there is no other alternative but "Death or Islam." The refractory conduct of the Hindus of the Doab necessiated drastic measures against them. They had to pay 50 per cent of the total produce of their land without making any deductions, and so rigorous was the assessment that not even a biswah of land was spared. A grazing tax was imposed upon cattle and a house-tax was also levied. The same regulations were applied to the (Khuts and the balahars Khut and balahar are obviously used for landed classes. Most probably they are used here for landlords and tenants). So as to save the poor from the heavy burden of taxation. So rigorously were the new rules enforced, that the *Chaudharis, Khuts, muqaddams* were not able to ride on horse back to find weapons, to get fine clothes, or to indulge in betel. The policy of the state was that the Hindus should not have so much as to enable them to ride on horseback, wear fine clothes, carry arms and cultivate luxurious habits. They were reduced to a state of abject misery to such an extent that the wives of the *Khuts* and *muqaddams* went and served for hire in the houses of the Musalmans. Barani speaks highly of Sharaf Qai, in some texts Sharaf Qaiyini the Naib Wazir of the emporar and says that he brought all provinces of the empire under one revenue law as if they were all one village".

In collecting the revenue he made one law applicable to all landed proprietors and their obedience became such that a single *chaprasi* of the revenue department would seize some twenty landed proprietors, chiefmen and agents and minister kicks and blows to them. He investigated all cases of embizlement and inflicted the severest punishments upon the wrong doers. If the ledger of the Patwari showed a single jital standing against the name of any officer, he was punished with torture and imprisonment. When an officer took bribe, either from a Hindu or Musalman, he was severely punished. The *amils* musarrifs and other functionaries of the revenue department were reduced to beggary and were thrown into prison for 500 or 1000 *tankas.*

The post of revenue clerk came to be looked upon as dangerous and only the bolder spirits offered themselves as candidates for it (Barani writes (Tarikh-i-Firuz Shahi) that the office of revenue clerk fell into bad odour that nobody would give his daughter in marriage to him, and the post of musarrif was accepted only by those who did not pay any heed to their lives. These men were frequently cast into prisons.)

(Ishwari Prasad - History of Mediaeval India - The Indian Press Ltd. 1940, pp. 237-239).

Tughlaq Dynasty

(A.D. 1320-1350 A.D.)

Ghiyas-ud-din Tughlaq 1320-1325 A.D.

His original name was Ghazi Malik or Ghazi Beg Tughlaq. According to Ibn Batuta and Shams-i-Siraj 'Afif' he came from Khursan to India during the reign of Ala-ud-din Khalji. It was generally believed that Malik Tughlaq a Turkish slave of Sultan Balban, married a women of the Jat tribe, and their son was Ghazi Malik who later became Sultan Ghiyas-ud-din Tughlaq.

After the defeat and death of Khusrau Ghiyas-ud-din ascended the throne. He had risen to high position by dint of personal merit and during the reign of Alauddin Khalji, had played and important part in wars against the Mongols whom he had chased out of India again and again. When he assumed the reins of office, the empire of Delhi was in a state of confusion and it was with great tact, prudence, and firmness that Ghiyas-ud-din restored order and recovered the moral prestige of the monarchy. The magnanimity of his nature showed itself in the generous treatment which he meted out to the relatives of Alauddin. He made a suitable provision for them and appointed them to high offices in the state. No just claim was ignored and no past service was forgotten. The claims of rank and birth were respected and many families that had been ruined were restored to their former dignity branch of the administration. It was no mean achievement to have successfully re-organised the administration which had been thrown out of gear during the reigns of the imbicile Mubarak and the unclean Khusrau. The following verse of Amir Khusrau is illustrative of the Sultan's excellent methods of government." He never did anything that was not replete with wisdom and sense. He might be said to wear a hundred doctor's hoods under his crown".

Death of Ghiyas-ud-Din

In the year of 1324 when Ghiyas-ud-din after suppersssing various rebel heads of Estates was coming back to Delhi he was killed by the fall of a pavillion which his son Prince Juna, had created near Afghanpur at a distance of six miles from the capital. The Prince was suspected of having planned the emperors death, for the hasty construction of such a palace was entirely superfluous. Whatever the real truth may be, there are strong reasons for thinking that the Sultan's death was the result of a conspiracy in which the royal Prince took part, and not of accident.

Administration of Ghiyas-ud-din

The administration of Ghiyas-ud-din was based upon the principles of justice and moderation, though the Hindus were still held in contempt and treated as inferior being. The royal order was that in the matter of revenue "there should be left only so much to the Hindus that neither, on the one hand, they should become arrogant on account of wealth, nor, on the other should they desert their lands and business in despair." The chiefs and headmen were allowed a fair share of the collected dues as their wages and were not allowed to take any additional or extra amount from the peasants. He took great pains to make the military system orderly and efficient. The soldiers were liberally paid and treated with kindness.

Estimates of Ghiyas-ud-din

He was a mild and benevolent ruler. He loved simplicity, and towards his quondam colleagues, he behaved with the same frank joviality which had characterised him in his earlier days. A pious and peace loving Muslim, he practised rigidly the observances of his faith, but he never presecuted the non Muslims. If the Hindus were treated harshly, it was due to political reasons and not to religious bigotry. His private life was free from blemish. His watchword was moderation. As long as he lived, he tried to promote the welfare of his subjects, and his beneficient activity extended to every.

Muhammad Bin Tughluq

(A.D. 1325 - 1350 A.D.)

Ghiyas-ud-din Tughluq was succeeded by his son Prince Juna, under the title of Muhammad Bin Tughluq in the year 1325 A.D. three days after the death of his father. His name was Ulugh Khan also called Jauna).

Mohammad Tughluq was unquestionably the ablest man among the crowned heads of the middle ages of all kings who had sat upon the throne of Delhi since the Muslim conquest, he was undoubtedly the most learned and accomplished. Nature had endowned him with a marvellous memory a keen and penetrating intellect and an enormous capacity for assimilating knowledge of all kinds. The versatility of his genius took by surprise all his contemporaries. A lover of the fine arts, a cultured scholar and an accomplished poet, he was equally at home in logic, astronomy, mathematics, philosophy and the physical sciences.

The Moorish traveller, Ibn Batuta who came to India in 1333 A.D. thus describes the Sultan:- "Mohammad is a man who above all others is fond of making presents and shedding blood. There may always be seen at his gate some poor person becoming rich, or some living one condemned to death. His generous and brave actions, and his cruel and violent deeds, have obtained notoriety among the people. Inspite of this, he is the most humble men, and the one who exhibits the greatest equity. The ceremonies of his religion are dear to his heart and he is very severe in respect of prayer and the punishment which follows its neglect. He is one of those kings whose good fortune is great and whose happy success exceeds the ordinary limit; but his distinguishing character is generosity. I shall mention among the instances of his liberality, some marvels, of which the like has never been reported of any of the princes who have preceded him.

Estimates of Mohammad Bin Tughluq

Throughout his life, he battled against difficulties and never abandoned his task in despair. It is true, he failed but his failure was largely due to circumstances over which he had little or no control. A severe famine which lasted for more than a decade marred the glory of his reign and set his subjects against him. The verdict that declares him a cruel and blood thirsty tyrant like Nero or Caligula does little justice to his great genius, and ignores his conspicuous plans to cope with famine and his efforts to introduce ameliorative reforms. There is ample evidence in the pages of Barani and Ibn Batuta to show that he was not fond of shedding blood for its own sake, and that he could be kind, generous and just even towards his enemies. He possessed an intellect and a passion for practical improvement, which we rarely find in mediaveal rulers. But his task was an extremely onerous one. He had to deal with the problems of an ever growing empire with a staff of officers who never loyally co-operated with him. He had also to reckon with the orthodox Ulama who clamoured for privilege and who resented his attempt to enforce justice and equality among his subjects.

Ibn Batuta was appointed Qazi of Delhi by Mohammad Tughlaq and admitted to his court, where he had close opportunities of acquainting himself with the habits character and acts of this most extraordinary and unfortunate monarch. The traveller dwells upon the Sultans generosity his hospitality his strict observance of the practices of Islam, his love of learning and his numerous other accomplishments in terms of glowing admiration. But he also gives a catalogue of the atrocities of the

Sultan, whom he describes as the "wonder of the age". The eight cases of murder of Shaikhs and Maulvis mentioned by Ibn Batuta are those of men who had either embazzled public funds or participated in seditious conspiracy. Ibn Batuta lived in India for 8 years and left the service of the Sultan in 1342 A.D. Ibn Batuta (Abu Abdulla Muhammad) commonly known as Ibn Batuta, was born at Tangier on the 24th February 1304 A.D. He reached the Indus on the 12th September, 1333 A.D. when he was 21 years old.

As stated earlier after the death of Ghiyas-ud-din Tughluq his son Mohammad Bin Tughluq ascended the throne in the year 1325 A.D. During 1325-27 transfer of the capital from Delhi to Daultabad took place. Introduction of the Token Currency was introduced in 1330 A.D. Ibn Batuta arrived in India in 1333 A.D. 1334-35 Rebellion of Jalal-ud-din Ahsan Shah in Mabar. 1336 Foundation of the kingdom of Vijayanagar. 1337 Rebellion of Fakhr-ud-din in Bengal. 1340-41 Revolt of Ain-ul-Mulk Multani. 1344 Revolt of Krishna Nayak. 1347 Foundation of the Bahmani Kingdom. 1351 Death of Mohammad Bin Tughluq and accession of Firuz Tughluq.

Death of Mohammad Bin Tughluq (1351 A.D.)

Hearing of the rebellion of Taghi the Sultan left Devagir for Gujarat. It was a mistake on his part to resolve to put down the traitor Taghi before dealing effectively with the foreign Amirs. In these depressing circumstances the Sultan had an interview with Barni whose advice he asked on matters of state. Barani suggested abdication, but the Sultan expressed his determination to punish his rebellious subjects. He told the historian clearly that he would touch the people obedience and submission by punishment. He pursued the rebel Taghi from place to place, but the latter succeeded including his grasp. He subdued the Rai of Karnal and brought the entire coast under his sway. From there he proceeded to Gondal where he fell ill and was obliged to halt for some time. Having collected a large force he marched towards

Thatta but when he was about three or four days march from that place he got fever and died on March 20, 1351 A.D. The empire which once contained 23 provinces and extended from Delhi and Lahore to Dvarsamudra and Mabar in the South, and from Lakhnauti and Gaur in the east to Thatta and the Indus in the west, broke up into pieces and upon its ruins arose powerful and wealthy kingdoms. Gujarat continued nominally a province of the empire, but elsewhere the imperial authority had ceased to exist. Such was the end of this unlucky monarch. All his life he battled against difficulties and never abandoned his task in despair. Firoz Tughluq ascended the throne (1351-1388 A.D.).

(Source: Ishwari Prasad - History of Mediaeval India. The Indian Press Ltd. Allahabad 1940).

ECONOMIC CONDITION

During the early days of the Muslim conquest the inhabitants of India were fleeced of their wealth by the Muslim invaders and Baihaki has mentioned the vast booty which was carried off by Mahmud of Ghazni from this country. The early Muslim rulers were occupied too much with work of conquest. Balban was the first ruler who paid attention to the maintenance of internal peace and order. He cleared the neighbourhood of Kampila and Patiali of robbers and highwaymen so that cultivation flourished and merchants could take their goods from one place to another without much difficulty. Under the Khiljis the economic conditions were radically changed. A famine occurred in Firuz's reign, and Barani writes that grain in Delhi rose to a jital per sair. The appaling hardship caused by the scarcity of food and fodder was so great in the Siwalik hills taht the Hindus of the country came to Delhi with their families and twenty or thirty of them drowned themselves in the Jamna when they found life unbearable. But it does not appear that the administration exerted itself to mitigate human suffering. The next ruler the greatest of the line, was a daring political economist and a bold tariff legislator. His soaring ambition of world conquest led him to build up an economic system which is one of the marvels of mediaeval statesmanship. There was no scarcity of wealth in the country and Alauddin's state entry into Delhi soon after his accession was marked by the distribution of rich gifts among the people. Five *mans* of gold stars were placed in a manjnig and were discharged upon the spectators who had thronged in front of the royal canopy. The revenue system was organised and the policy of thorough adopted by Sharaf Qai, the Naib Wazir-i-Mamalik, reduced the whole country of the Doab to a state of complete submission. The Hindus were required to pay 50 per cent of the produce of their fields, and in addition to this they had to pay a house tax, a grazing tax and a number of other cesses. The incidence of taxation fell upon cultivators who were mostly Hindus, for the Muslim whose number was small were largely employed in the civil and military offices of the state. The *Khuts, Chowdhris* and muqaddams were reduced to a state of abject poverty and Barni expresses great satisfaction at their miserable condition. The most remarkable achievement, however of Ala-ud-din was his tariff legislation. The Prices were so low that a soldier with one horse could live comfortably with 234 tankas a year, i.e. less than twenty tankas per mensam which will hardly suffice to meet even the cost of a horse in these days. Grain was stored in royal granaries and was sold to the people at low rates in times of scarcity. Ibn Batuta relates that he witnessed with his own eyes in Delhi rice which had been stored in the cellars of Ala-ud-din. The economic system of Ala-ud-din collapsed after his death, for it rested upon a complete disregard of all laws of political economy. The reaction began after his death. The bazar people rejoiced and sold their goods at their own price. The wages of labourers rose four times; and servants and menials who formerly got only ten or twelve tankas now demanded seventy, eighty, or a hundred tankas. The tariff laws of Ala-ud-din fell into disuse and Barni laments the disappearance of cheap prices; but there was no deficiency of crops, and the state never experienced any financial stringency. Nasir-ud-din Khusrau squandered the treasures of the state in order to win adheronts from among the nobles and yet Mohammad Tughluq found enough money to enable him to embark on costly experiments. Mohammad's economic measures failed disastrously, but his financial position remained unshaken. The failure of the token currency did not affect the stability of the state or destroy its credit for the Sultan at once repealed his edict and permitted the people to exchange gold and silver coins for those of copper. For about a decade, famine stalked the land and reduced the people to a state of utter helplessness. A vigorous famine policy was adopted by the administration, and Barani writes that in two years about 70 lakhs of tankas were advanced as Sondhar or taqavi to the agriculturists. Ibn Batuta dwells at length upon the Sultan's famine policy and says that was supplied from the royal stores and the Faquias and Qazis were required to make lists of needy men in each parish, which were submitted to the Sultan for orders. On another occasion when dire distress prevailed the Qazis, clerks and Amirs went from parish to parish and gave relief to the famine stricken people at the rate of one and a half western ritals per day. Large Khanqahs assisted the state in administering relief, and Ibn Batuta writes that hundreds of men were fed at the Khanqah of Qutb-ud-din of which he was the mutwalli and which contained a staff of 460 men. The state gave liberal encouragement to industry. There was a state manufactory in which 400 silk, weavers were employed and stuff of all kinds was prepared. There were also 500 manufacturers of golden tissues in the service of Sultan who wove gold brocades for the royal household and the nobility. Trade was carried on with foreign countries and Marco Polo and Ibn Batuta both speak of ports which were visited by merchants from foreign countries. Broach and Calicut were famous centres of trade, and Ibn Batuta says of the latter that merchants from all parts of the world came there to buy goods. The another of the Masalik-al-absar also writes that merchants of all countries "never cease to carry pure gold into India and to bring back in exchange commodities of herbs and gums." Foreign traders were encouraged by the state and Ibn Batuta makes mention of one Saiyyad Abul Hasan

Abadi who carried on business with royal capital and brought goods for the king from Iraq and Khorasan.

The trade conditions were favourable in the thirteenth and fourteenth centuries. Wassaf describes Gujarat as a rich and populous country containing 7,000 villages and towns and the people rolling in wealth. The cultivation was prosperous. The vineyards yielded blue grapes twice a year. The soil was so fertile that the cotton plants spread their branches like willows and plane trees, and yielded crops for several years in succession. Marco Polo also speaks of extensive cotton cultivation and says that the cotton trees were full six paces high and attained to the age of twenty years. Pepper, ginger and indigo were produced in large quantities. The local manufacturers prepared mats of red and blue leather inlaid with figures of birds and beasts and embroidered with gold and silver wires. Cambay is also described as a great centre of trade where indigo was produced in abundance. Merchants came with ships and cargoes but what they chiefly brought into the country was gold, silver and copper. The traveller writes: "the inhabitants are good and live by their trade and manufacture. Mabar was full of wealth, but much of it as Maro Polo says: was spent in purchasing horses which were very scarce in that country. The merchants of Kis, Hormes, Dofar, Soer—these are countries mentioned by Marco Polo - brought horses to Mabar and made a considerable profit. Bengal is described by Ibn Batuta in the fourteenth century as a rich and fertile province. Prices were cheap, and men could live in ease and comfort with small incomes.

Note: Ibn Batuta arrived in India in the year A.D. 1333 in the regime of Mohammad Tughluq also accessioned the throne in the year A.D. 1325-26 after the death of his father Ghiyas-ud-din Tughlaq. Mohammad Tughlaq transferred the capital from Delhi to Daultabad. In the year 1342 A.D. Ibn Batuta left India for his China mission. In the year 1351 A.D. Mohammad Tughlaq died and his son Firoz Tughlaq accessioned the throne.

(Source: Ishwari Prasad - History of Medieval India. The Indian Press Ltd. Allahabad, 1940, pp. 524-530).

SOCIAL CONDITIONS

The state encouraged conversions and in describing the reign of Qutb-ud-din Mubarak Shah, Ibn Batuta writes that when a Hindu wished to become a Muslim he was brought before the Sultan who gave him rich robes and bangles of gold. The orthodox party had such a great aversion for the Hindus that Barni on seeing their slightly improved condition under Qutb-ud-din Mubarak Shah, which was due partly to the relaxation of the rules of Alauddin and partly to the pro-Hindu policy of Khusrau laments that the "Hindus again found pleasure and happiness and were beside themselves with joy. There was no active persecution under the first two Tughluqs, but Firoz reversed the policy of his predecessors. He capped his measures against them by levying the Jeziya upon the Brahmans who had hitherto been exempted Afif writes that in Delhi it was of three kinds - (1) forty tankas; (2) twenty tankas; (3) ten tankas. When the Brahmans remonstrated against the step, the Sultan reduced the scale of assessment.

Ibn Batuta has given us an interesting picture of India in the fourteenth century, and from his narrative we learn a great deal about the social customs and manners of the time. The learned class had lost its prestige and Mohammad Tughluq who was terribly stern in administering justice, freely punished Shaikhs and Maulvis for their misconduct. Slavery was common but the State encouraged the practice of manumission. Men burried their wealth, as they do even now, and accepted nothing but coined money in their daily transactions. Ibn Batuta has given an interesting account of the law of debt as it prevailed in the fourteenth century and he is supported by Marco Polo who visited India before him. The creditors resorted to the royal court to seek the king's protection in order to recover their money. When a big Amir was in debt, the creditor blocked his way to the royal palace and shouted in order to implore the Sultan's help. The debtor in this embarrassing situation either paid or made a promise to pay at some future date. Sometimes the Sultan interfered and enforced payments. The practice of Sati and self destruction was in vogue but no woman could become sati without obtaining the King's permission. Riding on an ass was looked upon with contempt as it is today, and a man was flogged and paraded on an ass when he was punished for some offence proved against him. Men believed in witchcraft, magic and miracles as they did in mediaeval Europe, and the performances of the Hindu ascetics called Jogis by Ibn Batuta were witnessed even by the Sultan. A man like Ibn Batuta married more than four times in a most irresponsible manner and abandoned his wives one after another. The education of women was not altogether neglected and the traveller writes that when he reached Hanaur he found there 13 schools for girls and 23 for boys - a thing which agreeably surprised him.

He married four times in the Maldive Islands. He was already married to Hur Nasab, daughter of Jalal-ud-din Ahsan Shah. She was left by Ibn Batuta for he writes in one place: "I do not know what has become of her and the daughter she bore me."

Though women were treated with great respect, the birth of a girl was looked upon as an inauspicious event as is illustrated by Amir Khusrau's lament over the birth of his daughter. Seclusion was recommended for women, and Amir Khusrau in his advice to his daughter asks her not to leave the thread of the spinning wheel and always to keep her face towards the wall of the house and her back towards the door so that nobody might be able to look at her. The poet expresses his disappointment in his poem Laila Majanu, in these words: " I wish you were not born, and if you were, it would have been better, if you had been a boy. No one can alter the decrees of fate. But my father was born of a women and I am also born of a women:" The advice which the poet gave his daughter is also contained in his poem *Laila Majanu.*

Regarding the people of Malabar in his own day, Ibn Batuta says that among Hindu Princes in this part of the country the law of inheritance does not allow one's children to succeed to their father's estate. Even male heirs of the body are superseded by sister's sons.

From Ibn Batuta's account it appears that punishments in Malabar were extremely severe even for the pettiest offences. Theft was severely punished, and human life was sometimes taken for stealing even a coconut. (Ishwari Prasasd--History of Mediaevel India)

List of The Sultans of Delhi

Slave Dynasty (1206-1290)

1. Muiz-ud-din Mohammad Bin Sam
2. Qutub-ud-din Aibek (1206-1210)
3. Aram Shah (1210)
4. Shams-ud-din Iltutmish (1210-1235)
5. Rukn-ud-din Firuz (1235-1236)
6. Jalalat-ud-din Reziva (1236-1239)
7. Bahram (1239-1246)
8. Ala-ud-din Masud (1241-1246)
9. Nasir-ud-din Mahmud (1246-1265)
10. Ghiyas-ud-din Balban (1265-1287)
11. Bughra Khan (Governor of Bengal)
12. Muiz-ud-din Kaiqubad (1287-1290)
13. Shams-ud-din Qaiumurs

Khilji Dynasty (1290-1320)

13. Jalal-ud-din Firuz II (1290-1295)
14. Rukn-ud-din Ibrahim I (1295)
15. Ala-ud-din Muhammad II (1295-1316)
16. Shihad-ud-din Umar (1315-16)
17. Qutb-ud-din Mubarak I (1316-1320)

18. Nasir-ud-din Khusran, Wazir of Mubarak I (1320)

Tughlaq Dynasty (1320-1412)

19. Ghiyas-ud-din Tughlaq I (1320-1325) - Sipah Salar Punjab, Brother of Tughlaq I
20. Muhammad bin Tughlaq (1325-1351)
21. Firuz III (1351-1388)
22. Tughlaq II (1388)
23. Abu Bakar (1388-1389)
24. Muhammad III (1389-1392)
25. Sikandar I (1392)
26. Mahmud (1392-1394) (restored 1399-1412)
27. Nusrat Shah (1394-1399)
28. Daulat Khan (1412)

Saiyyad Dynasty (1414-1451)

29. Khizr Khan Saiyyad (1414-1421)
30. Mubarak II (1421-1433)
31. Muhammad Shah IV (1433-1443)
32. Alam Shah (1443-1451)

Lodi Dynasty (1451-1526)

33. Bahlal Lodi (1451-1488)
34. Sikandar Lodi (1488-1517)
35. Ibrahim Lodi (1517-1526)

Mughal Dynasty (1526-1857)

East India Company (1757-1857)

British Rule (1757-1947)

The Political Situation

(1270 A.D. - 1350 A.D.)
(A Chronology)

1210 A.D.-1235 A.D. Shams-ud-din Iltutmish who ascended the throne in 1210 A.D. was the greatest of the slave kings. He was the slave of a slave who rose to eminence by sheer dint of merit and it was solely by virtue of his fitness that he supperseded the hereditary claimants to the throne. He expired in the year 1235 A.D.

1235 A.D. Iltutmish who was well aware of the incapacity of his sons had nominated his daughter Raziya as his heir. But the nobles who had a prejudice against the succession of female placed upon the throne Prince Rukn-ud-din, the eldest son of Iltutmish, a notorious debauchee addicted to the most degrading sensual enjoyments. He was a handsome, open hearted, generous, pleasure loving fool, who took delight in the company of buffoons and fiddlers and squandered the riches of the state in ministering to his grosser appetites. So extravagant was he that often, seated on an elephant he would drive through the bazars of Delhi in a state of intoxication and scatter tankas of red gold among the populace. While the young prince was immersed in pleasures, the affairs of the state were managed by his mother Shah Turkan, an ambitious lady, who like Cathrine de Medici of France, had an inordinate love of power. But when mother and son brought about the cruel murder of Qutb-ud-din another Prince of the blood loyal, the Malik and Amirs assumed an attitude of hostility towards them. Malik Ghiyas-ud-din Mohammad Shah, the king's younger brother, who held Oudh, seized the treasures of Lakhnauti and plundered several cities of Hindustan. The governors of Badaon, Multan, Hansi and Lahore became openly hostile and disregarded the authority of the Central government.

1236 A.D. Shah Turkan, was taken prisoner by the infuriated mob. Her fall prepared the way for Reziya. The Turkish Amirs and nobles rallied round her and saluted her as their sovereign. Rukn-ud-din was also seized and thrown into prison, where he died on November 9, 1236 A.D. after a brief reign of a little less than seven months.

1236 A.D. After the death of Rukun-ud-din Sultan Reziya ascended the throne.

1239 A.D. Sultan Reziya married with Malik Ikhtiyar-ud-din Altunia (the rebel Governor of Sindh).

1240-Oct. 15 Sultan Reziya and her husband were killed. Reziya's reign lasted for three and a half years.

1240 A.D. Bahram Shah, brother of Reziya, who succeeded her, was a prince, fearless and full of courage.

1242 A.D. - May 10 - Bahram Sham was also assasinated.

1242 A.D. After the assasination of Bahram Shah the crown was offered to Ala-ud-din Masud Shah, a grandson of Iltutmish.

1246 A.D. - June 10 - Masud was thrown into the prison, where he was received into the Almighty's mercy a few days afterwards.

1246 A.D. The throne of Delhi now fell to the lot of Nasir-ud-din Mahmud Shah a younger son of Iltutmish. He was a pious, God fearing, compassionate ruler who patronised the learned and sympathised with the poor and the distress. He had a very able and strong willed minister in Balban who guided the domestic as well as the foreign policy of the state throughout his master's reign.

1266 - Feb. 18 A.D. After Nasir-ud-din's death on February 18, 1266 A.D. the mantle of sovereignty devolved upon Ghiyas-ud-din Balban.

1270 Birth of Sant Namdev Ji

1279 A.D. Tughrils rebellion in Bengal

1285 A.D. Death of Prince Muhammad son of Balban

1286 A.D. Death of Balban

1290 A.D. Jalaluddin Khilji's assumption of Royal Power

1291 A.D. Rebellion of Chhajju suppressed.

1291 A.D. Abdiction of Nasir-ud-din Bughra and accession of Rukn-ud-din Kaikus in Bengal

1292 A.D. Mongol invasion 'Ala-ud-din Khilji invades Malwa and raids Bhilsa.

1292 A.D. Ala-ud-din invades the Kingdom of Deogir, in the Deccan

1296 A.D. Murder of Jalal-ud-din Firuz Khilji and accession of Ala-ud-din Mohammad Khilji

1297 A.D. Conquest of Gujarat

1299 A.D. The Mongol invade India and are defeated before Delhi (The invasion of Qutlugh Khwaja)

1300 A.D. Siege of Ranthambhor. Rebellion of Akat Khan suppressed. Rebellion of Haji Maula also suppressed.

1301 A.D. Capture of Ranthambhor by Ala-ud-din. Accession of Shams-ud-din Firuz Shah in Bengal. Suhadeva sets up a government in Kashmir.

1302-03 A.D.	Capture of Chittor. Failure of an expedition to Warangal. Mongol invasion. Ala-ud-din lays his new capital at Siri.
1306 A.D.	Mongol invasion repelled by Ghiyas-ud-din Tughlaq. Death of Narasimha II of Orissa and accession of Bhanudeva II.
1307 A.D.	Expedition of Kafur (Malik Naib) to Deogir
1308 A.D.	Expedition to Warangal. Prataparudradeva submits and pays tribute
1310	Malik Kafur's South Indian Expedition. Death of Anantamalla of Nepal and accession of Jayananda deva. Ghiyas-ud-din Bahadur assumes sovereignty in East Bengal.
1311	Death of Maravarman Kulasekhara Pandya. Alai Darwaza built
1312	Defeat of Sankaradeva, son of Rama Deva of Devagir
1313	Shah Mir arrives in Kashmir
1314	Death of Ajayasimha and accession of Hammir in Mewar. Mithila army conquers Nepal.
1316	Death of Ala-ud-din Khilji and accession of Shihab-ud-din Umar. Death of Malik Naib. Deposition of Umar and accession of Qutb-ud-din Mubarak
1317	Mubarak's expedition to Deogir. Capture and death of Harapaladeva.
1318	Rebellion of Raja Har Pal Deva of Devagir
1319	Sundara Pandya ruled (South India) till A.D. 1319 or probably 1320
1320	Murder of Mubarak and usurpation of Nasir-ud-

	din Khusrav. Rinchana conquers Kashmir. Defeat and death of Khusrav and accession of Ghiyas-ud-din Tughluq (Ghazi Malik).
1321	Expedition to Warangal under Mohammad Jauna (Ulugh Khan). Rebellion of Mohammad.
1323	Second expedition to Warrangal under Mohammad. Capture of Prataparudradeva. Mongol invasion Death of Rinchana and accession of Udayanadeva Nasir-ud-din ascends the throne in West Bengal
1324	Ghiyas-ud-din Tughluk's expedition to Bengl and Tirhut
1325	Death of Ghiyas-ud-din and accession of Muhammad. Ghiyas-ud-din Bahadur restored in West Bengal. Harisimha of Mithila enters Nepal. Jami Masjid erected at Camby
1326	Rebellion of Gurushasp and invasion of Kampili. Ghiyas-ud-din Bahadur Shah conquers Tippera and Chittagong for Mohammad bin Tughlak
1327	Capital transferred from Delhi to Daultabad
1328	Rebellion of Kishlu Khan in Multan. Invasion of India by Ala-ud-din Tarmashirin. Death of Bhanudeva II of Orissa and accession of Narasimh III.
1329	Issue of fictitious currency of Mohammad Tughlaq
1330	Bahram acquires the Government of East Bengal
1331	Rebellion of Ghiyas-ud-din Bahadur in Bengal
1332	Death of the Ahom King Sukhangpha and accession of Sukhrangpha

1331	Arrival of Ibn Batuta in India
1334	Rebellion of Sayyid Jalal-ud-din Ahsan in Madura
1335	Mohammad leaves Delhi for Madura. He retires from Warangal. Revival of Hindu power in South India. Accession of Jam Unar of Sind. Rebellion in Lahore, Daultabad, Sarasuti and Hansi
1336	Foundation of the Kingdom of Vijayanagar
1336	Famine. Foundation of Sargawadi. Rebellion at Bidar, Kara, Gulbaraga and Awadh. Birth of Timur Accession of Harihar I and the foundation of Vijayanagar
1337	Rebellion of Fakhr-ud-din in Bengal
1337	Mohammad Tughluq's expedition into the Himalayas. Capture of Nagarkot. Failure of the expedition
1338	Fakhr-ud-din Mubarak Shah proclaims his independenc in Bengal. Death of Udayana and accession of Kota in Kashmir
1339	Death of Jalal-ud-din Ahsan Shah and accssion of Ala-ud-din "Udaiji in Mabar Shah Mir or Shamas-ud-din deposes Kota and becomes the king of Kashmir. Accsion of Ilyas Shah in Bengal
1340	Accession of Ala-ud-din Ali Shah in Bengal Bukka conquers Penugonda. Death of Udaiji and accession of Qutb-ud-din Firuz in Ma'bar. Death of Firuz and accession of Ghiyas-ud-din Mohammad Damaghani in Ma'bar
1341	Known regnal date of Vira Pandya

1342	Ibn Batuta leaves Delhi on his mission to China. Death of Shamas-ud-din of Kashmir and accession of Jamshid; deposition of Jamshid and accession of Ali Sher. Death of the Hoysala king Vira Ballala III.
1343	Mohammad's expedition into the districts of Sannam, Samana, Kaithal and Kuhran. Accession of the Hoysala Virupaksha Ballala IV
1344	Arrival in Delhi of the envoy of the Khalifa
1345	Rebellion of the centurions in Malwa, Gujarat and Deccan. Muhammad leaves Delhi for Gujarat and suppresses the rebellion. Rebellion in Daultabad: Ismail Mukh proclaimed king of the Deccan. Mohammad besieges Daultabad
1346	Known regnal date of Maravarman Kulasekhara Bukka conquers the Hoysala kingdom
1347	Rebellion of Taghi in Gujarat. Ala-ud-din Bahman Shah proclaimed king of the Deccan. Marapa of Vijayanagara conquers the Kadamba kingdom.
1349	Death of Fakhr-ud-din Mubarak Shah of Bengal
1350	Mohammad invades Sind. Ilyas Shah's invasion of Nepal. Bahman Shah invades Warrangal.

Source 1. The Delhi Sultanate—R.C. Majumdar-General Ed. Bombay-Bhartiya Vidya Bhavan, 1960. (History and Culture of Indian People, Vol. 6)

2. History of Mediaeval India by Ishwari Prasad, Indian Press, Allahabad, 1940.

Birth of Namadeva

India, the land of Ramayana, the land of Ashoka the Great, has been the pioneer in spreading the message of peace. The exponents of these great messages had never preached anything without realising the inner meaning of their significance. They knew the value of peace at a very high cost.

Ashoka the Great came to know what is meant by peace only after the ravage of Kalinga where thousands were killed in the battle. He was convinced of the utter uselessness of a war. Before Ashoka, Ratnakar a highway robber who used to kill people in dense jungle just to earn his livelihood left the henious criminal profession when he met a holy man who blessed him. The highway robber Ratnakar became a great Saint, Maharishi Valmiki and wrote the epic Ramayana after attaining solvation. It is recorded that when the holy man asked the robber to utter the name of Lord Rama the criminal could not do it. He was so sinful that the holy name would not come on his lips. So his guru asked him to utter repeatedly mara, mara (meaning dead) which finally comes to Rama. 'Mara' reads backwardly 'Rama'. The robber devoted himself so whole heartedly to the new task that days months and years rolled by and the fellow got completely covered by a hillock of white ant citadel. When the holy man came to check the progress of his disciple, he discovered this, got him released out of mound of white ant and saw the new glow of enlightement on his face. He named him Maharishi Valmiki and gave him the task of writing of Ramayana. The highway robber became a saint. And one of the greatest. The heart has a reason[1]. The cultural Heritage of India records - "Any strong emotional attitude towards God is sure to prove fruitful in the effort of the aspirant to realise Him. Intense love, warm affection like that of an infant for its mother, great fear, and even bitter hatred of God are all known to have been effective means of mystic experience. The emotion should be all absorbing, leaving no scope for any other emotion in the heart. There have been great devotees in Maharashtra, who might be sighted as illustrations of all these different methods of God realisation. Even the greatest sinners of enemies of God, the most confirmed atheists have been suddenly turned into great saints. It merely illustrates the psychological principle that strong emotion that invades the whole region of a person's consciousness drives away all other emotions. If such an emotion is deliberately developed, it has the inevitable welcome tendency of transmitting all other emotions auxilliary or adverse. Though there are not many instancs of conversion in the history of mysticsm in Maharashtra yet there are some typical ones. The later spiritual life of Namdeva was the result of such a conversion[2].

These are historic events - Ratnakar the robber who turned into Maharishi Valmiki. Ashoka, the great killer at Kalinga, who became Ashoka, the Great. Namdeva the way-lay robber who turned one of the greatest saints of India - all created history. Their role in the cultural Heritage occupy a supreme one each is important on merits[3].

According to Max Arthur Macauliffe Namdeva was the son of Damasheti a tailor, who resided at Narsi Bamani, a village near Karhad in the Satara district of the Bombay Presidency. Namadeva's mother was Gonabai, daughter of a tailor at Kalyan, in the same district. Both Namdeva's father and mother, and probably their ancestors for some generations possessed great devotional enthusiasm[4].

The author of the spirit of Indian culture - Saints of India wrote that this great saint of Maharashtra was born in 1270 A.D. in Pandharpur in the Sholapur district. His father Damaseta was a tailor by profession. His mother Gonabai was a highly religious lady. The ancestors of the Saint hailed from a little village Narasivamani, the modern name of which is Kalem Narasingpur in Satara district. Both the father and the mother were deeply devoted to the family diety Govinda. They never took their food without offering daily prayers[5].

About the low birth of the Saint of Pandharpur, a modern monk writes, "Often we hear, amidst the writings of the saints of Maharashtra, the echo that none by reason of caste, creed and by following a worldly pursuit shall be denied the gift of God realisation. If examples are necssary, look to Sena the barber, Kubja and Vidur the Sudras, Gora the Potter, Raidas the Cobbler, Savata the gardner, Narshari the goldsmith, Janabai the maid and Kanhopatra the dancing girl. Well did Chokha the untouchable bring out the point (when similarly condemned) in his inimitable style: a sugarcane may be croocked; a bow may be curved and yet arrow is not curved; a river may have windings and yet the matter has no windings. Chokha may be an untouchable, but his heart is not an untouchable. Namdeva has great difficulties even to enter the temple for his prayers because of his low caste. He gives vivid descriptions of his struggle in the abhangas. In one such song he laments the torture by the priests. He struggle to sing to the glory of God but he is thrown out because he did not follow the ritualistic drills and hailed from a low family.

One day Namadeva with heart bubbling with devotion came to the temple of the Lord.

In his enthusiasm he forgot all decorum and started his ecstatic dance before the Lord like a maniac.

Irritated at the insolenc, the Pujari pushed him out; Namdeva sore at heart complained. 'O Lord! You are responsible for my birth in a low caste which has brought all this insult on me." The Lord pleased with his devotee answered his prayer and turned round the frontal face of the temple. Pleased with this act of the Lord Namdeva started his song eulogising the Lord[6].

All the worshippers who had witnessed the miracle bowed to Namadeva and sought forgiveness for their affront."[6]

Namadeva: The incarnation of Udhav

The saints, Gurus and Mystics author have recorded about the birth of Namadeva that Lord Narayana invited Udhav and Shuka to see Him in his abode on the ocean of milk and said to them, "I wish you to become Avtars in the world of mortals: Shuka became Kabir and Udhav became Namdeva. There was one Damaji, a tailor, supremely pious pure through good deeds and perfect in his devotion to God. He took daily bath in Chandrabhaga and then had Darshan of Lord Panduranga. His wife Gonai was supremely pious and dutiful. One day Gonai asked Damaji, go to Panduranga and ask for a child". Damaji expressed his doubts about their having a child but Gonai insisted that he should try. He went to Panduranga temple and there prayed for a child. He had a dream in which Lord Panduranga told him that avtar of Udhav will be given to him on the bank of Bhima river. Next day as usual he visited the Bhima river and after taking bath he found a shell floating and when he opened it, he found a baby inside. He wrapped up the infant and took it home. He said to Gunai, "God has given us a son", Gonai took the baby in her lap and fed her lovingly. The infant was named Namdeva[7].

According to Bhaktavijaya's Mahipati - one day Narayan invited Uddhav and Shuka to see Him on the ocean of milk. Said he to them, I wish you to become avatars in the world of mortals. They replied to Him who dwells on the Ocean of Milk, We do not wish to be born in the natural way, O Vishnu, give us birth in an unnatural way. Listening to them, the life of the world turned them into infants, put them in shells, and dropped them down from raining clouds. One fell into the Bhagirathi river. One fell in the Bhimarathi river. As they flowed along with the stream they repeated the name of the God. Listen to what they said. The one in the shell that fell in the Bhagirathi river repeated the name Ram, Ram. The other who fell in the Bhimarathi river cried in his delight, Vithal Vithal. So Shuka became the worshipper of Ram, and Uddhava became the worshipper of Pandurang (Vithal) listened to the wonderful things that happened as they flowed along. There was a person named Damaji a tailor a Vaishnav supremely pious, pure through good deeds and perfect in his devotion to God, his knowledge, and his indifference to worldly things. After bathing in the Chandrabhaga he went to worship Pandurang. After completing this, it was his regular custom to take his morning meal. His wife Gonai was supremely pious and a dutiful wife. They both lived at Pandhari and were constant in repeating the names of the Lord of the World. Gonai had no child of her own, so she said to her husband, 'Go to Pandurang and ask for a son'. Damaji said to her, you are an ignorant woman. We are both now aged. Why should be expect God to give us a child. The wife replied, 'Lord of my life, you blame me for being unreasonable, but Gods power is supreme. Now I know that you are ignorant. When Ram was an avtar, He made stones float on the sea. What difficulty has He in giving us a child although we are aged? When Brahmadev carried away the calves He himself became cows and cowherds. What difficulty can He have, therefore, in giving us a son? Damaji said to his wife, I will go now to the temple and tell God the wish you hold in your mind. He therefore went to the great door of the temple and there prostrated himself before the God. He said 'My wife desires a son. Be pleased to give one Shri Hari. After saying this, he immediately fell asleep. The Life of the world came to him in a dream and said, I have given you the gift of a son. When at sunrise you go to bath on the bank of the Bhima a son will come floating down the stream. Take the baby up, and hasten back to your home with it. The Avtar of Uddhav will fill the three worlds with the glory of his deeds. He will be a saviour of the world and a supreme Vaishnava. He carries my name. Hearing this in his dream, he hurried back to his home. There he told his wife just what had happened. The next day Damaji came early to the bank of the Bhima. He quickly bathed and performed his daily devotions. Just then he suddenly noticd a shell floating down the Bhima. He waded into the river and took up the shell. When he opened the shell his eyes fell on beautiful baby, just as if at that very moment it had come from the womb of its mother. As he saw it his mind was troubled for he said, 'Who will nurse it? He wrapped up the infant in his garment and brought it to his home. He said to his wife 'God has given us a son'. Gonai took the child and immediately her breast filled with milk. Both of them though it very strange, that in her old age she should be able to nurse the child. She bathed the infant, and with great love fed it at her breast. Because they had made God pleased with them, and had asked for a son from the dark complexioned one, they therefore called him Nama, and they had intense love for the child[8].

The details of incarnations (Avtars) of Saint Namdev has been given his disciple 'Parsa Bhagwan, as under:

> Krityugi Nama Prahlad Pai Jhala-Stambhi Avtala Narayan
> Traitayugi Nama Angad Pai Asa Ramchandra-e-Syasi Alingla-z
> Danya to Nama Dhanya to Nama - Pareyi Purshottam Jeevahun
> Dwapri Nama Uddhav Gahan Narayan Na Vinsawe
> Kalyugi Nama sant sakar - Na Kale to par Brahmadika
> Chahuyugi Nama Bagala Nahi Jhala Mhnvuni Purla Narayan
> Vishnudas Nama Keshvi Rangla Dev Atma Jhala Mhne Parasa

It means that in satyug Namdeva had been incarnation of Bhagat Prahalad. To safeguard Prahlad from his father Harnakashyap, Narayan appeared in the Avtar of Narasingh. In Traita period Namadeva was born as Angad son of Bali. On the request of Sugriv Lord Rama had killed Bali. Afterwards Lord Rama took care of Angad and he devoted his entire life in the servic of Lord Rama. We bow our head in reverence to Sant Shiromani Namdev who was so dear to God Almighty. In Dwapar Period Namadeva was born as an incarnation of

Uddhav. Uddhav was a great disciple of Lord Krishna. In Kaliyug Namadeva was born as a saint in Maharashtra. In all the four Yugas, Namadeva had been attached with God Almighty. Being a disciple of Lord Vishnu Namadeva devoted Himself in the meditation and recitation of Lord Krishna. Says Parsa Bhagwan that Body and soul always remained one - this was the condition of Nama and Deva.

According to Fifth Avtar (incarnation) of Namdeva, the famous saint of Maharashtra 'Niloba' Maharaj says:-

"Jagatguru Tuka - Avtar Namayacha"

Shri Saint Tuka Ram Ji Maharaj was also the incarnation of Namadeva[9].

BRIEF LIFE SKETCHES OF ALL THE AVTARS

Prahlad

Hiranyakaship was the King of Daityas who were at war with the Devas. There are three worlds according to Hindu mythology—the middle world is inhabited by men and animals; the heavens are inhabited by gods or Devas and the under world is inhabited by Daityas.

Hiranyakaship declared himself to be the God of all the three worlds and began to demand worship for himself alone and strictly enjoined that no one should worship Vishnu.

Hiranyakaship had a son called Prahlad who was from his infancy devoted to Vishnu. Prahlad's father wanted to drive away this evil from the world and he sent his son to be taught by two teachers, Shanda and Amarka, who were strict disciplinarians and had injunction to the effect that Prahlad should never hear the name of Vishnu mentioned.

Prahlad would not study but would go on telling his classmates all the time about Vishnu. The teachers were frightened and they told this fact to the King who was greatly enraged. He called the boy to his presence and tried to dissuade him from the worship of Vishnu but the boy would not listen. The anger of the King knew no bounds and he ordered the boy to be immediately put to death.

Various diabolical means were adopted to kill the boy. He was ordered to be trampled under the foot of an elephant but that did not work. He was ordered to be thrown over a precipice, but he was not hurt, because Vishnu was protecting him. Several other methods such as fire, poison, starvation were tried but to no effect. At last the King ordered him to be tied with mighty serpents and from the under world he was thrown into the bottom of the ocean and became unconscious. Vishnu came to his rescue every time.

When Hiranyakaship found that all methods had failed, he was at a loss to know as to what to do. The boy was brought a second time before his father and was gently told to give up the worship of Vishnu. He was again sent to his old teachers but this time too Prahlad would not attend to his lessons and continued telling his schoolmates about Vishnu.

When his father came to know about it he was filled with rage and calling the boy before him abused Vishnu and threatened to kill Prahlad. But Prahlad still persisted in maintaining that Vishnu was the Lord of the Universe. Then the King roared in fury and ordered him to be tied to a pillar. If Vishnu is God Omnipresent, said the King, why does he not come out of this pillar? The King struck the pillar with a sword and instantly Vishnu issued forth from the pillar in the form of Narasingha—half lion and half man. All Daityas ran away terrified but Hiranyakaship gave him a fight and was vanquished and slain.

Thus blessing Prahlad, Vishnu disappeared and Prahlad was seated on the throne of his father to reign for a long time in peace[10].

Ram Bhakat Angad

Was a son of Bali. It is said that during her early age Mandodri gave birth to Angad. Angad was handed over to Bali and Mandodri was married to Ravana. Tara was the wife of Bali. She used to love Angad. The name of Bali's brother was Sugriv. On the request of Sugriv Lord Rama killed Bali. After the death of his father Angad became an orphan.

Lord Rama took Angad under him. Angad was a great disciple of Lord Rama. He devoted his entire life in the lotus feet of Lord Rama. Angad was a genious. Angad had blessing of Lord Rama. The duty to trace mother Sita was assigned to Angad. When Hanuman, Jamawent and other heroes were deputed to Lanka in search of mother Sita, Angad was the head of that deputation. During Rama-Ravana battle, first of all Angad was sent to Ravana as an Ambassador of Lord Ram. He scolded Ravana with full force. He reminded Ravana! - "dont creat enemity with Lord Almighty. Lay down in the lotus feet of Lord Rama, your life would be successful". Ravana did not acceded his request and ultimately killed by Lord Rama. When after the victory Lord Rama came back to Ayodhya - Angad accompanied Him. Reaching Lanka he started helping Sugriv to run the government[11].

Shri Krishan Bhakat Uddhav

The nephew of Vasudev, a great devotee of Krishna and always accompanied him. They loved each other very much. When Krishna dearted from Gokul to Mathura he sent Uddhav to console the Gopis and Nand and Yashoda. Krishna explained to him the knowledge of the soul as he (Krishna) passed away from this world. Then he went to Badrikashram in accordance with Krishna's command[12].

Sant Tuka Ram (1608-1650)

The Bhakti movement is perhaps the most glorious creative

upsurge of the Indian mind in this millennium. Tuka Ram epitomizes the liberal Hindu tradition of Bhakti in Maharashtra. He is something of a legend. Born as a Shudra, persecuted by the orthodox on account of the growing popularity of his rebellious social thinking. Tuka Ram, after mysterious end, became the most revered figure of his times. For over three centuries now he has exerted profound influence over the cultural life of the Maraathi people. In almost every generation his lyrics have been most widely sung, read and quoted as proverbs. The secret of his tremendous appeal lies in the intensely personal religion reflected in his lyrics. His morality is more relevant to our time than ever[13].

Controversy regarding Namadeva's date of birth

According to Madhav Gopal Deshmukh (Namadeva-Sahitya Akademi, New Delhi, 1990) Namadeva was born in Pandharpur on 26th October 1270. Doctor Mohan Singh Diwana has mentioned 1390 A.D. Doctor Bhandarkar, Professor Vasudev Balwant Patwardhan, Doctor Aruna Dixit is of the opinion that Namadeva's birth period is between 1370 to 1450 A.D. according to Bhagat Ram Namadevas' year of birth is 1363 A.D. Bansidhar Shastri is of the opinion that Namdeva's birth took place during 1393 A.D[14]. According to Winand M. Callewaert (The Hindi Padavali of Namdev. Motilal Banarsidas, Delhi 1989).

1270 A.D. (Suk Samvat 1192)
(Singh; 1906)
(Avati: 1908)
(Macau Liffe: 1909)
(Ranade 1933C)

26 October 1270)
(Mar. Enc.: 1985)

1309 A.D.
(Bhardvaj: 1898 (See Vaudeville; 1969d)

1390 A.D.
(Sari Bhakta Parichay 1696)

1370 A.D.
Bhagat Ram: 1936b

1364 A.D.
(Puranadas: 1888)

1443 A.D.
(Crooke: 1896 (in Marvar)
(Farquhar: 1920)

Shanivar, 11th Kartik Sudi, Suk 1192
(Macauliffe: 1909)
(Joshi: 1940)

Namdev will write a hundred thousand abhangas
(Avate : 1908)
(Macauliffe : 1909)
(Ranade : 1933C)

Born in Narasi Vamani, near the Krishna river
(Barthval : 1936)
(Joshi : 1940)
(Sharma : 1957C)
(Dikshit : 1970d)

Born in Pandharpur
(Avate : 1908 (Janabai abhanga)
(Bhandarkar : 1913b)

Namdev was born in Narasi Brahmani
(Prabhani District Marathvada)
(Dattatrey : 1723(?))
Karatkar : 1926)
(Pangarkar : 1933)

(Mar - Enc. 1985: Born in Naras in Marathveda where there is a smadhi and a temple in his name; an abhang is quoted. Narasi and Bamani are two different villages)

Namdev was born of a Virgin widow, daughter of Vamdev
(Priyadas : 1712)
(Chaturdas : 1800)

According to Madhu Malti - Namdev was born in a village in the Satara district of Maharashtra on Sunday, October 26, 1270. His father's name was Damsath and Gonabai was his mother. Both were very pious. They always sang songs in praise of Vitthal, their Lord. This had a deep impact on little Namdev who too, occasionally joined them[15].

Vankhade Guruji has quoted in his Hindi book entitled Sant Namdeva Charitavali that Sant Namdeva in one of his Abhangs Namdevaji was born during Shaka Samvat 1192 in the month of Kartik; Sunday dated 26th October 1270 A.D. This date has been authenticated by Doctor Ranade, Shripangarkar and Doctor Tulpule etc. etc.

Renowned hindi scholar Parshuram Chaturvedi, Vinay Mohan Sharma and English Scholar Macauliffe is all of the same opinion. European historian J.C. Powel. Price and A.R. Mcdonel and well known Indian historian Ishwari Prasad is also acknowledge the same date of birth of Sant Shiromani Namdevaji Maharaj[16].

According to Doctor Vivek Bhattacharya - Namdeva was born in 1270 A.D. in Pandharpur in the Sholapur district. His father Damaseta was a tailor by profession. His mother Gonabai was a highly religious lady. The ancestors of the Saint hailed from a little village Narasivamani, the modern name of which is Kalem Narasingpur in Satara district. Both the father and the mother were deeply devoted to the family diety - Govind. They never took their food without offering daily prayers[17].

Controversy regarding place of birth

As the different authors have different opinion about the date of birth of Namdeva, similarly there is a difference of opinion about his place of birth.

1. Anant Das the first hindi writer of Namdeva and Bhakatmal's author Mahipati have acknowledged Pandharpur as his birth place.

2. Namdeva in one of his Abhangs has mentioned Narsi Brahmani as his birth place. Regarding Narsi Brahmani there is a difference of opinion between the intellectual class. Doctor Bhandarkar is of the opinion that Narsi Brahmani is situated in the district of Sitara. A few Marathi writers like Madhav Appaji Mule, Pandurang Sharma, near about all the hindi writers including Ram Chandra Shukla, Acharya Vinay Mohan Sharma, Parshu Ram Chaturvedi, Doctor Aruna Dixit and English author Macauliffe is also of the same opinion.

3. Majority of the Marathi writers are of the view that village Narasi Brahmani is situated in the Prabhani district upto the year 1936 A.D. Narsi Brahmini was a part of Sitara district. In the year 1926 A.D. an article by Keshav Ram Kertkar appeared in a periodical published by Bharat Itihas Sanshodhan Mandal that Narsi Brahmini is situated in the Parbhani district. Since than it has been acknowledged by the entire scholar community that Narsi Brahmini is the birth place of Namdeva in the districtd of Parbhani. J.R. Ajgaonkar, Pangarkar Bhave Tulpule etc. etc. are all of the same opinion.

4. Ramchandra Janarden the author of Kavicharit is of the opinion that village Gopalpur nearPandharpur is the birth place of Namadeva.

5. According to Gasanad Tasi Gwalior was the birth place of Namadeva[18].

Importance of Pandharpur

Mahipati in his book Bhaktavijaya has recorded that Pandharpur the sacred city for deliverence, is the treasure - house of all the sacred bathing places and if one should look all over the world, another like it cannot be seen. A jivanmukta (one free while living) and a wise man and chief among the bhaktas was the muni pundalik. He sat down for contemplation of the most supreme Krishna and the river Bhima flowing towards the south gives the necter of immortality. She is the mistress of an abundant joy and shines with the water of that supreme joy. Anyone who sees this Chandrabhaga river from a distance will not have to return to rebirths. When the Bhagirathi river looked at her (the Chandrabhaga) she felt ashamed and hid away. The Bhagirathi feeling a sense of fear joined with the ocean, and the Bhagvati hastened with extreme speed to the lower regions. In such a sacred city my servants have lived continually day and night, and in the joy of their love they unceasingly shout my names. With joy filling his heart Nama danced in the Kirtans in the name of Hari. When one goes in search through the three worlds for such joy he will not see it anywhere else. The good being also said to the Brahmans, he who with his lips repeats My name, whether with some desire in his heart or without a desire, such an one is my dearest friend and relative. I love him more than I love myself and I will not put him away. He is my family deity whom I worship in reverence.

So putting aside your pride, make your mind pure through repentance. Perform those acts which your reputation will increase in both worlds. Go to Chandrabhaga river, and there bath accompanied by the rites of repeating the mantras[19].

Family Background

From the family tree of Namadevaji Maharaj it is learnt that one Yaduseth was one of the known ancestor of this dynasty. He was called Yaduseth alias Relkar. He was born in a village named Narsi Bamani, in the district of Parbhani in Maharashtra. He was a cloth merchant. His wife was very loyal and faithful. Yaduseth was a person of cool temperament. The couple was true devotee of Vithal Bhagwan. In their sixth generation Namadevaji Maharaj was born.

It is said that Namadevaji's father Damseth was only two year's old when he started uttering the name of the Lord. He was a sweet nature person and faithful to his parents. He was a kind hearted person. After his schooling Damseth was put in the family business.

After some time Narhar Seth; father of Damseth alongwith his wife and son went to Pandharpur. At that time Damseth was eighteen years old. Reaching Pandharpur they performed Pooja.

On the Dwadashi day Narhar Seth and his wife Limabai fell ill. Keeping in view critical position of both the persons Narhar Seth summoned his son Damseth and said - Dama! very shortly we are leaving for our heavenly abode. After my departure, you have to complete my unfinished tasks. After few seconds they breathed their last. Damseth was terribly upset at the sudden demise of his parents. After the Poornamasi function Damseth went back to his village. When his maternal uncle came to know about this incident he was also saddended. He took Damseth to his village. After some time Damseth was married with Gonabai daughter of Govind Seth, the resident of village Kalyan.

In one of his Marathi Abhangs Namadevaji has narrated the occasion of his father's marriage as under:

A resident of Kalyan the devotee of Hari, Goma was a Chhipai. His wife's name was Uma; who always devoted herself in the meditation of God Almighty. She gave birth to a daughter named Gonabai was married to Damseth; who was a resident of Narsi Bamni village. Their ancestors belonged to Gadhij or Bhardwaj Gotra. Gonabai gave birth to a daughter who was named Aaobai. Afterwards Gonabai prayed the God to be blessed with a son. Namdevaji said that whatsoever is the desire of Vithal Bhagwan, just to fulfill that Gonabai always prayed the same.

It is clear from this Abhang that the name of Namadeva's

grandfather (mother side) was Gomaji and grand mother's name was Umabai. And the name of Namadeva's father was Damseth.

Damseth was a follower of Bhagvad. He was the staunch follower of Vitthal. Being a house holder he was leading his life like a saint. This couple first of all was blessed with a daughter namely Aaobai. Gonabai had a great desire for a son, she was much pained to have a daughter. She continued her prayers to Vitthal Bhagwan to bless her with a son. For a long time her desire was not fulfiled. After all they left Narsi Brahmani and settled at Pandharpur and devoted their full time in the service of Vithal Bhagwan. Here on 26th October 1270 A.D. Namdeva was born.

Naming ceremony

On eleventh day of his birth naming ceremony was performed. The family members proposed the newly born child's name. Then Babaji Brahman proposed the name as Namadeva. The fvamily circle started calling him as Nama. On his birth Damseth was quite happy. On completion of his Janam Kundali Babaji Brahman told Damseth that this son of your will be a great follower of Vitthal Bhagwan. Afterwards he would be famous as Namadeva throughout India. On this occasion Damseth had invited all the nearer and dearer ones.

Bhakatraj Sant Namadevaji Maharaj's Janam Kundali was prepared by Shri P.R. Moonga Gyan Mandir of Bombay in the year 1937.

Before Namadeva's birth a maid servant named Janabai was living with his parents to help house hold jobs. Later on she herself came to light as a famous saint. In one of his Marathi couplet she had recorded that :-

Mother Gonabai resident of Pandharpur was a devotee of Vithal Bhagwan. Pandharpur is also the resident of Vitthal Bhagwan and mother Rukmani. Gonabai prayed to Vithal Bhagwan to bless her with a son. Thus by the kind of blessing of Vitthal Bhagwan Namadeva was born. On the birth of Namadeva his father Damseth as well as Janabai were quite happy.

As stated earlier Janabai was working as a maid servant in Namadeva's house before his birth. Namadeva had the pleasure and honour to play in the lap of Janabai. Namadevji himself in one of his Abhang has apprised his eldest son Narayan about his birth. The meaning of which is as follows:-

Babaji Brahman has prepared my horoscope whatsoever is written in it, please listen very carefully. In the Shalibahan Shake Samvat 1192, at the time of sun rise,Kartik Ekadashi, Sunday. Pramod namely Samvat Shalibahan Shak I was born.

At the time the God Almighty wrote on my tongue that Namadeva will write 100 crore abhangs. Namadevji further said that according to my horoscope my life time is 80 years and I will devote my entire life in the propagation of the sacred name of Vithal Bhagwan.

We have already mentioned the opinion of different authors of his date of birth and place of birth, and his parents[20].

According to Mahipati the well known biographer of the saint, poets of Maharashtra says Namdev was among the saint. Poet who in their teachings placed a special emphasis upon purity of heart, humility, self surrender forgiveness and the love of God, they severely condemned religious practices which concerned the body only and all mechanical rites and ceremonies; and they strongly enforced the absolute necessity of striving for the attainment of pure devotion to God." (Bhaktavijaya, which contains 40,000 lines of beautiful Marathi poetry and is rightly regarded as one of the classics of the language).

Born in a Maharashtra village, Namadev was a Vaishnavite adherent of the bhakti sect, whose members are united in seeking to reach God through bhakti, or loving devotion.

According to one account, he bore like many other saints from his infancy the marks of saint hood. The first words he spoke were "Shri Vitthal". He learned nothing at school, for he cared for nothing but Kirtans.

Vitthal is one of the several synonyms of God used by Namadev in his hymns. Among the others are Ram, Shyam, Gobind, Madho, Mir Mukund, Jadavraya, Jasrath Rai and Shri Rang[21].

Education

He was sent to school at the age of five. When the teacher wrote alphabets on the slate, the child asked him to write the name of Lord Vitthal on it. He learnt nothing at school for he cared for nothing but "Kirtan"[22].

Outside the village of Narsi Bamani stood the temple of Kashiraj (Shiv), of whom Damasheti was a devout worshipper. He never omitted to pay a daily visit to the temple and make an offering to his God. Namadev's mother when pregnant used to request everybody she met to repeat the name of her favourite God. At the age of three years the young saint used to ejaculate the name of the local god of his devotion. At the age of five years he was sent to school, but he made no progress in learning. Whenever he found an opportunity, either in the absence of his teachers or otherwise he set his school fellows singing songs to his favourite god, in which he joined both with voice and cymbal accompaniment. It is said that he loved God even from the day of his birth, and his divine love and devotion increased with his years.

At the age of eight years Namdev was betrothed to Rajabai, daughter of Govind Sheti. His father finding that he made no progress in learning apprenticed him to his own trade. It very soon became manifest that Namdev paid no attention to practical business but spent his time consorting with religious mendicants, visiting the temple of his god, and performing the devotions usual in such cases.It was then decided to put him to commerce.

To this he consented, but represented that he possessed no capital. This was procured from a friendly banker whom Namadev found himself in the possession of funds, he gave a great feast to Brahmans which exhausted all his money. At this both his parents and the money lender were greatly distressed. His mother bitterly reproached him for his recklessness and extravagance - Was it for this I carried thee about for nine months? Was this misery kept in store for my old age? O! why did I not rather remain a barren woman than give birth to such a son? Art though not ashamed of thyself? People laugh at thee for thy madness. Have some respect for thy mother. Look at my grey hairs. Think of the misries of thine aged father. What wilt thou gain by this madness? There are also other worshippers of Keshiraj. Why cansl thou not act like them? What merits wilt thou obtain from this god? All who cared for him were ruined.

Namadev's mother finding her remonstrances and objurgations useless, appealed to the priests of the temple to remonstrate with her son and lend him to a right understanding of his worldly position. From them, too, no hope was received of the youth's amendment. They urged in reply to her representations that she was a fortunate mother, and that the good deeds of her previous births had ripened,and she had obtained a saint like son.

One day when Namadev's father was absent, the son took the daily offering of the family to the temple. It consisted of milk, which the youth had just milked from his cow. He thought that the god would freely partake of the offering on which he had lavished so much care. The stony idol, however, would not vouchsafe to do so. Upon this Namadev began to cry, threw himself down at the god's feet and uttered passionate supplications. In due time the god relented and accepted the boy's offerings. He celebrated the event in the following hymn in the Bhairo measure:-

> Nama having milked his brown cow took
> A cup of milk and a jug of water for the idol

Drink milk and my mind will be at ease;
Otherwise my father will be angry.
A golden cup filled with milk
Nama took and placed before the idol -
The saints alone abide in my heart-
On seeing Nama the god smiled;
On giving milk to the idol the worshipper Nama went home
And God appeared unto him[23].

Hari said to Nama, 'By no means tell anyone about this event'. After making obeisance to God Nama returned to his home. His mother said to him, Whom did you give that offering to? Nama said, 'O mother the god ate the offering. Now next day Damaji returned from the market. After inquiring of his wife what had happened he heard the whole story about the offering. Damaji became much perplexed; it seemed to him a very extraordinary thing. He said to Nama, How was it that the god ate? Let us both go to the temple, and show me what took place. They took with them the materials for worship, and both came to the great door of the temple. There they bowed to the Savior of the world, and began at once to worship, and fittingly offered incense and lights. Nama said to the eagle bannered one,' Be pleased to eat. The god said to Nama, Damaji has come with you; I shall never appear to his sight. I will meet with you. Nama said to God, Thou art a deceiver, Thou sayest Thou will not meet with my father. Thou seemest to me, O God, to use deception. Hearing Nama's remarks the life of the world began to laugh. He gave Damaji a sight of him and ate the offering. The father said to Nama, You have been born in my family line, therefore God in His love has given me this vision. Thus sataisfying his doubts, the father bowed prostrate before the god. He took Nama by the hand, and returned to their home. He told the whole story to his wife. The Lord of the Heaven truly ate the offering. We must no longer call Nama a relative, because he is God's bhakta. Gonai then said, God had mercy upon you, and gave you a son though born in an unusual way'.

Thus with their doubts settled they bestowed great love to Nama. After searching for one who would be a helpmate he was married[24].

Like Shri Ramakrishna, who would offer sweets to Mother Kali and would not leave the temple till she accepted it. Namadeva would offer milk to Govinda, Accept this offering O dear Govinda Delay not. And what is important is the description of the Saint of the acceptance of this offering by the Almighty. In an abhanga he confirms it. Namadeva says:-

Soyan Katouri Amrita bhari
Lai Namdev Hari agay dhari
Ek bhakta merey hridaya basoi
Namey dekho Narayana honsoi
Dudh Pibaya Namay ghar gaya
Namey Hari Ka darshana bhaya

Seeing this devotion of his devotee Nama (in whose heart He dwells) the Lord Hari smiled and accepted it.

To the Lord it was verily nectar.

The Lord out of compassion moved by the lament and seeing the determination of His devotee, Namadeva, set aside his hesitation and drank the milk; Namadeva was very happy and with joy returned home[25].

Marraige of Namadev

Wankhade Guruji in both of his hindi books entitled." Sant Namadeva tatha unka Hindi Sahitya and Sant Namadeva Charitavali published by Publication Division and Sant Namadeva Shodh Sansthan, New Delhi in the year 1970 and 1983 respectively has mentioned.

Namdevji was eight years old, then one day his father Damseth determined to arrange marriage for his beloved son Namadev. He gave it a serious thought that if by chance his son inclined towards Vitthals meditation, one day he may refuse to plunge in the married life. Incidentally during the same period one Govind Seth Sadavrate visited Pandharpur and met Damseth. During his childhood days Namdev was quite famous for his meditation during entire Maharashtra. He determined to married his daughter named Raja Bai with child devotee Namdev. After giving a serious thought to his idea he approached Damseth and expressed his feelings to him. Damseth approved the proposal. The family pandit when through their horoscope and gave green signal to solmnize their marriage. Thereafter marriage was solmnized with great pump and show.

Janabai in one of his Marathi Abhang has given the details of his family as under:

Gonabai - Mother in law

Rajabai - Daughter in law

Damseth - Father

Namdeva - Son

Narayan Mahadeva
Govind Namadev's sons
Vitthal

Ladabai - wife of Narayan

Godabai - wife of Mahadeva

Yesabai - wife of Govind

Sakhrobai - wife of Vitthal

Limbabai - Daughter of Namadeva

Aubai - sister of Namadeva
and
Janabai - Maid Servant

There were fourteen persons in Namadevaji's family except Jonabai. Rajabai has also mentioned in his poetry about 14 members of this family.

Towards esceticism

Namadeva has completely devoted himself in the meditation of Vitthal and his relations with worldly affairs were receding day by day. Financial position of the family had worsen very badly. It has become difficult for the family members to make their both ends meet properly. His parents wife and children were facing starvation. It is said that while the family was passing through grave situation, one day his father said to Namadeva that I am now an old man, to run and look after the family is my duty. To sew clothes and selling it, is our profession. You must go to bazar for the sale of clothes. He further said, perhaps you don't know after long prayers to the God Almighty we have received you? It is ironical that you are paying back to us in these coins. Even now, is the time, you can save us from desister. You please start going to bazar.

It is said that on the admonition of his father Namadeva went to bazar to sell clothes. He also positioned in the bazar where other cloth merchants were sitting. Instead of pursuing customers he devoted himself in the meditation of Vitthal. So question of any sale did not arise. In the evening all the hawker surrounded Namadeva started cutting joke for his inefficiency in the trade. He did not mind it. In the evening he went to a Dharamshala. In the morning he proceeded to Pandharpur. In the way he noticed a number of stones scattered in the field which were wet due to morning dew. Namadeva was a kind hearted person, he assumed that these stones may be feeling cold. He covered all the stones with cloth whatsoever he was keeping in his bundle. Pointing towards a covered stone he said, "Ganoba", I know you do not have money to pay to me today. Nothing doing He thought that today's sale is enough but without money he was much frightened from the anger of his parents. He told 'Gonoba' stone, when next week I will come to bazar, you manage to make the payment to me. Nearby a big stone which was also covered by him naming him "Ghandoba' said you are a witness to it. After this programme he reached home. His father enquired about the sale of the cloth. He replied in the positive. Next week they will make the payment. Reaching at the temple he narrated the whole story to Vitthal Bhagwan.

After the expiry of eight days he demanded the price of the cloth from the witness stone. The stone did not reponded to his request. He said, if you unable to make the payment than you have had to accompany with me to my house. Saying so he picked up 'Ghondi' stone to his residence. Rajabai was closely watching all the development. Damseth and Gonabai had gone to have a bath in the river Chanderbhaga. Namadeva had left for Vitthals temple. When his parents entered the house Rajabai related the whole story to them. His father advised Rajabai to depute some one to summon Namadeva from the temple. His both the sons namely Narayan and Mahadeva rushed to the temple. Seeing them Namadeva understood the facts of life that his father must be very angry. Namadeva started staring at the statue of Vitthal Bhagwan. Vitthal said to Namdeva! Don't worry you will pass this test! When Namdeva reached home, his father Damseth said, "Namdeva! un-necessarily you have imprisoned a stone in the house? You have done a very good business. You have spoiled the entire amount for nothing. Now, please do one thing - throw this stone out of the house. On the advice of his father Namdev took the stone out. From coming out it converted into the gold. All the family members started whispering among themselves. Gradually this news spread like wild fire in the entire village. The owner of the field came rushing to Namdeva to collect the stone. He threatened him, either to return the stone or ready to face consequences. Namdeva requested the farmer to pay the price of the cloth and take the stone back. There should be no quarrel. In the presence of the members of the Panchayat the farmer paid the price of Namadeva's cloth and took the stone to his house. On reaching home he found the golden stone again converted into the real shape of the stone. He put the stone near main gate of Namadeva's house. It is learnt the same stone is lying in the Namadev's temple. This stone is still worshipped.

There is another story regarding Namadevji's business. One day his mother Gonabai said to him - My son! you don't do any work. It is very difficult to make both ends meet properly of the family members. It has become very difficult to run household affairs properly. He told his mother that without money nothing can be done. What I can do? Gonabai said, if this is the problem, I will manage for the money.

There was a money lender named Dada Sahukar in Pandharpur. Gonabai approached him. Though he was a Brahmin by caste but he was a miser by nature. He never spent a single penney even on the death ceremonies of his father. Whosoever approached him for financial help, without mortgaging anything he never loan a single rupee to anyone. Gonabai approached him empty handed. But in the name of Namadevaji he agreed to loan her a loan of Rupees Two thousand. She promised to repay the entire amount within six months. Reaching home she handed over the amount to Namadeva and apprised him of the terms and conditions of the repayment of loan. He agreed to abide by them and assured her mother to do the needful whole heartedly.

After receiving the amount Namadeva gave it a serious thought that profit and loss is must while one invest in the business. He planned that if money is invested in the feeding the Brahmans there would be no chance of any profit and loss. He thought if he implented his plan in Pandharpur, his parents would not tolerate it. He determined to execute his plans at the banks of river Godavari. He took the money from his mother reached Vitthal Bhagwan's temple for his blessing. Namadevaji preceeded towards Rakshasbhuvan. Whosoever met him during his journey he invited them to the feast. In this manner while performing Kirtan he reached his destination.

When the news of Brahmbhoj reached to money lender Dada he approached Namadeva at Rakshasbhuvan and requested to return the money with interest. Namadeva started meditating desperately. He prayed the God Almighty to help him to face the situation. When he was praying in this manner an idea came to his mind and requested the money lender to have a bath in the river Godavari, take food and have your money. Money lender accompanied Namadevaji for a short distance. He thought I am a thin and weak person while Namadeva is a healthy and stout built person.He doubted that Namadeva may throw me in the river forcibly. He was much frightened and stop moving. Seeing this Namadeva catch hold his hand and took him in the river water. When he plunged in the water he reached some other place. This happened due to the miracle by Lord Vitthal. Money lender noticed a Musim king was sitting there. Actually Lord Vitthal was sitting in the shape of a king. He was seen surrounded by a beautiful garden and Darbar scenes of the king were visible. Money lender was upset to see all this. He remembered Namadeva. He prayed in his mind that if he could get rid of this situation he would never demand a single paise back from Namadeva. In the meantime he saw Namadeva there. To see him he cool down. The king requested him to take meals. The money lender said, Sir, being a Brahman, I cannot take food from a Muslim. If you wish to feed me you can give me some raw mate4ial to enable me to cook food for myself. His request was acceded. Before taking food he went to Godavari to take bath. The moment he plunged in the river he fell out of the Chanderbhaga. Now he found himself in Pandharpur. He was so confused that could not reach to some conclusion whether he is asleep or awakened. He left it to the God Almighty. From there he proceeded towards his house. He left the material there, which he got from the king. In a wet lion cloth he reached his residence. Family members inquired whether he has got the money or not? He said, thank God that my life is saved. He tried to clean the cloth in which he had kept the flour etc. A piece of cowdung fell down from its bundle of clothes. When he took it up, he was horrified to see that it was a gold. Seeing this he repented and said how foolish I am it would have been in the fitness of things, if I could have brought home entire lot of cowdungs. What, what to do now?[26]

One day Gonabai said to Namadeva Both of us are now aged. You are engaged in the contemplation of God. Day and night you mediate. Your thoughts are always occupied with his name form. Not for a moment do you think of yourself. You are holding the Lord of Pandhari in your heart. In your domestic life, we require everything but you have become indifferent to worldly things. What I can do? At these words of his parents he was agrieved and went to the temple. He bowed and prostarted before the God and said, " O Hari, who dwelled at Pandhari why didst thou put me in this domestic life? Why hast Thou deserted me in the sad sea of this worldly existence? Hearing Namadeva's pitious plea, God said to Him, "Who is that is troubling you? Namadeva said, O God, it is my parents who are troubling me".

A devotee named Parissa Bhagavat propiated Rukmini and got a stone which could convert iron into gold. Parissa's wife gave the stone to her friend, Rajabai one day. Rajabai showed the stone to her husband and said that his bhakti was of no use and was inferior to the bhakti of Parissa Bhagvat. Namadeva threw the stone into the river. Next day Parissa came to know of everything and took Namadeva to task. Namadeva showed Parissa the place where he had dropped the stone. Parissa searched for the stone and found not only one stone, but a whole lot. Parissa was wonder struck. He admitted the spirit of renunciation and the spiritual powers of Namadeva.

Namadeva felt it increasingly difficult to take interest in household affairs and in his parents, wife and children and no amount of persuation from all those people of his friends was successful in bringing him back to the worldly life. To him there was only one interest and that was Lord Vithoba. He used to spend time after sitting before Vithoba, talking to him, discussing spiritual matters with him and doing bhajan/kirtan. To Namadeva, Vithoba was the beginning and the end of every thing.

God Disguised as Keshav Shet

Namas wife experienced much trouble in her home, and said to her mother-in-law, For me you have given birth to a pure crystal but unfortunately our home is poverty stricken and I see no way to battering our domestic state. At this Lord of Pandhari had mercy on them and decided to visit them as a merchant by the name of Keshava. He filled a bag with gold coins and said to his eagle. Take the form of an ox and go to the house of Namadeva. On his way he asked the way to Namadeva's house. Hearing this question, the town people laughed. They said, There is no food to eat at Namadeva's house. Who can be this guest that has arrived". They added, Do you see younger Tulsi alter with bright banners; that is Namadeva's house. Keshav came outside Namadeva's house and Krishna said to Rajabai, "Some guests have come to your house". Hearing these words Rajabai was perplexed, "Where could a guest come from?" She, therefore, attempted to send him away and said, "The master of the house is not here." To the neighbours, who assembled, she said, "These guests have nearly taken my life; what am I to do?" Sri Hari was standing at the door and listened to this. He said loudly "My name is Keshav Shet, I love Namdev dearly and I have come with gold coins to help him. Hearing this Rajabai came outside and offered the guests a seat. The Lord Hari said to Rajabai, "Do not do anything now to trouble Namadeva". I have brought a bag ful of money. Give my regards to him. So saying Vithoba hastened to go away.

Gonabai's complaint to God

Gonabai had gone out, when Lord of the Lord visited her house as a Keshava Shet; and she knew nothing of what had happened. She had gathered some grain and was returning to her house. She thought to herself, "Namdeva has sulked and gone off. I will go to the temple, console him, and bring him back". Thus saying, she hastened to the great door of the temple. She bowed to the God on the eagle platform and saw God before her sight. Gonabai said, 'O God, turn Thy face this way towards me. Then hast Namadeva love Thee greatly, and so we are looking in our worldly affairs. By association with Thou, O God, he has neglected his house and business. By lack of things in our domestic life, we are laughed at by the evil mind. His wife is in great distress at home." God smiled at this and consoled Gonabai in various ways. However, Gonabai replied, 'O my life of the world. O Provider of the Universe, the Delight of the hearts give me my son Namadeva and let love of worship still remain.' Lord Hari remained silent. Gonabai then implored upon Satyabhama and Kalindi to have reasoning with Lord Keshava and tell him to free me from my trouble.

Gonabai then turned to Namadeva and said to him, "why are you sitting here? I will take you away by force in the very presence of the God." Gonabai said further, "O life of the world, Provider of the Universe, ornament of bhaktas why does my plea not come to your mind? Give Namadeva back to me and thus may Thy fame increase in the world." Hearing her say this, the Husband of Lakshmi spoke as follows:

Listen to me, Gonabai. Take your son and go away. You are making a vain attempt to frame a charge against me. Take your son and go back to your house."

As they walked along the road his mother said to Namadeva. You have deserted your business and have gone to the Lord of Pandhars as a supplaint." Hearing this charge of Gonabai Namadeva hung his head and tears of love flowed from his eyes.

Namadeva sickens of Fortune's sight

Rajabai started cooking many kinds of delicious food and said to herself. The life of the world has done a very remarkable thing. Namadeva saw with displeasure various pots and ornaments which had been given to his wife. Namadeva seeing this wealth became sad at heart. He asked his mother where has all this wealth come from? Namadeva's wife told him "God had bestowed all this as a favour". Namadeva enquired from his wife, where did you bring this bag full of wealth from?" Rajabai kept quiet but Janabai Nama's maid servant, related the whole story. On hearing this tears flowed from Namadeva's eyes. Praising God for his kindness and mercy, he called the Brahmans of the town and gave them the money, the ornaments and garments.[27]

Gora Tests Nama

There was the extraordinary story of how hands sprang from Gora's arms and now the husband of Rukmini brought back the dead child to life and gave it back to its parents. Gora then joined his hands palm to palm, and said to the saints come to my home and purify my abode. Seeing his great desire the saints replied that they would come and they at once set off. The Vaishnavas walked along to the home of Gora and were filled with joy while with love in his heart Gora bowed to them with love. Gora gave them grass mats to sit upon and began to wash their feet. And as he drank the water in which their feet were washed his mind felt satisfaction, worshipping them and using the sixteen materials, he gave them all a meal of six juices and the tulsi leaf for the purification of their mouths. Nivritti, Gyandeva, Sopan, Nama, Savata and other Vaishnavas, also Muktabai the store house of all goodness, all sat in their appointed places. Gyandeva now said to Gora, You have placed the jars (the saints) on their seats. Now separate those that are unbaked from those that are baked, and tell me your experience. Gyneshwar having saith this by his own reason Gora understood what he meant. Gora then took in his hand the potter's paddle, and with it he rapped the skull of all the saints who were present. All accepted it in silence. But when he reached Nama, he (Nama) cried out 'Why do you strike me needlessly? 'God replied' This vessel is as yet raw and unbaked. Muktabai said to him, O Gora, how did you know this? You are good and an expert examine. I have without a doubt discovered that Jewellers are expert in their examination of jewels, so also a potter by a mere glance recognize a jar (as baked or unbaked). A person sick with disease is easily recognized by a doctor, so you by a mere glance know what is baked and what is not baked. Listening to what she said, all the saints broke out into a hearty laugh. But Nama was sorry at heart and was much troubled. Therefore raising from the assembly, Namdev came to Pandharpur, and there meeting the Husband of Rukmini he began to tell him the secrets of his heart. His throat chocked and tears flowed from his eyes and he said to the God, 'I have been greatly insulted. My heart is full of anger. The life of the world laughed and gave Nama an embrace and said He, who insulted you? Please tell me without hesitation. Nama replied, O Harishi Keshi (the Lord of the heart), one should tell others of the praise he receives but the criticism he receives should be kept to himself.' The husband of Rukmini replied, I know the feelings of your heart. But I see no one so good and dear to me, aside from you. Do not be ashamed to tell your secrets to your dearest friend. Thus spoke Adhokshaja (Krishna) to Nama in love. Nama replied, Listen to my story, O God Gora - the potter, Thy bhakta, took all the saints to his house, and he did a very astonishing thing. He seated them upon grass mats and lovingly worshipped them. Then Gyandeva motioning to him said something to him. Gora than took his potter's paddle in his hand and rapped everyone on the head. All received it silently and no one replied to him. But when he came to rap me I was afraid, O Lord God, I said to him, after remembring Thy feet, "Go away". Hearing me say this, all the saints laughed, and Gyandev together with Muktabai began to make fun of me. Gora than said about me, He is still raw and unbaked "and all the saints still laughing I became ashamed. I then arose quickly and came to tell Thee. As Nama said this, Lord Krishna replied - You need a Guru.

Need of a Guru

The Life of the world said to Nama, what he has said about you is quite true. He who does not go as a suppliant to a guru is spoken of as one who is not ripe. As the holder of the disk (Krishna) said this to him Nama's spirit gave way. Just as salt dissolves in a moment when water is poured upon it; or as where water is poured upon sugar it at dissolves away so at the words of the cloud dark one (Krishna) the God loving bhakta became very troubled in thought. When a storm comes from the South, the clouds melt away so at the teaching of the Lord of the world Nama became sad. He then replied to God, 'I came here to tell

Thee my complaint, because I thought Thou wouldst take away my pain. But Thou hast shown me disfavour, and hast talked to me as they did. Now O Lord of the world, I know of no place to go to. If the earth feels troubled, where should the trees go? If a mother casts away her child, who will care for it? The Lord of Pandhari than said to Nama, 'Your heart and mine are one. Go now as a suppliant to a good guru and put an end to your thoughts on duality. Nama said, O God supreme, why do I need a Sadguru? Listening to Nama Lord Krishna replied 'O Nama, listen to me. When I was the avtar of Ram, I went as a suppliant to Vashishta to question on self knowledge. When I was the Krishna avatar, I went with reverence to Sandipani and from him I obtained self knowledge. So, if you will listen to me, you will to acceptable to all the saints. As the life of the world said this Nama grasped His feet.[28]

Meeting with Gyandeva

When Namadeva was about twenty years of age, he met the great saint Gyandev at Pandharpur. Gyandev was naturally attractive towards Namadeva as a great devotee Vithoba. He persuaded him to go with him to all the holly places on pilgrimage. Namadeva did not want to go as that would mean separation from Lord Vithal of Pandharpur. However, he agreed and accompanied Gyandeva on pilgrimage, which extended to all holy places in different parts of India.

Many miracles are associated with this holy pilgrimage when they reached the desert of Marwar. Namadeva became vey thirsty. With great effort, they found a well but the water was at such a low depth that it was impossible to get it.Gyandev proposed to assume the form of a bird by his Saghima Siddhi and bring the water up in his beak. But Namadeva proved superior to him. He prayed to Rukmini. The level of the water rose miraculously to the surface. The well is seen even today at Kaladji ten miles off Bikaner.

Namadeva and Gyandev came to Naganathpuri. Namadeva

started bhajan in the temple. There was a huge crowd. The temple priests were not able to enter the temple. So they became angry. Namadeva went to the western gate of the temple and spent the whole day in doing the kirtan. The image of the temple itself turned to his side.

A Brahman of Bidar invited Namadeva to sing bhajan in his house. Namadeva went there with a large number of devotees. The local sultan mistook them for rebel troops and sent General Kasi Pant against them. The General reported to the Sultan that it was only a religious party. But Sultan was adament and he ordered that Namadeva should be arrested and presecuted. Namadeva was put up before Sultan who asked him to embrace Islam or bring to life a butchered cow. Namadeva refused to embrace Islam and preferred to give life to the dead cow. Namadeva's mother was in great grief and advised Namadeva to embrace Islam but Namadeva did not relent. Namadeva raised the dead cow to life. The Sultan was struck with amazement and admiration.

Meeting with the great Contemporary Minds

During their extensive travelling, Namadeva and Gyandeva met Narsi Mehta at Junagadh, Kabir, Kamal and Mudgalcharya at Kashi. Tulsidas at Chitrakoot, Pipaji at Ayodhya. Nanak at a place in the Deccan and likewise Dadu, Gorakhnath and Matsyandernath in other places. The pilgrimage lasted for five years and during this period Gyandeva repeatedly advised Namadeva to adopt a Guru so that he might be in a position to realise completely the manifestation of the all pervading God.Namadeva did not relevant because he considered Vithoba his Guru and guide.

Adoption of a Guru

The author of the Bhakat Vijaya has related the story differently under the title of Gora tests Nama and Need of a Guru; which has already been mentioned in the previous pages of this book. This is another author's narration which I am also including for the information of the readers of this book.

One day, Gora another saint and a potter by trade, was asked to ascertain which of them were half baked, i.e. had not become a realised Brahman. Gora took a small flat wooden board such as he used to prepare or test the pots and began to put on the head of everybody. When he came to Namadeva and potted on his head, Namadeva cried aloud thinking he was hurt. Immediately, all others in the company began to laugh saying that Namadeva was only half baked and had not become fixed in his spiritual position. Greatly mortified Namadeva went to Vithoba and complained to Him of his humiliation. He said that he saw no necessity for him to have a Guru as he had intimate relationship with Lord Krishna himself. Lord Krishna said that Namadeva did not really know him. Namadeva protested Lord Krishna asked to identify him that day and Lord Krishna took the form of a Pythan and passed from that place. Namadeva could not recognise him. Lord Vithoba asked him to take a Guru and suggested him the name of Vishoba Khichar.

Vishoba Khichar was one of the disciples of Gyandev and was living at that time at a village called Avandhya. Namadeva proceeded to the village immediately and arrived there at about noon. He took shelter at a temple in order to take some rest. There he saw a man sleeping with his feet on the diety itself. Namadeva was shocked, woke up that man and rebuked him for this sacrilege. The man was no other than Visobha himself. Vithoba replied, "O Namadeva, why did you woke me up? Is there a single spot in this world which is not permeated by God? If you think that such a spot can be found, kindly place my feet there." Namadeva took the feet of Visobha in his hands and moved them to another direction, but the diety moved along with it. Namadeva could not find any direction or spot where he could place the feet of Visobha without treading on the diety. God was everywhere. He had his first lesson that God was everywhere. Visobha advised Namadeva, "If you want to be absolutely happy, fill this world with bhajan and the sacred Name of the Lord. The Lord is the world itself. Give up all ambitions and desires. Let them take care of themselves. Be content only with the name of Vithal. You need not undergo any hardship or penances in order to go to heaven. Vaskunth will come to you by itself. Do not be anxious of this life or of your friends or relatives. They are like the illusions of a mirage. One has to spend a short space of time here like the potter's wheel which goes on rotating even after the potter has left."

"Pandharpur was established on the bank of river Chandrabhaga as a sort of God for people to cross safely this occean of life. Pandharinath is the boatman. Incharge to take you to the otherside, and the most important point is that he does this without asking for any fee". In this way he has served millions of people who have gone to Him in surrender. If you surrender to Him, there is no death in this world". After initiation by Visobha, Namadeva became more philosphical and his vision was widened.[29]

Impact of Visoba Khechar on Namadeva

After meeting with Visoba Khicher Namadeva alienated from the worldly affairs. He started his whole time in the meditation of Vithoba and Kirtan. He devoted himself in the meditation of his Lord that he often forget to take meals. He never remember his parents and kith and kin.

This was the mental position of Namadeva. He was of the opinion that Vithal is every where. Namadeva always used to live in the vicinity of Lord Vithoba. To meditate and worship Vithoba was the mission of his life. In the public eyes he was known as a mad man. By tying a string of small bells worn round the ankle and had a kartal in his hands and Vina (a large instrument of the type of the lute) or lute player; a title of the goddess Saraswati as patron of the art) on his shoulders he used to meditate the God Almighty and devote his full time in Kirtan. He completely forgot his family life and responsibilities. His alienation from worldly affairs one day his mother Gonabai reminded him:-

"Namadeva!!! You know! you are my son that is why I am reminding you that you completely forgotten your responsibilities about your family and other family members and you have completely devoted yourself in the service of your God. I wonder, what you are demanding from him and what he will give you after, I don't know? Can't you see how the neighbours sons discharging their family responsibilities and on the contrary you are bent upon to spoil everything. You are such an unfortunate person that leaving aside everything you have devoted your entire energy in the service of Pandurang. You have gorgotten every thing - wife, children, parents, relatives and house hold responsibilities. I wonder, what kind of your meditation is? This attitude of yours have completely spoils the lives of entire family members.

Namadeva was the only son of Gonabai. He was the only hope of their old age and family members and he in the eyes of the world was functioning like a mad man. Seeing the deplorable condition of his only son Gonabai was terribly upset. She went to the temple and prayed the God Almighty, 'O Lord of Lords, kindly give me my Nama back to me, otherwise I will lay down my life beneath your feet.

The financial position of the family of Namadeva had gone bad to worse due to his twenty four hours devotion towards Vithal Bhagwan. The hut in which they were putting up was in a torn condition. In the absence of four walls the family members in general and children in particular have had to face chilly and hot winds. They were also short of proper clothing. Seeing her family members starving, Gonabai and Rajabai was much pained.

In one of his Abhang Rajabai had said:-

The wives of other person are laden with gold ornaments. On the contrary I have nothing to wear. My family is facing famine and I am unable to relate my misfortune to any one? Other women always wear beautiful clothes while I have to pass my life in torn clothes. My hut is also in bad shape, cold wind is unbearable. My griefs have no bound. I am much pained. I wonder to whom should I go to share my griefs? I do not know about the beautiful bedding and fine furniture. I have only one quilt in a very torn and bad condition. There is scarcity of food, clothes and utencils - but unfortunately my shameless husband even in these deplorable condition, forgetting his responsibility used to dance before the diety in the temple. Rajabai was unable to feed a family which was consisting on 14 persons. She was fed up with poverty. One day she planned to commit suicide along with her children. She alongwith Mahadev and Narayan (her sons) jumped into Chanderbhaga river. It is said that Vithal Bhagwan reached there to help and save them . Rajabai, pointing towards Vithal Bhagwan said - O, Lord Vithal what kind of Lord you are - neither you permit us to live like a human being nor you allow us to commit suicide? What kind of Bhagwan you are! tell me. When she was on way back home, she found a body of a cobra lying in the way. She took that while assuming that it contain poison. On reaching home after boiling it we all will take the poisonous soup and kill ourselves and get rid of the miserable condition. Reaching home he put it in a kettle for boiling. After sometime when she checked it, she found piece of gold instead of a cobra's body. In the meantime Namadevaji reached home and he distributed entire gold among the poor people.

Namadevaji's mother used to devotee her time in the meditation. His father Damseth also devoted his time in the service of the suffering mankind; though he was very cold. They were much worried and pained to see their only sons alienation from the world. They tried their level best to indulge their son in his family life but they miserably failed.

The wife of Namadevaji also meditate Vithal Bhagwan. She had also authored a few Abhangs. But she disliked Namadeva's always sitting in the temple. In her residence the sadhus of Barkari sampardai used to do bhajan/kirtan also. She also did not like that. Inspite of all her differences she had a great regards for Vitthal and Rukmini. One day Rajabai said to Rukmani, O Mother Rukmani, please ask Vithal Bhagwan to have mercy on him, and told him not to act as a mad man while in his meditation. Her requests to Rukumani fell on deaf ears. She also prayed her family Devtas, but of no use. Had quarrelled with Lord Vithal but without result. She failed on every front. In the end she vowed her head in the interests of her husband and started to devote her time in the meditation of her God. Gradually the parents of Namadeva and his sons devoted themselves in the meditation of Vithal Bhagwan. They all compromised with Namadeva and Vithal Bhagwan and became his disciples.

Now Namadeva had reached spiritually upto such an extent that no untowards incident, no short comings could frightened him because he had completely devoted his all senses in the lotus feet of Vithal Bhagwan. He was so devoted to his beloved Lord that his heart and soul had became pious, stable and fully satisfied. He had started distributing the pious Ganga of love and affection among the devotees of his Lord. Through his actions and deeds he had become a source of love and affection to everybody whosoever came in his contact, plunged in the sea of eternal peace of love and affection.[30-]

Notes and References

1. Cultural Heritage of India. Vol. IV - pp. 368-369.
2. The Spirit of Indian Culture. Saints of India pp. 145-146.
3. Ibid.
4. Max Arthur Macauliffe. The Sikh Religion, Vol. VI. pp. 17-18.
5. The Spirit of Indian Culture - Saints of India. pp. 146-147.
6. Ibid.
7. Namadev-Saints, Gurus and Mystics. pp. 236.

8. Mahipati - Bhakatvijaya - pp. 57-60.

9. Sant Namdev Charitavali K.G. Vankhede Guruji p. 38 (Hindi).

10. Saints and Sages of India (Authors Publishors) pp. 36-37.

11. Sant Namadeva's Chitravali by Vankheke Guruji - Sant Namadeva Shodh Sansthan - New Delhi.

12. Mahipati Bhakatvijaya - Appendix I.

13. Tukaram - Bhalchandra Nemade, Sahitya Akademi, New Delhi 1997.

14. Sant Namadeva Charitavali by Vankhede Guruji. Sant Namadeva Shodh Sansthan, New Delhi, 1983.

15. Namdev - The Saint - Poet: Edited by Jagan Nath. Namdev Mission Trust, New Delhi - An Article entitled Namdev - The Light Bearer by Madhu Mali, 1983, p. 35.

16. Sant Namdev Charitavali - Vankhede Guruji - Sant Namadev Shodh Sansthan, New Delhi, 1983 pp. 54.

17. Famous Indian Sages - Their immortal Messages - Dr. Vivek Bhattacharya. Sagar Publications, New Delhi, 1982 pp. 422-423.

18. Sant Namadeva Charitavali by Vankhede Guruji. Sant Namadeva Shodh Sansthan, New Delhi, 1983 pp. 55-56.

19. Mahipati - Bhakatvijaya pp. 227-228.

20. Sant Namadeva Wankhede Guruji - Publication Division. Govt. of India, 1970.

21. Namdev - The Saint Poet (Saint Poet of the People by Jagan Nath) Namdev Mission Trust, New Delhi, 1983, pp. 30-31.

22. Namdev - The Light Bearer by Madhu Malti (Namdev - The Saint Poet Ed. by Jagan Nath - Namdev Mission Trust, New Delhi, 1983, p. 34).

23. The Sikh Religion by Maculiffe, 1963. Bhagats of the Granth Sahib - Namdev.

24. Nahipati Bhakatvijaya.

25. The Spirit of Indian Culture - Saints of India (Saint Namadeva 1270 A.D. - 1350 A.D.) by Dr. Vivek Bhattacharya Metropolitan, Delhi 1980.

26. Sant Namadeva. Vankhede Guruji (Hindi) Publication Division, Ministry of Information and Broadcasting, Govt. of India, New Delhi, 1970, pp. 20-22.

27. Courtsy the author/publisher of the book entitled, Saints, Gurus and Mystics pp. 237-241.

28. Bhaktavijaya.

29. Courtsy the author/publisher of the book entitled, "Saints, Gurus and Mystics. pp. 241-244.

30. Sant Namadeva - Vankhede Guruji - Publication Division - Ministry of Information and Broadcasting, Govt. of India, New Delhi (Hindi).

Sant Gyaneshwar

(1275 A.D. - 1296 A.D.)

The oldest reliable biography of Jnaneshwar is written by his contemporary saint Namadeva. According to him Jnaneshwar's ancestors lived at Apegaon, on the bank of Godavari, 13 kilometers from Paithan, the then famous seat of Sanskrit learning in the Deccan. Jnaneshwar's grandfather, Govindpant and grandmother, Nirai were disciples of Gorakhnath. This pious couple got a son and named him Vithal after their dear deity of Pandharpur.

Vitthalpant had a deep religious bent of mind from his boyhood. He studied sacred sanskrit scriptures and with the permission of his parents went on a pilgrimage. He happened to visit Alandi, situated on the bank of Indrayani, 21 kilometers from the present Pune city and had darshan of Siddeshwar Siddhopant, the kulkarni of Alandi gave his daughter Rukmini in marriage to Vitthalpant. The married couple went to Apegaon and lived happily for some years gladdening the hearts of their parents. After the death of his parents, both of them went to stay at Alandi.

Gradually Vitthalpants' heart became restless. He yearned for self realisation. One day he left his wife, went to Varanasi and got himself initiated as a sanyasi by one Sripadswami who named him Chaitanya. After this incident Sripadswami left Varanasi for pilgrimage and on his way visited Alandi. There Vitthalpant's wife Rukmini was circumbulating a sacred Aswatha tree. When she saw Sripadswami she bowed down to his feet. Swami gave her blessings saying: "Let pious sons be born to you". But to his dismay Swami found on the face of Rukmini only the sign of ironical smile that concealed her hearts anguish. When he knew the cause of her grief he was reminded of his new disciple and wondered whether he was the same person for whom Rukmini was pinning. He returned to Varanasi. After inquiry he was convinced that Chaitanya was no other than Vitthalpant. He ordered him to give up sanyas, to go back to Alandi and had a householder's life with his wife. He gave his blessings saying Don't fear, God will always help you. So Vitthalpant returned home and led the life of a householder.

Orthodox Brahmins of Alandi excommunicated him and he was greatly harassed for having given up sanyas. Twelve years passed and Rukmini gave birth to three sons and a daughter. Nivrittinath was born in Saka 1195 (1273 A.D.), Jnaneshwar in Saka 1197 (1275 A.D.), Sopendeva in SAka 1199 (1277 A.D.) and Muktabai in Saka 1201 (1279 A.D.). All these children were pious spiritual gems but orthodox people of Alandi thought it a bad omen even to look at them. Dejected with these adverse circumstances, Vitthalpant went to Tryambakeshwar (near Nasik) with his wife and children when Nivrittinath happened to enter a cave where Gahininath dwelt and was initiated by him. When returning to Alandi, Vitthalpant asked the Brahmins to tell him some way of atonement. He was told that there was no other remedy except sacrificing his life. So one day, leaving his wife and children he went to Prayag and ended his life by throwing himself into the sacred Ganga. Some months later Rukmini also follwed her dear husband and did the same thing. Yet the orthodox Brahmins were not satisfied. They wanted a certificate of purification from the Pandits of Paithan. Nivrittinath, with his brothers and sister went to Paithan accordingly. But the Pandits ridiculed them. It is said that they were silenced only when Jnaneshwar caused a buffalo to recite Vedic hymns in their presence.

While returning to Alandi all of them halted at Newase on the bank of Pravara in the present Ahmedanagar district. There on the command of his brother and Guru, Nivrittinath, Jnaneshwar delivered extempore the exposition of Shrimad Bhagvadgita in Marathi. It was taken down by his disciple Sachhidanand Baba. This happened in Saka 1212 when Jnaneshwar was only a lad of fifteen. After this commentary called Jnaneshwari, Jnaneshwar also wrote an independent Philosophical work Amritanubhava.[1]

From there they hastened to return to the town of Alandi. Muktabai said to Nivritti, We must see the place where we were born. When all arrived at Alandi, all people there felt very happy. With feelings of love they worshipped their feet and embraced them. The people had already heard what had happened at Paithan. In addition Sopan showed to the Brahmans the letter he had brought with him. Listening to it all were amazed. It was clearly written in the letter that the three brothers were the incarnation of god. Hearing this, the Brahmans were lost in wonder and accepted the contents.[2]

Namadeva and Gyandeva go together on Pilgrimage

Once Gyandeva came to Pandhari and conceived the desire meeting with Namadeva. When he entered into the house of Namadeva he saw him from a distance. Namadeva paid his obeisance to him and embraced him. He worshipped him with ritual and said, I am fortunate enough today as a genious among the wise men has very kindly visited my house. I have the honour to meet Pandurang in a visible form.

During this pilgrimage they used to discuss various aspects of meditation. Namadeva put his doubts before Gyandeshwar and he replied them. Gyaneshwar asks about 'Bhakti' from Namadeva. To this request of Gyaneshwar, Namadeva gave reply, 'Listen then with reverence to my experience. One should have the determination to be indifferent to all earthly passions. One should have unchanging compassion on every creature. One should not have the troublesome thought of 'I am thou'. One should not have any perplexities about the earthly life. As soon as one reaches this condition his worship may be called pure. And if he does not have those characteristics, why adop useless means of acquiring them. One can bow outwordly and at the same time remember the faults of the person bowed to; just as a man with keen appetite may eat dainty food along with - fly in it. Not to have in mind the superior and the common, that should be regarded as unceasing worship, for there is no cessation of the supreme divine joy in the heart. God fills the universe. He pervades the universe. With that fixed thought, one should keep his mind steady. This is called contemplation, and it is an everlasting cloud of joy. Namadeva's method of Bhakti is never understood by others.

Such were their daily and occassional discussions, as they walked along full of joy. Suddenly in their wanderings to sacred places they arrived at Hastanapur (Delhi). Namadeva in his love was singing of God's goodness. As he came near the city every one looked at him. As they listened to Nama's most unusual expression of love, they prostrated themselves before him. Having heard of Namadeva's kirtan an innumerable number of people gathered.

Mohammad Tughluq (1325 A.D. - 1350 A.D.) was the king of Delhi. When he came to know about the arrival of Namadeva in the capital and the impact of his kirtan on the general public he got angry. He decided to meet Namadeva personally. One day, suddenly the king reached the Kirtan Place. At that time Nama who was filled with love, as he was describing the attributes of Shri Hari. The sky reverberated with the sound of the cymbals, the drum and vina. To that was added the loud hand clapping. The enthusiasm was without limit. Now what did that King do in the midst of the enthusiastic kirtan? He killed a cow. And he said to Nama, "What is it you are singing, you heretia? If you will raise this cow again to life. I shall regard your songs as true. If you do not bring the cow to life, I shall kill you with my own hand.' When this evil doer said this, the men and women became greatly concerned. Their minds were thrown into confusion and the enthusiasm of love melted away. They sat silent in their places, as they could do nothing else before the king. The King said to Nama, tell me when are you going to raise this cow to life? Give me some evidence of your truth, and then go on praising Hari'. The noble Vaishnava having heard him replied, 'O king, it will certainly take me four days from today to do it. Having heard him saying this, the king went back to his palace. Namadeva brought Hari to his mind and earnestly asked Him to come to his help. Thus Namadeva filled with enthusiasm of love expressed his mournful thoughts in the midst of the kirtan. His throat choked with emotions. Tears flowed from the eyes. The large assembly of those who came to hear him began also to weep. For a whole day they sat there. Namadeva took the heard of the cow in his lap and wept. He cried out and said, 'O Lord of Pandhari, Shri Hari come quickly to help me. The earth was sprinkled by the tears that fell from his eyes. Hearing his moving appeals the God Almighty immediately came and manifested Himself in Namadeva's heart. He at once raised the cow to life and then said to Namadeva, Awake to consciousness and opened his eyes and looked, the cow was sitting besides him raised to life.

Seeing this amazing thing, the people reported the matter to the King. Hearing this most extraordinary news the king arrived on the scene. Seeing the cow whose head he had cut off now raised to life, the king made namaskar to Namadeva. All the people felt great joy and exclaimed Namadeva arose and revently worshipped Lord Krishna. (Courtesy - Mahipati - Bhakatvijaya).[3]

Notes and References

1. Devotional Poets and Mystics Part I (Cultural Leaders of India) - Jnaneshwar by B.P. Bahirat - Publication Division, Ministry of Information and Broadcasting, Govt. of India, New Delhi, 1983.
2. Mahipati - Bhakatvijaya.
3. Ibid.

Journey to Religious Places

Vankhade Guruji in his book Sant Namadeva tatha unka Hindi Sahitya has related an interesting story regarding the pilgrimaes of Namadev alongwith Sant Gyaneshwar as under:-

One day Sant Gyaneshwarji saw in a dream while he was sleeping during night time in the Alandi area.He saw in the dream that he has been surrounded by a group of most beautiful and uptodate women. When Gyaneshwarji inquired them about their whereabouts, one of the lady said, 'I am Krishna, this is Yamuna,' This is Ganga, this is Bhagirathi and this is Saraswati. Whatsoever pilgrim places are there, those exists in all of us. Gyaneshwarji further enquired from them, how and why you have took trouble to come to this place. They replied - Gyaneshwarji, you are fully aware that all sinful wicked and guilty persons to get rid of their sins take bath in the pilgrim places. We all are over burdened with the load of their sins. This load has increased manifold and we are unable to bear that. That is why we have come to you with the request that for God sake, please do come to have bath in us, so that we may get rid of this unbearable load of sinners. Saying so, all those gentle ladies disappeared from the scene.

One day Sant Gyaneshwar dreamt to go on for pilgrimage of all the pilgrim places. He disclosed this idea to Nibritinath, Sopandev, and to Muktabai; who were brothers and sister of Sant Gyaneshwar and used to live with him. When Gyaneshwar determined to go on pilgrimage he thought that it would be in the fitness of things if some Bhagvad devotee could accompany us.He immediately decided to include Namadevji in this pilgrimage. On one auspicious day they started their journey and after some days they reached Pandharpur.

In one of his Abhang Namadevaji has narrated this incidence of meeting with Sant Gyaneshwar as follows:-

"Gyaneshwarji went to meet Namadevji. Namadevji with due regards and embrace welcomed them with Arti and proper worship. Namadeva said, today I am very happy and my mission in life has been fulfilled, because I happened to see and meet Sant Gyaneshwarji at my residence.

Gyaneshwarji said to Namadeva that to show the real path to those who have completely indulged themselves in the materialistic world - is only duty of yours. So, please accompany us in this pilgrimage.

After this meeting they departed from Pandharpur. From Mangalweda the discipile of Namadeva namely Chokhamela also accompanied them. From Aaran Madi, Sawanta Mali, from Pandharpur Narhari Sunar, also accompanied them.

They saw many sacred bathing places in the different countries through which they hastened. They visited Badrikaashram in the Himalaya and arrived in the Himalaya mountains. They visited Jagannath of Odhya where God lives in the form of Buddha; and even in the Kali Yuga seemingly impossible miracles still take place here today. After visiting Onkar and Amaleshwar they reached Kedarnath. From there they visited Mahakaleshwar at Ujjain. After seeing that place they came back and visited Paralivalijnath and arrived at Somnath. Their next place was the mountain of Shri Shaila where the Husband of Parvati lives (in a Shiva temple). For sixty years he had been waiting for these bhakats to come there. After visiting this place they hastened on to see Ghrishneshwar. I am not able properly to describe the great glory of the sacred bathing place Saval. From there they came to Nasik and Trimbak where they bathed in the Kushavart pond. After worshipping the five faced one (Shiva) they departed from there.

They had a view of the western ocean and then arrived at Bhimashankar where they worshipped Janardan. From there they started for Rameshwarm. After that they visited Ayodhya, Mathura, Kanti, Banaras, Dwarawati, Avanti and Maya, the seven cities as givers of salvation, were lovingly visited with repentant hearts.

Nama and Gyaneshwar at Nagnath

After visiting Rameshwarm both returned from there. The God loving bhakats Nama and Gyandev, finally arrived at Nagnath. The fourteenth of the dark half of the moon in the month of Magh (February) is the special night for the festival in honour of Shiva. On such an occasion Nama and Gyandev arrived at that place.

Namadeva then stood before the main gate of the temple and started a kirtan. He took in his hands the cymbals and vina and loudly shouted the names of God. Bringing into his mind the image of Vitthal he closed both his eyes. He had no longer the least consciousness of possessing a body. He put aside the thoughts of honour and insult and the proud ways of men. He put aside every form of desire and in his love performed the kirtan. A great crowd of people came with the desire to listen. In listening to God's goodness, in their joy of love, tears fell from their eyes. Their throats choked with emotion. As they listened to the character and deeds of Shri Hari they all lost consciousness of body. As they brought into their minds the Lord of the world, they clapped their hands in joy, they shouted aloud the names of Vitthal and their minds were unable to contain their happiness.

Brahmans angry with Namadeva

When Namadeva's kirtan was going on the Brahmans came from bathing and reached the main gate of the temple. They saw there Nama was performing his kirtan, singing and dancing in the joy of love. An enormous number of people were assembled there and the Brahmans could see no way of getting through them. They were filled with anger and spoke roughly to the people. They shouted at them. Why are you singing here uselessly? Such doings are acceptable at Pandhari only. Nagnath does not enjoy such things. Go off to Pandhari and have dance there putting aside all shame. On the out brusts of the Brahmans the people assembled there, replied, you should bear in mind that Hari and Hara (Vishnu and Shiva) are not different from one another. Listening these words the Brahman lost their temper and said, These low cast people with pride in their hearts are preaching to us. We do not approve of the principles preached by Nama. Now get away from here at once. If not agreed we shall punish you. No one responded to their threat. We have already been delayed in our worship of Shiva and there is no way open for us to go into the temple, said one. Another said, Beat out Nama at once Brahmans suddenly walked into the midst of Nama's kirtan. Addressing angrily they said toNama, why are you needlessly making all this noise here? Now go and stand at the back of the temple, and there you may sing without any shame. Namadeva having listened to their demand, bowed to the Brahmans. He replied, 'I will do so'. And the noble Vaishnava went away from there. The enthusiasm of the kirtan immediately melted away, and the people followed him. In company with Namadeva they retired behind the temple of Shiva, and sat down there for kirtan. But one thing was lacking there. Nagnath was facing the other way. He has turned his back on this kirtan in honour of Hari. I do not know what wrong has been committed by me. Why does not the Husband of Rukmini came to my aid? Why does he hold his anger against me? Lord Shiva is sitting in His temple, with his back turned towards me. Now look upon me with the eye of mercy and come to my help, O Lord of the Universe. Thus Nama full of love, mournfully pleaded in the midst of his kirtan. Suddenly an extra ordinary wonderful thing took place there.

The temple facing East turns West

The temple that had faced the east, suddenly turned around to the west. Every one present there expressed their astonishment. Seeing how forceful and great was the bhakti of Nama, the people became full of joy. Nama remarked to them, The doer of this is the merciful Shri Hari. This most extraordinary kirtan of Nama was seen as being performed in front of the temple with the joy of love. After the worship the Brahmans came out of the temple and saw the kirtan of Nama was being performed in front of the temple with the joy of love. After taking bath when they sought to make oblation to the sun, then they remarked The sun seems to have arisen in the west or we have lost all sense of direction. Everything was there it was the temple alone that had turned and was now facing Nama.

Repentence of the Brahmans

Seeing this, the Brahmans were astonished and remarked. Even Brahmadev and the other God could not understand the limits of Nama's power. Being proud of our own deeds, we have needlessly punished him. Thus repentant they came to the place where the kirtan was being performed. The Brahmans pointing towards Nama said, our whole hearted blessing to you being a real God living noble Vaishanav - the incarnation of Udhav. This we now truly understand. The miracle performed and shown to us by you is never seen by us. O Nama, blessed in your mother. They paid their obeisance to Nama.

When the Brahmans of Pratisthan (Paithan) persecuted Gyaneshwar, then he made the buffalo repeat the Vedas. In the same manner you made possible the impossible thing. You have actually turned the temple of the Shiva round. Nama then opened his eyes and became choked with emotion. He with greatest regards made a prostrate namaskar and then distributed the sweetmeats. The temple of Lord Shiva that was turned round about that time is even in the same direction today. As among all the gods, the Husband of Rukmini is the most supreme, similarly among all the Vaishnavas, Nama bhakat stands first.[2]

Gyandev and Namadeva went to Pandhari

In the previous pages you have read a delightful and moving story of how the temple of Avandhya Nagnath was turned round and how when all the Brahmans witnessed the marvel they were overcome with amazement. After Gyandev and Namadeva had made a namaskar to the Lord of the heaven Kailash, both left that place and returned to Pandhari. When they approached Pandhari they saw the dome from a distance. As soon as they saw Pandhari they made a prostate namaskar. They embraced one another and both felt very happy and performed kirtan in Honour of their beloved Hari. Reaching at the main gate of the temple, they again made a prostrate namaskar. On the door steps of the temple Nama fell down there and became unconscious. Gyandev helped him to regain his consciousness. When they entered their Lords' bed room they vowed their hands. It is said that the Lord of the Lords descended from His throne and came forward to meet them and embraced Nama. Seeing his Lord he filled with emotions and could not control his tears. He placed his head on the lotus feet of his god almighty and spoke with a sweet voice. O Lord of the Lords I am dead tired. Please have mercy upon me. Being an ignorant man, I am wondering from place to place but I fail to see even in my dreams as best as Pandhari. No doubt, India is full of sacred bathing places with high reputation, but I am sentimentally attached to the Chandrabhaga. To this the Lord Vitthal replied, I was also upset. I could not sleep properly while waiting for you; Nama when you were far away, this place called Pandhari seemed a desolate city. But my heart never forgot you a single moment.

In the meantime some noble Vaishnavas came to see Him; Nivritti and Gyaneshwar, Sopan, Visoba Khecher and Narhari. They prostrated on the ground and embraced Nama.

Nama was advised by his god that to complete his

pilgrimage you must feed Brahmans. It is said that Lord Krishna went himself alongwith Nama to invite Brahmans. After the grand feast Lord Krishna with his own hands gave gifts to this servant of Vishnu.

Krishna shook the Brahmans when He ate with a feeling of foodness what Nama had left on his plate. Seeing this, all the Brahmans were astonished, and feeling shocked they hung their heads down. The Brahmans considered it a strange act, and discussed it among themselves. What are we to think about it? He has truly violated the religious rules His doings are unfathomable. He seemed different from the four castes. How is it that we forgot this when seeing His acts that are beyond comparison? Now we must regard this as certain that He is Nama's mother and father and that He loves him in body, mind and speech. He took the rice in His yellow garments and sprinkled it over Nama's head, and when the offering of food to the god was to be performed He made him the leader in it.[3]

Macauliffe has related the story of Namadevas journey to religious places in the following words:-

Gyandev[1] a disciple of Vishoba Khechar, hearing of the fame of Namdev, went to Pandharpur to visit him. Gyandev was a Vedantist and pantheistic philospher who relied on knowledge, while Namdev was thoroughly convinced of the superiority of devotion of spiritual love to one God. The Brahmans deem Vedantism more orthodox as having been originally propounded in works which they accept as divine revelation. When a man becomes a Vedantist, he rejects religious observances and believes himself saved during life. Namdev now totally repudiated this belief. At the same time there was nothing to hinder a Pantheist from consorting with a monotheist and both saints became fast friends; Gyandev proposed to him that they should go together to visit holy places. Namdev replied that he was in the hands of Vitthal, and his permission must first be obtained. This preliminary having been arranged, Namdev fainted at the thought of leaving his God. Gyandev tried to console him, and said that as he was incarnation of Vitthal, the god could have no cause for regret.

In the course of their conversation Gyandeva asked him to indicate the way of devotion and explain how man could make Vitthal his own. Namdev replied, The strength of contempt of the world should be in the body as an unchanging companion. Man should lay aside the difference between himself and others and feel no anxiety for things of this world.

The object of the saints was most probably rather a thirst for information than a desire to make a religious pilgrimage. Had the latter been their object, they would have gone first to Banaras and endeavoured to obtain the hall-mark of orthodoxy and the favour of the great Hindu priests who resided there. The two saints set out from Pandharpur to Hastinapur, the name by which Dihli was then known. The Emperor Muhammad bin Tughlak hearing of Namadev's influence with the people, and suspecting that it would lead to an insurrection, resolved to arrest his career. The following hymn in the Bhairo measure gives the result:—

The emperor said, Ho, you Nama.
Let me see the deeds of your God.
The emperor had Nama arrested—
Let me see your God Vitthal;
Restore to life this slaughtered cow,
Otherwise I will strike off thy head on the spot.
Your majesty, how can that be?
No man can reanimate what is slaughtered.
All I could do would be of no avail;
What God doeth taketh place.
The emperor fell into a passion,
And set a huge elephant at Nama.
Nama's mother began to cry—

Why dost thou not abandon the God of the Hindus and worship the God of the Musalmans?

Namdev: I am not thy son, nor art thou my mother;

Even though I perish, I will sing Gopd's praises.

The elephant struck him with his trunk.

But Nama was saved by the protection of God.

The king said, The Qazis and the Mullas salute me,

But this Hindu trampleth on mine honour.

The Hindus said, O king, hear our prayer;

Take Nama's weight in gold.

If I take a bribe I shall go to hell;

Shall I amass wealth by abandoning my faith?

While Nama's feet were being chained

He sang the praises of God and beat time with his hands.

The Ganges and the Jamna may flow backwards,

But Nama will repeat God's name.

When seven gharis were heard to strike,[1]

The Lord of the three worlds had not yet arrived.

God afterwards came mounted on His garur.

Which beat the air with its wings.[1]

He took compassion on His saint.

And came mounted on His garur,

Say but the word and I will turn the earth on its side;

Say but the word and I will upturn it altogether.[2]

Say but the word and I will restore the dead cow to life.

So that every one may behold and be convinced.

Nama said, Spancel the cow.[3]

They put the calf to her and milked her.

When the pitcher was filled with the milk the cow gave,

Nama took and placed it before the emperor

And the time of trouble came on him

He implored Namdev through the Qazis and the Mullas—

'Parden me, O Hindu, I am thy cow.'

Nama said, Hear, O monarch,

Hath this credential been exhibited by me?
The object of this miracle is
That thou, O emperor, shouldst walk in the paths of truth and humility—
Namdev, *God* is contained in everything.
The Hindus went in procession to Nama.
And said, If the cow had not been restored to life,
People would have lost faith in thee.
The fame of Namdev remained in the world;
He took saints with him to salvation.
All trouble and sorrow befell the revilers—
Between Nama and God there is no difference.

Namdev continued to preach that God and his idol were one, as holy water and ordinary water have the same appearance, as a lamp and its light, as a flower and its fragrance, as the sun and its rays, as the cloud and water, as sweetmeats and their taste as a musical instrument and its melody, as an object and its shadow are all inseparable. His teaching again involved Namdev in serious difficulty, and he had to hastily retreat to save himself from the indignation and violence of the Muhammadans.

Namdev and Gyandev next proceeded to Kashi (Banaras) where they met the renowned Sanskrit scholars of the age. Thence they travelled to Priyag. Thence they went to Gaya, where Budha in days long past performed his heroic penance and renunciation. Thence the two saints proceeded to Ajudhia the birthplace of the god Ram Chandar. They then went to Mathura, the birthplace of the god Sri Krishan, thence to Gokal and Bindraban, thence to Jagannath, the temple of the lord of the world, on the shore of the Bay of Benal. From there they made the long journey to Dwaraka by the shore of the Arabian Sea, the scene of Krishan's retreat from the battle in which he was defeated by King Jarasandh.

The two saints having thus proceeded to the utmost limit of India resolved to begin their homeward journey, and in due time reached Marwar. They tarried for a night in Kolad, probably the modern Koilath near Bikaner. Here occurred an incident which is related by the Marathi chronicler. Namdev and Gyandev both felt thirsty. There was a well in the neighbourhood, but it was very deep and they had not the means of drawing water. It is said that Gyandev by the aid of jog science assumed a minute body descended into the well, and quenched his thirst. He then challenged Namdev either to assume a minute body and descend into the well or drink water from his hands. Namdev who was no believer in the efficacy of jog, declined the challenge, and said that if his god Vishoba were there, he would supply him with water. Upon this, it is said, the well filled to the brim with sweet water and Namdev's desires were in every way gratified.

Namdev and Gyandev then departed for Rameshwar in the extreme South of India, memorable as the place whence Ram Chandar set out on his expedition to Ceylon. After seeing the temple of Oamkar the two saints proceeded to Kalapadhara and thence to Dhara. In the latter place they visited the temple of Audhiya Nagnath. When Namdev arrived at the temple, he began to sing hymns with a loud voice. This attracted a crowd of people, so that the Brahman ministrants could not gain entrance without suffering the pollution of being touched by men of lower caste, deemed unworthy of salvation. Upon this they asked Namdev to cease singing and retire to a spot at the rear of the temple where he might continue his ministrelsy if he chose. Namdev told them that in God's temple there were no higher or lower castes, and that no one's touch could soil those who performed heartfelt worship. The Brahmnans were not convinced; they struck Namdev, deprived him of his cymbals and insisted that he should leave the temple. He went and sat down behind it and thus addressed God, I have no asylum but in Thee, and I want nothing if Thou show Thyself to others and not to me, lend Thine ear at least to my songs. He then began to sing verses full of self-reproach and abasement.

It is said that God, on hearing Namdev's tuneful worship,

was moved with kindness and compassion, and caused the temple to turn round so that the door remained opposite His saint. Namdev has versified the incident in the following hymn in the Rag Malar:—

> I went, O Lord, with laughter and gladness to Thy temple,
>
> But while Nama was worshipping, the Brahmans forced him away.
>
> A lowly caste is mine, O King of the Yadav,[1] why was I born a calico-printer?
>
> I took up my blanket,went back.
>
> And sat behind the temple
>
> As Nama repeated the praises of God
>
> The temple turned towards His saint.

Namdev returned to the subject in the following hymn in the Bhairo measure:—

> Forget me not, forget me not.
>
> Forget me not, O God!
>
> Those misled Brahmans of the temple were all furious with me;
>
> Calling me a Sudar they beat me and turned me out; what shall I do, Father Vitthal?
>
> If Thou give me salvation when I am dead, nobody will be aware of it; save me now.[2]
>
> If these pandits call me low, then, O God, Thine honour will be in the background.
>
> Thou who art called the compassionate and the mericful, altogether unrivalled is Thine arm—
>
> God turned round the front of the temple towards Nama, and its back towards the pandits.

From Audhiya Nagnath the party proceeded to Paithan. Salivahan's capital on the margin of the Godavari in the present state of Haidarabad, and thence to Deogiri, once the capital of the Maratha kingdom in the vicinity of the famous caves of Ellora, where they met Sadhna, who hospitably entertained them and then joined them in their peregrinations. They visited several places in the neighbourhood of Nasik, and thence proceeded to Junagarh in the Province of Kathiawar.[4]

Notes and References

1. Vankhede Guruji - Sant Namdeva tatha unk, Hindi Sahitya New Delhi Prakashan Vibhag of Suchna Aur Prasaran Manatralaya, Bharat Sarkar, New Delhi, 1970.
2. Mahipati - Bhakatvijaya.
3. Ibid.
4. Max Arthur Macauliffe. The Sikh Religion - Its Gurus, Sacred writings and Authors.

Namadeva in the Punjab
(1325 A.D.)

While travelling in Northern India Namdeva reached in a village named Bhattipal in the year 1325 A.D. when he was about 55 years old. He used to stay outside the village. One day a women was going to her fields to serve his husband with food. She met Namdeva in the way. She was so impressed to see him that she offered the food to Namdeva. As courtesy Namdeva took a small portion of food for himself and the remaining one she took for her husband. In the manner she started daily feeding Namdev.

One day she was late to bring food. Namdevaji enquired the reason of delay. She told, Maharaj! there is no well in the village. I have had to go a far off place to bring drinking water. That is why I am late today. After digging the soil Namdevaji prepared a well to enable the people to have drinking water. The same well still exists.

It was harbouring time of the wheat crops. Every body was busy. One person approached Namdevaji and requested him to help in harbouring the crop. Namdevaji started cutting the crop. When the work was over, everybody started making bundles and took the bundles on their heads. In this work one person Jallo was also involved. The farmers taking the bundles was proceeding towards their homes. Namdevji was following them. Jallo was so impressed by the personality of Namdeva that he became his disciple.

Arrival in Ghumman

Reaching Ghumman Namadev went to a nearby jungle. At

that time Ghumman was not a town. It was surrounded by a dense jungle. Even in day time one could listened the roars of wild animals. Namdeva used to stay there. With wild fruits he used to fill his empty stomach. When after leaving village Bhattiwal he stayed near Ghumman, the residents of the said village were terribly upset. One day some villagers while grazing their cows and buffalows reached there. After meeting Namdevaji there they were much pleased. Jallo had permanently settled there and devoted himself in the service of his guru.

Just across the river Satluj there was a village in the Doaba area named Ghurachi. In this village Ghumman caste Jats were putting up. Once upon a time there was a famine in the area. The residents started leaving the village. After travelling a long distance the people reached to this place where now Ghumman situated. The place was full of greenery, therefore they decided to settled there. They were even not aware of the owner of the land. They were also afraid whether the owner of the land may evict them from there. One day while grazing their animal they went to Namdevaji. Assuming Namdev as owner of the land they said, we are outsider in this area and we are famine stricken. Please allow us to stay here for a few days. Namadeva said Yes you can stay here without any fear. The people constructed hutments there. They also constructed a beautiful Kutiya for Namadevaji. Jallo used to devote his full time in the service of Namadevaji.

This piece of land was the property of the Rajputs of village Madi. When they came to know they reached at the spot and inquired that who had permitted you to settle here? They apprised them that we are Jats of Doaba area and victim of famine and living with this saint. Listening this they thought that how can we remove them from here? They approached Namadevaji. Namdevaji told them that they are famine victims. You should help them. The Rajputs replied that we don't want anything from them but in case we need milk or curd they have to supply us. This was settled amicably.

Among these Jats of Ghumman who were putting up in this jungle there was an old man named Sallo. He was the chief of these Jats. He had a son name Ghirnar who used to graze cows throughout the day. He had great regards for Namadevji. During summer season the rehabilitants had to face shortage of drinking water in this area. Both the father and the son had to go alongwith their cows and buffalows for feeding water to them. One day during noon Sallo and Ghirna were going alongwith their animals. It was burnign heat. They were covered with sweat. The dried pool of Namadevaji was filled with water after minor digging. They started bathing and feeding water to their animals from this tank.

The Rajput Gujjar of village Madi was a glorious person. He was the owner of this piece of land. He had a daughter. Her marriage was arranged on that occasion he required milk and curd. According to the agreement the villagers of Madi demanded these items. The Jats were fed up of the day to day demands of the Rajput's. The Jats planned to cut joke with these Rajputs. They filled up the pots with cow dung and pour a small portion of milk and curd on it and sent these pots to them. They accepted these pots with great pleasure. When they opened these pots their anger needs no bound. They fully armed started to attack them. When this news reached in the Jat campus they were much frightened. They rushed to Namdevaji for help. They apprised Namdevaji about the entire incident. He consoled them. They fought each other. A number of Jats killed in this dispute. Ghirna was killed in this battle. It is said, that where the memorial had been built up, this is the same place where battle took place. It is also said that Ghirna continued the fight even without his head. Rajput fled the place after their defeat outside the Madi village the body of Ghirna had fallen. The same place had been marked the boundary of the village when the villagers of Ghrachi came to know about this battle a number of them reached there for permanent settlement.

Alongwith these Jats a Mirasi (Bard) named Jamman had

also came. He was a fool by birth. One day he approached Namadevaji and as a joke or to test His spiritual power he put a branch of Beri tree in the earth and requested Namadeva to convert it in life and greenery. He was admonished several times but with no result. He stayed there for complete three days without eating any thing and water. It is said that ultimately this branch of Beri tree started sprouting. Even today this Beri tree is known as Khundi Sahib.

The place where Ghuman village has been set up, there was a dense jungle at that time. Namadevaji after constructing a small hut had started his religious preaching. It is said that the place where Namadevaji's temple exists these days this is the same place where first hut (Kutiya) was constructed by Namadevaji. Some Akalis of Punjab are of the opinion that the place behind Namadevaji's temple and called 'Taptyana' Namadevaji used to meditate at this place. A few years ago a Gurdwara has also been constructed. But there is no mention of any meditating place in any of the old books.

Regarding Namadev Memorial Temple of Ghuman, one renowned author Bhai Kahn Singh of Nabha has mentioned in his dictionary that this temple was constructed by Jassa Singh Ramgarhia in the year 1770 A.D. There is a mention of this Gurdwara in Gurubilas. Guru Hargobind the sixth Sikh Guru has been kind enough to offer some gifts to this Gurdwara. The Babas of Ghuman are of the opinion during Muslim period 'Alamshah' who was known as Allaudin had constructed this temple. To meet the requirements of drinking water a well was also digged up. In the Samvat 1503 (Vikarmi), the foundation of the temple was laid down. Afterwards a tank was also dug there. According to the elders of Ghumman that this work was done in the presence of Namadevaji. But according to historical facts it did not seen correct, as there is no document is available to support these views.

After staying in Northern India for a few years and preaching Varkari Sampardayas ideals, returned to Pandharpur. (Source : Sant Namadeva by Vankhede Guruji)

Contemporary Saints of Namadevaji Maharaj

Hazrat Nizamuddin Auliya

(1238 A.D. - 1325 A.D.)

The greatest saint of the 14th century was Nizamuddin Auliya. He was one of the greatest saints of the land. During his long life of eighty seven years the saint made Delhi the spiritual centre of attraction for thousands. Even today the Dargah of Nizamuddin is a holy pilgrimage for people belonging to different religions. He was the greatest among the desciple of Baba Farid (1173 A.D. - 1265 A.D.).

Hazrat Khwaja Nizamuddin Auliya was born in the year 1238 A.D. at Badaun, Uttar Pradesh. His father Khwaja Syed Ahmad was a scholarly person. The saints' grand father belonged to Bukhara. His mother Bibi Zulekha was more devoted to God. When he was five years old he lost his father. It was left to the helpless widow to appoint suitable teachers for the young child.

The father had named his son as Mohammad. Young Mohammad was put under the charge of Shadi Muqiri who had specialised in the Holy Quaran. Like his guru Baba Farid, young Auliya too mastered the whole of the scripture by heart.

The young Auliya was an incarnation of humility and a symbol of purity. According to Dr. S.A.A. Rizvi, around 1253 A.D. when ordered to put on a turban as a sign of his graduation, Nizamuddin was without funds to buy one. His mother, however, assisted by her slave girl spun some yarn and a neighbour speedily wove material for a turban. With some sweets he went to Maulana Alauddin, who supplemented some more food from his own house in order to make a feast. On this occasion, Ali Maula a great Saint was invited. After the meal, the Maulana took the turban and asked 'Ali Maula to wrap it around Shaikh Nizamuddin's head. At each winding, Shaikh Nizamuddin placed his head at the feet of Shaikh Ali. So touched was the Shaikh that he prophecised Shaikh Nizamuddin's future prominence as a saint. There were two reasons which prompted this. Ali Maula said: firstly Nizamuddin had prostrated himself before his elders; and secondly his turban was completely made of cotton, without a silken thread, thus proving his simplicity and piety."

One day he heard of the presence of an enlightened soul Baba Farid. There was a thrill in his whole body and mind of young Muhammad who was at that time hardly twelve years old. The new dream of the child was only a meeting with Baba Farid. Nizamuddin would constantly remember the unseen hero of his heart and his biographers tell us that "after each prayer he began to repeat the name of Baba Farid".

Nizamuddin suddenly found himself one day an orphan in the big capital city of Delhi when his mother left for her heavenly home. There was no body to look after him. After that event he became a wandering monk. He at once set in for Ajodhan to meet Baba Farid ... what a meeting! the ocean mingles with sea! Baba was waiting for him it seemed. The Saint embraced his dear one.

He was welcomed with a great deal of honour and warmth by Baba Farid who offered him a bed in jama at Khana. Nizamuddin was immediately initiated and his head shaved. The Baba urged him to become fully involved in ascetic exercises on his return to Delhi. He was sent to Delhi, mainly to spread the divine message of universal love, compassion for mankind. Very shortly Nizamuddin left Delhi and joined his guru Baba Farid at

Ajodhan. Baba Farid himself taught Nizamuddin not only the six important chapters from the Holy Quran, he taught him some classic scriptures like the works of Abu Shakar Sulami. He had to leave again to Delhi.

When Nizamuddin met Baba Farid in 1257 he was just a young lad of nineteen. More than eight years had passed and not a day passed that Nizamuddin had not uttered the holy name of Baba Farid at least a thousand times with the prayers from Quaran.

The time was ripe and Baba Farid sent for Nizamuddin Auliya from Delhi in summer 1265 A.D. He was given Khilabatnama by Baba Farid. This was more than a convocation or initiation. This meant Nizamuddin Auliya also had the power of attorney to initiate any body to the teachings of Baba Farid. On the happy occasion, Baba Farid said, "You will be a tree under whose shadow the people will find rest... You should strengthen your spirits by devotion. I have hundred over all those things to you for at the time of my death you will not be present".

Nizamuddin Auliya's mission in life was to present to the lay men in Delhi the message of Baba Farid.

Nizamuddin Auliya had no dwelling place in Delhi. He was living for some time with the relation of Amir Khusro. The relations were staying out of station. When they returned it created a problem for the Darvesh. He shifted to a small village named Ghiyaspur. Melons were available free in plenty. But how long one can get them? The rest of the year he could hardly get a single chapati.! His face to face struggle against starvation made him a very perfect friend of the poor and the down trodden. Even when he got sufficient food later on as presents from hundreds of disciples, the Saint did not change his habit. He would take very little. How can I take so much when so many people near my mosque are sleeping on the streets with empty stomachs.

He identified himself with his teachers message of compassion, Dard. When his admirers once praised him for his deep learning and great popularity, the Saint opened his heart by saying. No one in the world is as sad and unhappy as I am. Huge number of people come to me and tell me of their misery and troubles. All this afflicts my heart and soul. Strange is the heart which listens to the sorrows of Muslim brethern and is not touched by it. The saints who retire to the mountains or jungles are free of these problems.

His main teachings to all was one must feel for others. One should always distribute his surplus things to the poor. The Saint introduced free kitchen langer to feed the poor, irrespective of their religion - Hindus or Muslims. The Saint drew big crowds - Hindus and Muslims of Delhi and people from far and near used to throng his mosque just to listen to his learned discources. He never distinguished between one religion and another. Nizamuddin Auliya also made it clear that it was not necessary, rather possible for all to be ascetics. What was necessary was a higher value of life to be practised in our daily lives.

The life of Nizamuddin Auliya cannot be complete without some references to the most illustrious disciple Khusro who was a creation of the Saint. The poet lived and died for the God man.

Hazrat Nizamuddin lived for eighty seven years and saw the reign of seven Sultans of Delhi, namely—

1. Ghiyasuddin Balban (1265-1287)
2. Muazuddin Kaikbad (1287-1290)
3. Jalaluddin Khilji (1290-1295)
4. Ala-ud-din Muhammad (1295-1316)
5. Kutubuddin Khilji (1316-1320)
6. Ghyasuddin Tughlaq (1320-1325)
7. Mohammad Tughlak (1325-1351)

while most of these emperors were devoted to the Saint, two of them Kutubddin Khilji and Ghyasuddin Tughlaq at the instigation of jealous ulemas turned against him. In trying to harm and humiliate him they met their own tragic ends due to the miraculous spiritual powers of the Saint. On account of his piety and spiritual attainments the Saint earned the title of Mahboob-e-Illahi, Beloved of God. The Saint maintained celebacy and remained a bachelor throughout his life. Like his illustrious father who refused the offer of Qazi's post, the Saint refused all royal patronages. He hated lust for Gold and spurned a royal Jagir offered by Alauddin Khilji.

About the spiritual power of the Saint there are many ancedotes. The most famous one is about the emperor Ghyasuddin Tughlaq. The emperor built Tughlaqabad about five miles from the old city. It is on way from Badarpur to Faridabad. It was a well built city, yet failed to attract people. There is a popular belief among the local people that the city was deserted due to a curse of the Great Saint Nizamuddin Auliya. When the city was being built the Saint requested the labourers to dig a water tank for the benefit of the tired travellers.

The labourers were in a fix, what should they do? They had to listen to the Saint whom they loved but at the same time they could not ignore the royal order. They decided to build the city during the day and dig the tank at night. It was near the prayer hall of the Saint. The construction of the city was delayed. Many workers even defied the order of the king's men. They refused to construct the big walls around the new city. Ghyasuddin was in Bengal and was told of the Saints immense popularity. He could not tolerate the defiance of the construction workers. He felt insulted. So the king himself led an army against the Saint. He had been warning the workers in advance.

The follower of the spiritual leader were in great worry. They did not know what to do. How will an unarmed poor God. Man stand the royal wrath? All the well wishers of the Saint advised him to flee away before the king returned. But it seems Hazarat Nizamuddin paid no heed to any of them. Completely unalarmed, calmly and quietly he would only ask the workers to continue their work. He would simply smile and say Delhi hanuz dur ast Delhi is yet at a distance.

Ghyasuddin came to Afghanpur just one day's march from Delhi and the Saints followers only started counting beads. They were sure the king would kill him. And yet calmly he would say 'Delhi hanuz dur ast'! At Afghanpur a pavillion fell on the king and killed him. The Saint escaped his vengeance.

The new city of Tughlakabad was soon deserted because the Saint had hurled his curse. He did not like the royal arrogance against common man's welfare. He said "The city of Tughlakabad will become an abiding place only for the jackals and the Gujars"! It came true.

The historic tank is still there near the shrine. Its water has great mediciual quality. The tank is a holy pilgrimage for millions.

The grave was just built by the Saints admirers immediately after the Saints death but the rest of the building was done later. There are marble arches surrounding the grave. They are simply charming. Akbar II built the dome. The tomb is just adjacent to the pictureque mosque built by Allaudin Khilji. This is known as Jamat Khana. The Saint was very much fond of this mosque and chose this spot for his tank nearby. Shahajahan also built the marble screen, popular jali around he courtyard of the tomb. The work is very fine.

Many great personalities wanted to be buried near the Saints tomb. Among them were Begum Jahanara, Amir Khusro, the great Urdu poet, Mirza Ghalib and others.

(Courtesy: Dr. Vivek Bhattacharya)

Amir Khusro

(1253 A.D. - 1325 A.D.)

Amir Khusro is perhaps the first poet of Delhi who could leave a permanent mark in the history of Indian literature. He is better known in the literary circles of Delhi as Tut-i-Hind (तूती–ए–हिन्द) (Parrot of India) Delhi is proud of Khusro. Delhi is proud of Urdu. It was in Delhi that Urdu was born, nourished and flourished.

Khusro was born in 1253 A.D. Maulana Saduddin took care of the child. Khusro was not much interested in studies. He would prefer muttering self composed rhymes. The Maulana used to give full attention to the orphan child. One day the Maulana had to attend an invitation in a respectable family. The Mulana used to attend literary sitting invariably with one disciple or another. That day he took with him young Khusro. Khwaja Aziz Sahib an eminent contemporary scholar was also present there. Aziz was equally a poet of repute. But what made him more famous was his wide outlook and a kind heart.

All were busy in discussion. Young Khusro, as a matter of habit was muttering his self composed favourite rhymes. The dreamy eyes were kept absorbed in his own thoughts and the child did not even notice what was going on in the meeting. His thoughts were lost in the clouds. The Khawja was observing him. The boy was muttering something. His lips were moving. Aziz Sahib noticing this boy for a quite a long time.

The learned scholar got interested in the boy. He concentrated his full attention on the boy. The poets and scholars were left to themselves. The Khawaja could not check his curiosity. He patted the child and with a touch of affection asked him what he was muttering.

Khusro's guru the Maulana got perturbed. What an indisciplined boy. Muttering poems in a gathering like this! With much humility he told the learned Khwaja that it was more or less a habit with the child always to mutter something or the other within himself, Gustakhi Mauf (गुस्ताखी मुआफ). The toddler composes his own poems.

What Aziz was thinking was not far from truth. He was thinking on similar lines. He could recognise the gem at first sight. Aziz requested him to recite some of them loudly. For the first time Khusro recited four self composed poems one by one.

The whole gathering was stunned. In one voice they welcomed the young poet. Aziz Sahib stood up in excitement embraced the child and showered on him his blessings. In the history of Indian literature a new name was added Abdul Hussain alias Amir Khusro. Balban's son Bugra Khan became a great admirer of Amir Khusro. He would arrange musharas in honour of Amir Khusro where all the important poets used to be invited. One day he was presented with one big plate full of mohars (gold coins) by Prince Bugra Khan. That enraged his guru Kitlu Khan so much so that he left the royal court. What? observed Kitlu Khan, "When I am supporting him and am still alive he accepts royal honour?"

The poet returned the royal present and asked pardon of his preceptor. But Kitlu Khan never changed his mind. So Amir took shelter under the prince who accepted him as an intimate friend.

Bugra Khan was killed by Timur who imprisoned also the poet. When released the poet described the death of the prince in a long poem. The emperor fainted. The whole court was in tears.

Amir used to spend restless nights in search of truth. He had no earthly problems. According to traditions of the day, he was given pearls and jewels equal to his weight but that did not help him to solve his real problem. For that he would sit at the feet of Saint Nizamuddin Auliya.

Amir Khusro was the court poet of eleven emperors of Delhi. Once the emperor Jalaluddin Khilji wanted to go to the prayer hall of the Saint secretly. The emperor did not admire him.

He was jealous of his great popularity. Jalaluddin called the poet and disclosed his desire. It was to be kept a close guarded secret.

Amir was in a fix. What to do? On one side is the emperor, on another the preceptor. He preferred to save the life of his guru. Risking his own life, he disclosed this to the Saint. So when the emperor came to the hamlet of the Peer, he was missing.

The emperor was enranged. No third man knew of this royal adventure. So the poet was to explain. Very boldly he admitted everything.

On one side is the emperor and on the other is the spiritual guru. If the king is angry the head will be off the shoulders. If the Saint is angry the whole spiritual force will vanish. I prefer the first, he replied.

Saint Hazrat Nizamuddin Auliya was so much fond of the poet that before he passed away he told his disciples the following ancedote.

"You see when I go to heaven and Kornish the Lord he would ask me, well Nizamuddin what have you brought for me from the earth"? Then what shall be my reply?

Some of the disciples shouted "fragrant flowers".

The Saint noded his head, "No, no, I shall tell him I have brought for you a world fame poet whose heart is as clear as a diamond, a crystal clear piece. His name is Amir Khusro".

Amir Khusro composed poem for more than sixty years. During his life time of seventy two years (1253 A.D. to 1325 A.D.) as said earlier, the poet had the opportunity of serving as many as eleven emperors of India as their court poet. Khazame-ul-Fateh gives a historical account of Ala-ud-din Khilji's reign. Tughlaq Nama gives us an eye witness story of the reign of Ghiyas-ud-Din Tughlaq. Ashiquah marrates a royal romance. He has noted with much care and painsome of the spiritual lessons of the Saint Nizamuddin Auliya. These conversations with the most enlightened soul of the age reveal the great reverence that the poet had for his Master.

Inspite of so many important royal assignments the poet would long to be in the company of the affectionate guru. When the great Saint passed away, the poet was away from Delhi. On his return to Delhi with a broken heart the poet wrote:-

"The fair one lies on her couch,
With her black tresses over her face;
O Khusro, come here now
For night has fallen all over the world".

The night had really "fallen all over the world" and the poet could keep his promise. Within less than six months of the Saints death the poet too joined him in the other world!

(Courtesy: The Spirit of Indian Culture—Saints of India, Dr. Vivek Bhattacharya)

Ramananda

(1299 A.D.-1411A.D.)

There are conflicting traditions about the time when Ramanand flourished. Bhandarkar suggested that he was born in A.D. 1299-1300 and died in A.D. 1411. But of the tradition that his disciple Kabir lived at the time of Sikandar Lodi (A.D. 1489-1517 A.D.) is genuine, even these dates must be regarded as doubtful. It seems better to refer Ramananda's birth to the fourteenth, and his death to the fifteenth century. He is said to have been born at Prayaga or Allahabad and to have studied the Visishtudvaita system of Ramanuja at Varanasi at the feet of a teacher named Raghavananda. After some time he gave up some practices followed by orthodox Vaishnavas (e.g. taking food without being seen by anybody) and founded a new school of Vaishnavism based on the gospel of love and devotion. The most important reform attributed to him is the abolition of considerations of caste among his followers. He made no distinction between a Brahmana and a member of the lowest castes. He was himself a Brahmana, but had no objection to dine with member of the low castes if they were Vaishavas. He took pupils even from the so called degraded castes. According to traditions his first twelve disciples were:—

1. Asananda
2. Surasurananda
3. Sukhananda
4. Parmananda
5. Mahananda
6. Pipa (a Rajput ruling chief)
7. Kabir (weaver)
8. Bhavananda
9. Sena (Barber)
10. Dhanna (Jat, peasant)
11. Sri Ananda
12. Ravidas (Cobbler)

Although a spirit of sympathy for the low castes was a feature of Vaishnavism, the earlier Vaishnavas did not put sufficient emphasis on this point. Ramananda, however made it a fundamental tenet of his doctrine. The use of the vernacular instead of Sanskrit was another reform introduced by Ramananda. The third important reform attributed to Ramananda is the introduction, on a firm basis, of the cult of Rama and Sita in place of the worship of Krishna and Radha. Ramananda borrowed ideas from the various religious schools that flourished before him, but vitalized them with the love and devotion of his heart, and founded a new path of spiritual realization. It is this path which Kabir and others followed later and decorated with their lives and sayings. Ramananda may be said to have begun what is known as the religious renaissance in Medieval India.

Ramananda occupies a unique place in the history of religion in Medieval India. Although brought up in the traditional school of Vaishnavism founded by Ramanuja, he gave an altogether new turn to it by its reforms and was mainly instrumental in ushering in the new epoch of medieval mysticism to which reference has been made above. He has not left behind any written records of his new message, but his disciples and their successors embodied in this lives and teachings the new way of spiritual realization revealed by him. One of his songs presumed in the Sikh scripture Granth Sahib, may be taken as the gist of his teachings. I had an inclination to go with sandal and other perfumes to offer my worship to Brahman. But the guru revealed that Brahman was in my own heart. Wherever I go, I see only water and stones (worshipped); but it is Thou who hast filled them all with Thy presence. They all seek Thee in vain among the Vedas. My own true guru, Thou hast put an end to all my failures and illusious. Blessed art Thou! Ramananda is lost in his Master, Brahman, it is the word of the guru that distroys all the million bonds of Action".

Other disciples and followers of Ramananda

The most famous disciple of Ramananda was Kabir (A.D. 1398 - A.D. 1518). He met Guru Nanak during the year A.D. 1496 Guru Nanak's period have been (A.D. 1469 - A.D. 1539). According to legends, Sikandar Lodi, the bigoted Sultan, tried by various means to kill Kabir, but the latter was miraculously saved each time. Both Hindu and Muslim legends make Kabir a contemporary of Shaikh Taqqi; the former represent them as rivals, while the latter regard Taqqi as the Pir or religious guide of Kabir. Taqqi is said to have been the Pir of Sikandar Lodi also. So we may take Kabir as a contemporary of Sikandar Lodi who ruled from A.D. 1489 to 1517. It is doubtful whether all the twelve disciples mentioned above were really initiated by Ramananda. Some of these were probably attracted by his ideas and teachings, but joined his order after his death. That was the case with Anantanand, who founded a sect. His grand disciple, Nabha, an untouchable, was the author of the Bhaktamala or

Lives of Devotee's which is one of the most important source books for the history of the medieval saints.

Another famous follower of Ramananda thought not an actual disciple, was Sadna a butcher by caste, two of whose songs are included in the Grantha Sahib.

Among the twelve disciples mentioned above, Ravidas occupies a high place on account of his exalted spiritual life and purity of heart. He is reputed to have been the spiritual guru of Jhali and Mirabai, two queens of the Sisdiya Rana family of Chitor. His religious ideas followed the same lines as those of Kabir. We need not dwelt at length on the other disciples of Ramananda, each of whom gathered round him a devoted band of followers. The monasteries founded by some of them still attract devoted pilgrims.

(Source: The History and culture of the Indian People - The Delhi Sultante General Editor R.C. Majumdar. Bombay, Bharatiya Vidya Bhavan, 1960, pp. 560, 561, 565, 566).

The following is the hymn of Ramananda found in the Granth Sahib. An invitation had been given him to attend a religious service of Vishnu to which he replied:-

Basant

Whither shall I go, Sir? I am happy at home
My heart will not go with me; it hath become a cripple
One day I did have an inclination to go;
I ground sandal, took distilled aloc wood and many prefumes
And was proceeding to worship God in a temple
When my spiritual guide showed me God in my heart
Wherever I go I find only water or stones
But Thou, O God, art equally contained in everything.
The Vedas and the Purans all have I seen and searched
Go thou thither, if God be not here.
O true guru, I am a sacrifice unto thee
Who hast cut away all my perplexities and doubts.
Ramanand's Lord is the all pervading God;
The guru's word cutteth away millions of sins.

(Source: Sikh Religion. M.A. Macauliffe, pp. 105-106).

Sadhna

Sadhna is believed to have been born in Sehwan in Sind and to have been a butcher by trade. He was a contemporary of Namdev. He embraced a religious life by listening to the instructions of holy men. Sadhna never killed animals himself, but purchased those killed by others and then retailed their flesh. He wiped out the sins of previous births and became purified like fine gold which resists the touchstone. His idol was the salagram or ammonite stone worshipped by Hindus. With this he weighed out meat to his customers. However much or little they required, they received the weight of the salagram.

A Sadhu, or holy man, on seeing the use to which the salagram was applied, thought it ought no longer to remain with a butcher, and resolved to take possession of it. Sadhna gave it up without hesitation. After some time, however, the Sadhu took back the salagram to Sadhna and told him that, though he had bathed it in the five ambrosias, worshipped it with sandal, sweet basil, and so forth his worship was unacceptable. The salagram is pleased with thee, said the Sadhu and I have sinned by taking it. By this time, however, Sadhna's thoughts took a different turn. He became wrapped up in the love of God, abandoned everything he possessed, and bent his steps towards the forest to enjoy the uninterrupted worship God.

On the way he saw some of his relations at a distance. He concealed himself and avoided them by taking another route lest any of them should pressure on him to return. On arriving in the evening at a village, he went into the house of a married man and asked for something to eat. The lady of the house on seeing Sadhna young and handsome fell in love with him. She prepare exquisite food for his repast and induced him stay. At night she proposed to elope with him. Sadhna spurned her, and said he would not do such a thing even though she were to cut his throat for refusing. Understanding by this that, if her husband's throat were cut, Sadhna would be ready accede to her wishes, she forthwith went and killed her husband. On returning to Sadhna she told him what she had done, and repeated her immoral proposal. Sadhna replied, 'O unworthy woman, that hast lost thy reason; how can I agree to what they proposest? In her despair she raised loud cries and invented a false accusation against him; believed this person to be a holy man, and accordingly entertained him. He hath now killed my husband and made improper overtures to me. Sadhna was arrested and taken before a magistrate. When asked what he had to say, he with the meekne and unwillingness to throw blame on others, while have characterized so many Hindu saints, pleaded guilty to the charge. He thought to himself, 'Since God hath placed me in this position, no one will accept my denial.' He then composed the following hymn:—

> Even though Thou, O God, consign me to hell, I shall not dispute it or turn away from it.
> Even though Thou bestow heaven on me. I shall not rejoice or praise it.
> If Thou reject me, I cannot constrain Thee; if Thou accept me, I shall not be puffrd up with excessive joy.
> He by whom Thou standest shoulder to shoulder is dyed with Thee.
> Let him whom Thou orderest cheerfully burn his body.
> My mind desireth not death, yet Thou mayest, if it please Thee put me in the fire.
> What the Beloved desireth ought to be the heart's desire also.

The judge sentenced Sadhna to have his hands cut off. The punishment was duly carried out, and Sadhna was then discharged. He got out without a frown on his forehead notwithstanding his barbarous mutilation.

There is a tradition, which, however, is not found in the Bhagat Mal, that the woman who had brought the false accusation against Sadhna of having killed her husband with the object of abducting her, burned herself on her husband's funeral pyre. On seeing this Sadhna said, "No one knoweth the way of a woman; she killeth her husband and becometh a Sati'. However this expression originated, it has passed into a proverb.

Sadhna devotions proved so successful that, it is said, new hands then sprouted from his body, and he was released from all pain of future birth. So efficacious, says the author of the Bhagat Mal, is the love of God. In the Mahabharat it is stated that, even were a man to study the four Veds, it would not avail him unless he loved God. And God said, Even though a man be the lowest social outcast, yet if he be a saint of Mine, he is dear to Me and worthy of worship.

There is a legend to the effect that Sadhna became the object of further persecution. A king, who was probably incensed against him on account of his religious opinions, ordered him to procure meat for him at an unusual hour of night. Sadhna was unable to do so, and the king thereupon ordered that he should be put to death by being built alive into a wall. While the wall was closing round him. Sadhna is said to have composed the following hymn in the Bilawal measure:—

On account of a king's daughter a man assumed the disguise of Vishnu.

> For love of her and for his own object; but his honour was saved.
> What merit hast Thou, O Guru of the world, if my sins be not erased?
> What availeth it to enter the asylum of the lion, if he allow the jackal to clutch me?
> For want of a drop of rain the chatrik suffereth agony;
> When its life is gone, even were an ocean at hand, it would be of no avail.
> Now that my life is weary and abideth no longer, how shall I be patient?
> When a man is drowned, even if a boat be obtained, say whom shall you put into it?
> I am nothing, I am nothing, and I have nothing.
> At this conjuncture Thy slave, Sadhna, prayeth Thee to protect his honour.

Sadhna's tomb is at Sarhind in the Panjab, but the sadhu in charge of it can give no information regarding him. (M.A. Macauliffe)

Trilochan

Trilochan, a name which literally means three eyed, that is, seer of the present past, and future, was a celebrated saint of the Vaisya caste. His birth is said to have taken place in the year A.D. 1267. He either lived at or visited Pandharpur in the Sholapur district of the Bombay Presidency, and was a contemporary of Namdev, who mentioned or addressed him in his hymns. Inquiries at Pandharpur and the neighbouring city of Barsi have, however, failed to furnish any information regarding Trilochan. The following legend passes for history among his admirers. He had a perfect faith in and love for saints, but they visited him in inconveniently large numbers, and there were only he and his wife to attend and wait on them. He thought that they were not served as he could have wished, so he resolved on engaging a servant if he could find one who was accustomed to minister to holy men. He continued to search for such an attendant, but not finding one became sad at heart. It is said that God was not pleased at the sorrow of his saint, and sent him a candidate for service. Trilochan asked the candidate who he was, whence he had come and whether he had parents and a house and home. The man replied that he had no parents or home. He had merely come to be engaged as a servant. He could wait on the saints of God without assistance from others, as his life had been spent in such service. He gave his name as Antarjami which interpreted means Searcher of hearts. Trilochan was high pleased and ordered his wife to engage him and cheerfully supply all his wants. She was cautions to consider his pleasure as her first duty.

Antarjami performed menial services for the saint such as cooking, drawing water, washing their feet shampooing and bathing them in such a manner that Trilochan's house became famous for its hospitalaity and a large crowd of saints began to live with him and consume his substance. Thirteen months passed in this way, until one day Trilochan's wife went to visit a female neighbour. The latter inquired who she was so dirty and looked so miserable. She replied that her lord had taken into his employ servant who required so much attention that she had to spend all her days grinding corn and cooking for him. This was reported to Antarjami and he promptly disappeared.

When the time came to wait on the saints, Antarjami could not be found. Trilochan became very much grieved, and, rebuking his wife, told her that it was through her indiscretion Antarjami had left their service. When Trilochan's grief had lasted for three days it is said that he was comforted by divine interposition. He consequently applied himself to the praise and contemplation of the one true God. His sorrow was then dispelled.

The following hymns of Trilochan are found in the Granth Sahib:—

SAIRAG

Trilochan admonishes mortals.

> The heart feeleth great worldy love, O mortal, through which man forgetteth old age and the fear of death.
> O fool, thou art pleased on beholding thy family, like a thief on espying his neighbour's house.
> When the powerful myrmidons of Death come with a rush,
> I cannot withstand them.
> May some friend come and speak to me!
> Come to me, my God, throw Thine arms around me!
> Come to me, my God, and rescue me!
> In various pleasures and royal state, O mortal, hast thou forgotten God, and deemest thyself the only immortal one in this world.
> Deceived by mammon thou hast not thought of God, and hast lost thy life, O heedless man.
> Mortal, thou must tread a difficult and terrible path where neither sun nor moon hath entrance.
> When man hath abandoned the world, he forgetteth his worldly love.
>
> Today it hath become clear to mine understanding that Dharmraj will keep his eye on man.

There his very powerful *myrmidons* will rub men between their hands, and none may withstand them.
If any one give me instruction, *let it be this that* God is contained in every place.
O God, saith Trilochan, Thou knowest everything.

GUJARI

A Hermit, a Sanyasi, a Brahmin called Jai Chand a Jogi, and a Kapria held a religious discussion in which each maintained the superiority of his own sect. They came in the heat of their arguments to Trilochan, and he, knowing that they were all hypocrites addressed them each in turn as follows:—

To the Hermit.— Thou hast not cleansed thy heart from filth, although thou wearest the dress of a hermit.
To the Sanyasi.—In the lotus of thy heart thou hast not recognized God; why hast thou become a Sanyasi?
To the Brahmin.—Thou hast gone astray in error. O Jai Chand. And not recognized God the Primal Joy.
To the Jogi.—Eating in every house thou hast fattened thy body; *thou wearest* a patched coat and beggar's ear-rings for gain.
Thou hast rubbed on thyself the ashes of the cremation ground, but being without a spiritual guide, thou hast not found the Real Thing.
Why mutter *spells*? Why practise austerities? Why churn water? Remember *God* the Dweller at ease, who hath created the eighty four lakhs of existences.
To the Kapria.—O Kapria, why carriest thou a waterpot? Why wanderest thou to the sixty-eight *places sof pilgrimage*?
Saith Trilochan, hear, O mortal, having no corn why layest thou a threshing floor?
Last thoughts determine man's future state.
At the last moment, he who thinketh upon his wealth and dieth in that thought,
Shall be born again and again as a serpent.
O my friend, forget not God's name.
At the last moment, he who thinketh of a woman and dieth in that thought.
Shall be born again and again as a prostitute.
At the last moment, he who thinketh upon a boy and dieth in that thought.
Shall be born again and again as a hog
At the last moment he who thinketh of a mansion and dieth in that thought.

Shall be born againand again as a sprite.
At the last moment he who thinketh upon God and dieth in that thought.
Saith Trilochan, shall obtain salvation, and God shall dwell in his heart.

DHANASARI

Trilochan engaged in his devotions, neglected his worldly calling and this led to his straitened domestic circumstances. Thereupon his wife became discontented and upbraided God. The following is Trilochan's remonstrance. He endeavoured to console her by telling her that her distress was the result of her sins.

Why slander God, O erring and ignorant woman?
Thy woe and weal are according to thine acts.
Though *the moon* is attached to Shiv's forehead, and daily batheth in the Ganges;
Though *Krisan the avatar* of Vishnu became incarnate in the moon's family;
Yet the stain contracted on account of his misdeeds is ineffaceable from his head;
Arun, the charioteer, whose lord is the sun, the lamp of the earth, whose brother was Garur, the king of birds, was born without feet on account of his sins;
Shiv, the remover of many sins, the lord of the three worlds, wandered to many places of pilgrimage, but never reached the end of them:
The act of *cutting off Brahma's* head was never effaced from his person.
Although ambrosia, the moon, the all-yielding cow, Lakshmi, the miraculoustree, the steed with seven faces and the physician arose from the ocean, the lord of rivers.
Yet on account of its deed the brackishness of the ocean departeth not:
Although Hanuman who burnt the fortress of Lanka and uprooted the park of Rawan, took the wound-healing plant to Ram Chandar and made him happy.
Yet on account of his act of theft the curse *that he should never have more than* a loin cloth was not effaced from his person.
The result of past acts is never effaced, O wife of my house;

Wherefore repeat for me the name of God;
Trilochan repeateth God's name. (Courtesy: M.A. Macaullife)

Contemporary of Namadev

1. Hazrat Nizamuddin Auliya (1238-1325).
2. Dyandev (Gyaneshwar) (1275-1296)
3. Acharya Ramanand (1299-1410)

Other Maharashrian Saints

1. Eknath (1533-1599)
2. Tukaram (1598-1649)
3. Ramdas (1608-1681)
4. Mukteshwari (Second half of the 16th century)

Scholar Poets

1. Vaman Pandit (1618-1695)
2. Moropant - (1729-1794)
3. Shridhar (1678-1729)
4. Raghunath Pandit (Author of Nal and Damyanti)

Prominent Social Reformers

1. Gopal Hari Deshmukh (1823-1892)
2. Jotirao Phule (1828-1890)

Prominent Prose writers (modern age)

1. Gopal Ganesh Agarkar 1885-1895) Editor of Kesari and Mahratha and Founder of Sudharak Weekly.
2. Lokmanya Bal Gangadhar Tilak (1856-1920). The pioneer of Freedom is my birth right - and the editor of Kesari and Mahratta.

3. Shivaram Mahadev Paranjpe (1864-1929) - The Founder Weekly Kall (Time)

   Achyut Balwant Kalhatkar editor of the weekly Sandesh, C.V. Vaidya, V.K. Rajwade, K.A. Kaluskar and Rajaram Shastri Bhagwat.

Poetry and Drama (1866-1905)

1. Keshavsait (1866-1905)
2. Narayan Vaman Tilak (1865-1919)
3. Ram Ganesh Gadkari (1885-1919)
4. Balkavi (Tryambak Bapuji Thombro) (1890-1918)
5. Bee (Narayan Muralidhar Gupta (1872-1947)
6. Bhaskar Ramchandra Tambe (1874-1941)
7. Govind Ballal Devals (1855-1916)
8. Shripad Krishna Kolhatkar (1871-1934)
9. Krishnaji Prabhakar Khadil Kar (18722-1948)
10. Ram Ganesh Gadkari (1885-1919)
11. Narasimha Chintaman Kalkar (1872-1947)

The Novelists

1. Hari Narayan Apte (1864-1919)
2. Nathmadhav (Dwarkanath Madhav Pitale) (1882-1928)
3. Dr. Shridhar Vyankatesi Katkar's (1884-1937)
4. Vishnu Sakharam Khandekar (1898-1976)
5. Gajanan Tryambak Madholkar (1899-1976)
6. P.Y. Deshpande (1899-   ) etc.

(Source: Marathi Literature: An Outline—P.N. Paranjpe, Nishikant Nirajkar, Maharashtra Information Centre, Govt. of Maharasthra, New Delhi).

Principal Disciples of Namadeva

Janabai

Sant Janabai was born in a village named Gangakhed, at the bank of river Godavari, in the Nander district of Maharashtra. Her father's name was Dama and mother's name was Karund. Janabai's parent were the blind followers of Vitthal Maharaj. They used to visit Pandharpur every year. When Janabai was only five years old she accompanied her parents to the pilgrimage of Pandharpur. When she had a sight of Lord Vitthal's statue she lost herself. She give up the idea to go back to her home alongwith her parents. She was persuaded a lot but failed miserably. She decided to stay there permanently. Seeing this her parents handed over to her to Damseth the father of Namadeva. She became member of Namadeva's family. She used to work in their house as a maid servant. To sweep the house, cleaning of utencils washing of clothes and to bring drinking water was her duty. In her Marathi Abhangs she has used word maid servant for herself. While putting up in the family of Namadeva she was influenced by the Bhagvadgita. Service to the members of the Namadeva family and meditation of the God Almighty was the only mission of her life. Hence maid servant Janabai one day became a famous Marathi poet. She had confessed that she was fully influenced by the spiritual powers of Namadeva and she was completely influenced by him.

She had also confessed that being a maid servant of Namadeva, she blessed by Vitthal Bhagwan. Janabai looked after Namadeva in his childhood. She loved him like her younger brother. She did not marry in her life. She devoted her complete life in the service of Hari. She had been a selfless worker. She used to meditate Vitthal Bhagwan without any selfish motive.

She always prayed to Lord Krishna that O Lord bless me with such a power that I should always busy in reciting your pious name. My eyes should be blessed with your Almighty's darshans. I would always devote myself dancing in repeating your kirtan. It is my earnest desire to have your darshan in every breath of my life. Please help blessed 'O' Hari with this blessing. When the entire day was over while singing she had a 'darshan' of her beloved Vitthal. Her meditation reached to such an extent that she used to see her Vitthal in every thing. She said most humbly to her Vitthal:— I have devoted everything to my Lord and I see my Lord in every thing. My Lord is every where. Wherever she goes her Vitthal accompained her. Her Lord helps her in every affair. When she used to go to fetch water from the well her Lord fill up her pot with His pious hands. Whenever she goes to jungle to collect cow dung she realised the presence of her Lord behind her. When she starts cleaning rice, her Lord help her in that job also.

Being an ordent disciple of Vitthal she was always blessed by Him. She always devoted every thing in the name of her Lord. She was of the firm opinion that in discharging house hold duties her Lord had blessing in every thing. She always discharge her duties in that spirit. Her firm belief in Vitthal had purified her personality in every direction while going through her Marathi Abhangs one could easily feel that she could not tolerate the seperation of her Vitthal even for a moment in life. Whenever she find him missing she used to start weeping bitterly like a innocent child.

She used to say - O! My Lord! I could not live without you. I am unable to control my emotions and conscious. O Lord! you are my beloved mother. Please come rushing to me and arrange meeting with my mother (Vitthal). She always prayed to saints. In some of his Marathi Abhangs she had expressed her views in most philosphical manners. She said:

I have tied the thief of Pandharpur with a string in His neck and I have converted my heart as a jail and locked Him there. I have prepared a strong chain of words and have placed in His hands and feet. When I started penalising Him with the word 'SOHANG' He had become loyal to me. I have firmly told Him - O Vitthal now throughout my life I would never release you from the jail of my heart.

About 350 Pads of Janabai have been traced. They are so beautiful that one could never satisfied singing them again and again. They are so much appealing and full of emotions that while singing one feels him or herself in the lap of Vitthal Bhagwan.

Janabai also breathed her last alongwith Namadevji in the year 1350 A.D.

Parisa Bhagwat

A Brahman called Parisa Bhagwat lived in Pandharpur. He had a philosopher's stone-paras-the word from which his name was apparently derived. His wife Kamalja one day went to the adjacent Bhima river and there met Rajabai, Namadeva's wife. The latter complained that her husband Namadeva would do no work and that in consequence the family was in very straightened circumstances. Kamalja said she possessed a philosopher's stone which she would lend her. It would convert everything into gold, and she would no longer be indigent. Rajabai, it is said, took the philosopher's stone and produced much gold by its agency. When Namadeva heard of this, he took the stone and threw it into the river. When Kamalja remonstrated with him, he dived into a water and brought up two handfuls of gravel which he threw in front of her. On looking she fancied that every bit of the gravel was a philosopher's stone. On this she left her home and became a disciple of Namdeva.

There is another story about Parisa Bhagwat by Wankhade Guruji:-

Sant Namadeva had a number of disciples. Among them one Parisa Bhagwat. He was a Brahman by caste. Parisa is a Marathi word. It means please listen. He used to recite Bhagwat in front of Mahadwar in Pandharpur and used to request every body to listen Bhagwat. That is why people called him 'Suno Bhagwat' (Parisa Bhagwat).

No details are available about his birth, birth place, parentage and date of death. He has enriched Marathi literature by contributing a few impressive and full of emotions Abhangs. He accompanied Sant Namdeva and Sant Gyaneshwar in their first pilgrimage. He had great regards for Sant Namadevaji.

Chokhamela

Chokhamela belonged to Mhar caste of Maharashtra. He was a resident of Mangal Bedha Tehsil of Sholapur District of Maharashtra. Being a follower of Vitthal he used to go to Pandharpur as a pilgrim. He regards Namadeva as his guru. He used to attend his kirtans regularly. From his very childhood he was a simple and God fearing person. To fetch dead animals out of the locality was his profession. While discharging his duty he used to devote himself in the meditation of God Almighty. Being a low caste he had to face humiliation on various occasions, but he never turned his face from his meditation. Sant Janabai has said about him —" Every body is a devotee but Chokhamela is a supreme devotee.

Under the influence of Namadeva not only Chokhamela but also every member of his family became devotee of Vitthal and all became saints and poets. His wife Soyarabai, sister Nirmalabai, son Karmmela, son-in-law Banka Mhar etc. etc. all were devotee of Bhagvad. Unfortunately not a single Abhang of Karmmela is available. Soyarabai's one Abhang is available —

" O Lord! After having your 'darshan' my all desires have been fullfilled.

My heart is clear. I have no feeling about untouchability. No proud, no superiority complex, of any kind. I have lost every worldly relations and have become a free bird. This Abhang is an exemplary Abhang of Barkari sect. Thus an illetrate Mharn lady express herself.

Once in village Manglabedha the repair work of village Parkota was in progress. Thousands of peoples were working there'. Chokhamela was also one of them. All of sudden Parkota fell down. So many Mhars also died. In this incident which occured in the year 1338 A.D. Chokhamela lost his life. Namadevaji took his ashes to Pandharpur and in front of the maingate built up his Samadhi. This samadhi still exists. Whosoever Barkari used to go to Pandharpur until and unless pay his or her obeisance to this samadhi did not consider pilgrimage of Pandharpur complete.

Keshav Kaladhari

In a village named Tara in district Gurdaspur (Punjab) one person named Keshav lived. Some intellectuals are of the opinion that he was a celibate throughout his life. The author (Wankhande Guruji) had the occasion to visit this village. He happened to meet one of his relatives. He was the last member of his family. He told that Keshav was a family man but in his later age he left his house.

It is said that he had some chronic disease. The family members did not paid any heed to look after him. His family members has left him on the mercy of God. In these circumstances he decided to commit suicide and left his house and reached Ghumman. Namadevaji was putting up there. He paid his regards to Namadevaji, and apprised him of his patahetic story. Namadevaji had mercy on him and kept him there. Namadevaji advised him to take bath daily in the nearby pond. Gradually he get rid of his skin disease. He became disciple of Namadevaji. Afterwards he became chief disciple in Punjab of the Namadev's followers. When at the time of departure to Maharashtra Namadevaji left Punjab, he nominated his chief disciple Keshav Kaladhari as the Chief Bahawalpur State to preach Bhakti Marg in that area but to his preaching of Namadeva sect, there was a great impact on people of Northern India. When after partition of India (1947) Bahawalpur became the part of Pakistan, the Mahant Jamnadas Gosai of Bahawalpur centre shifted to Bhiwani, district Hissar. Near Bhiwani Railway Station he has built up Namadeva temple there.

Laddha

There is a village named Sukhowal near Ghumman. There lived a Bhagvad Bhakat named Laddha. He was a Khatri by caste. Though he was a poor man but he used to look after sadhus, whosoever comes to him. He had a grocers shop. He came to know that some Mahatma is putting up in the nearby jungle. One day Laddha went to meet Namadevaji. He made up his mind to offer something to Him. Being a poor person, he was unable to offer anything to Him. After serious thought he reached to the conclusion that he should daily light a lamp in the hut of Namadeva. While going back to his village he used to light the lamp daily. One day it happened that all the stock of mustard oil in his shop was sold out. There was no mustard oil in his shop and the lamp was also empty. He did not enter the hut of Namadeva and from a distance he paid his regards facing Namadevaji's hut and proceeded towards the village. In the meantime Namadevaji called him - Laddha! What is the matter why are you going from a distance? He was much ashamed. He went to Namadeva and said - Maharaj due to the non-availability of the mustard oil I have to take this step. Namadevaji said to Laddha - Laddha! You are telling a lie. There is enough oil in the lamp? It is said that when Laddha checked up the lamp it was full to capacity. Laddha was stunned to know. From the same day he became a ardent disciple of Namadeva.

At the outskirts of village Sukhowal there is a Samadhi and temple in memory of Laddha. Recently this temple had been converted into a Gurdwara. Due to the paucity of funds this temple was in a deplorable condition. On the occasion of Maghi Mela people visit this place in Ghumman.

Bohardas

(1424 A.D. - 1523 A.D.)

Bohardas was a resident of village Bhootpind. He lost his father in his very childhood. His mother's name was Alodi. She looked after Bohardas. One day Namadeva visited this village. He stayed outside the village under the shadow of a tree. One day Bohardas approached Namadeva there. Gradually that meeting converted in friendship. Afterwards Bohardas started staying with Namadeva. Sometimes his mother took him her home. Similarly time was going on. One day all of a sudden Bohardas expired. Somebody informed Namadeva about Bohardas's death. Namadeva reached his home. It is said that when Namadev put His hand on his head he got up. From that very moment Bohardas became Namadeva's disciple. His childhood name was Bala alias Baloden. When by the blessing of Namadeva he again regained consciousness he was known as Bohardas.

After this miracle Bohardas left his village. He was much upset. One day Namadeva deputed Jallo to bring Bohardas to his village Bhootpind. To know the message of Namadeva he was much pleased. On the permission of his mother Bohardas accompanied Jallo and reached to Namadeva. His mother also accompanied them. For Bohardas a hut was built up near the Kutiya of Namadeva. A village also came into being nearby. It is said that now where store is situated this was the place of Bohardasji's Kutiya.

In a village named Mard there was a women named Dharma. She had one daughter named Sulakhani. Dharma expressed his desire to marry his daughter with Bohardas. Marriage date was finalised. Marriage procession reached in the village Mard. People went to see the Barat. In the Barat there was one blind person. He fell down due to some obstacle. His foot was hurt and started weeping. Namadeva summoned him through Jallo. Namadeva touched him with his hand and all his pain vanished and he became alright. It is said that the same blind man went to the village pond for washing his mouth he regained vision of his eyes. Barat (Marriage procession) came back. Bohardas started living in village Ghumman. According to the elders of the village Bohardas was born in the year 1424 A.D. Though no confirm date has been traced out about his death but it is believed that he most probably expired in the year 1523 A.D.

According to Punjab writers Namadevaji expired in the year 1450 A.D. According to them after the expiry of Namadeva Bohardas remained alive for 70 years. But this period has not been confirmed by any other author. His Samadhi is in village Ghumman. Elders of Ghumman say they are the members of Bohardasji's family. Bohardas has three sons:-

1. Padarthdas
2. Durga Ram
3. Bal Chand

They also have three sons, one each:-

1. Bhogi Ram
2. Rakha Ram
3. Dayal Das

After this the family tree of Boharda's family is not available.

Jallo

Near the village of Ghumman there is a village named Bhattiwal. Jallo was the resident of this village. He was a carpenter. He had great regards for Namadeva. He became disciple of Namadeva. On the occasion of Namadevaji's first journey (pilgrimage) he accompanied Namadeva to Pandharpur. There is a mention of this incident in Namadeva Marathi Abhangs. His memorial has been built up in village Bhattiwal. No details are available about his birth and death. Sant Namadeva had visited Bhattiwal once. Namadev has built up a Tank in this village. It is known as Namainya.

Vishnu Swami

He was a resident of Mathura or Brindavan. When Namadevaji travelled Northern India he accompanied him. He was one of the prominent disciples of Namadeva among North India. More details are not available. In Bhakatmal Nabhadas has given the following order in Acharya traditions:-

49. Swami Namadeva

50. Vishnu Swami

51. Laxmibhatji

It is said that he remained alive for many years after the death of Namadevaji.

Trilochan

He was a contemporary of Nmadev. A few writers are of the opinion that he belonged to Maharashtra. But there is no mention in Marathi literature. The followers of Trilochan sect are of the opinion that he belonged to Hardwar area. He met Namadeva somewhere in Northern India. Nabhadas in his book Bhakatmal had included his whole story. Trilochan has used word Vitthal in his Abhangs:

Namdeva told Trilochan - My dear friend I use my hands and feet and recite Ram Nam by my mouth. I have devoted myself in the meditation of my Lord Almighty.

Nibritinath

Sant Nibritinath was the elder brother and Guru of Gyaneshwar and staunch follower of Vitthal Bhagwan (Lord Krishna).

The ancestors of Nibritinath used to live at the bank of river Godavari about four kilometers from Paithan in the village Ape Gaon. When he was 55 years old his wife Nirabai gave birth to a son, who was named as Vitthal Pant. Vitthal Pant was a great intellectual. He had studied all the Vedas. He was a well read and devotee of God. From his very childhood he was a Nbrit Marg. After studying the Vedas with the permission of his father he started for pilgrimage. He went to Somnath, Dwarabati and Pandharpur and reached Alindi. At Alindi there lived a brahman named Siddhopant. He was also a great scholar. When he met Vitthalpant, he was fully impressed by his personality. He married his only daughter with him. Rukmanibai, name was given to his bride.

He had no interest in married life. To live with his wife he deemed it a burden. He was eager to become a sanyasi but it was not possible without the permission of his wife. One day when Rukmani bai was busy in his house hold works he told her Rukmini I want to go to Ganga snan. Innocent Rukmini said my beloved! please must go. Considering this as her permission he left the house, and reached Kashi. Took sanyas with the blessing of Shripad Swami and became Chatinya Swami.

When he was putting up at Kashi as a sanyasi his wife Rukminibai did her best to search him. She came to know after a long period that her husband has entered in Sanyas Ashram. Then she also started meditation at her home. After few years Shripad Swami alongwith his disciple was going to Rameshwaram via Alandi. Like other devotees she also went to pay her regards to Swamiji. She paid her obeisance. Shripad Swami blessed her by saying "Be a mother of a son". Hearing this Rukminibai started laughing. When he asked the reason of her laughing she replied "Gurudeva! You have permitted to my husband to join 'Sanyas Ashram'. In these circumstances how your blessings would be materialised?

Hearing her logic Shripad Swami aboundended his idea of Rameshwaram pilgrimage, he alongwith Siddhopant and Rukminibai came back to Kashi. Reaching there he advised Chaitanashram Swami Vitthal Pant to rejoin his family life (Grahasth Ashram). He alongwith her wife Rukmibi came back to Alindi. Their family circle discarded them from the Society. In this manner they became parents of three sons and one daughter namely - Nibritinath, Gyaneshwar, Sopandev and Muktabai.

Nibritinath was the eldest in the family. He was born in the year 1273 A.D. He had authored so many Abhangs. He loved Gyaneshwar very much. When Gyaneshwar went to his heavenly abode he during Samvat (Vikarmi) 1296 A.D. in Trimbkeshwar area through yog took Samadhi while he was alive. There is a memorial temple built up on that spot in his memory. Nibritinath was invited by saint Gaininath in the Nath Sampardaya and Nibritinath initiated his brothers and sister in this sect.

Sant Gyaneshwar

Maharashtra has produced so many poets and writers but Gyaneshwar was topmost among them. He was born in the year 1275 A.D. about 4 kilometer from Paithan Gaon on the Northern bank of river Godavari. Nibritinath's teaching were different from Gyaneshwar. He was not pained or worried when they were discarded from the society. Gyaneshwar has devoted himself in Varun Ashram. He said to Nibritinath and Sopandev - "Let us approach Brahmans for purifications and perform thread ceremony. For this purpose they went to Paithan. All these kids presented themselves in the Brahman Sabha. Their request was not acceeded. In the meantime a Brahman saw a Buffalo and started joking - The Brahman pointing towards Buffalo said its name is also Gyaneshwar. All the Brahmans started laughing. Gyaneshwar replied cooly this buffalo is also my soul. Brahmans were adament to test him. It is said that Gyaneshwar made the buffalo to recite Vedas from its mouth. Seeing this miracle all the Brahmans paid their obeisance to all of them.

From Paithan Gyaneshwar alongwith his brothers and sister set out for Alindi. During this journey in a village named Niwasa authored Gyaneshwari. From there they went to Apegaon and staying at Alindi they went to Pandharpur. They met sant Namadeva there. On the request of Nibritinath, Gyaneshwar authored book 'Amritanubhav', Dasham Granth. Afterwards he accompanied Namadevji in his pilgrimage. The mention of this pilgrimage has been made in his book entitled 'Tirthawali' in 59 Abhangs.

Gyaneshwar, except Gyaneshwari, and Amritanubhav have authored hundreds of Abhangs. In the year 1296 A.D. at the age of 21 in the village Alindi Gyaneshwar took alive samadhi.

Sopandeva

During Samvat 1334 Kartik Shukla Poornima during night time Sopandev was born. Like Nibritinath and Gyandev he resemble like a living person. His character has mixed up with Gyaneshwar's character which could not be seperated. In one of his Abhangs he has recorded that if as one light mix up with other light and very difficult to distinguish them, similarly my life has become a part and parcel of Gyaneshwar's life. According to Sopandev God is one, one says Shri Hari, the other Shri Krishan and Vitthal - and same is Gyaneshwar. Sopan says I have devoted my everything in Him.When Gyaneshwar went to his heavenly abode by taking live Samadhi after one month's period in a place named Saswad while performing Hari Kirtan Sopandev also breathed his last.

Muktabai

Gyaneshwar's sister Muktabai was born during Samvat 1336. Like his three brothers she has also devoted her life in the service of God Almighty. She was fully aware of Yogmarg. Changdev become his disciple.

Once upon a time that Muktabai was taking bath. By chance Changdev reached there. To see Muktabai in this position he hid his face with a piece of cloth and went away. When Muktabai came out she said in the presence of her three brothers. You are an old man of 1400 years but you fail to remove aberration of your mind! You have gone through the procedure of hathyog even than you fail to recognize yourself. There is no difference between sexes among intellectuals. Changdev put his head on the feet of Muktabai and prayed "forgive me my mother". Muktabai realised Changdev his spiritual powers. After five months of Gyaneshwar's going to heavenly abode she breathed her last on the banks of river Tapi.

Changdev

He belonged to Shukal Yayurvedi Brahman caste. He was a complete yogi. It is said that owing to his yogic powers he lived for 1400 years. His Math was situated on the bank of Godavari in a village named Puntamba. Gyaneshwar, Nibritinath, Sopandev and Muktabai had visited this place after taking clearance certificate from the Brahman of Paithan. Changdev met all the three brothers and their sister.

There is a folklore that Changdev alongwith his 1400 disciples riding a dreaded tiger with a snake like hunter in his hand reached Alindi. At that time all the four brothers and sister were sitting in a broken platform. To give a stunning shock to Changdev they ordered platform to move he was badly shaken. He get down from the tiger and threw away the snake hunter and laid down in the feet of Gyaneshwar. To give him a lesson Gyaneshwar wrote 65 obiyan, which are called Paisashti. After taking live Samadhi by Gyaneshwar during Samvat 1353 Changdev also expired.

Vesoba Khechar

He was a resident of nearby village of Paithan. Afterwards he settled at Aundha Nagnath area. About 50 kilometers away there is an ancient Shiv Temple namely Aundia Nagnath Shiv Temple. It is one of the 12th Jyotarlingam. He was a Yayurvedi Brahman.

He was the guru of Namadevaji. In his Marathi Abhangs he has appreciated the greatness of his guru. It is said that due to his spiritual Powers he could fly in the air. That is why he is called Khechar. It is learnt from his Abhangs except yogmarg he had full control on Gyanmarg and Bhakti Marg. Harishchandraakhyan authored by him is still available. He died in the year 1309.

Sanwata Mali

About 10-12 miles away from Pandharpur there is a village named Arnmendi. Sanwata was the resident of this village. He was born during Shak Sanwat 1172. He used to work as a gardner and send Vanmali to Vitthal. He was a firm believer in the recitation of Ram Nam. In one of his Abhangs he said, "Hari Nam is so powerful that I don't fear from anybody and beat the Kalikal (death messenger) with full force. By singing the name of Vitthal and by dancing we call Vaikunthpati in our kirtan. Similarly we celebrate our Diwali and catching that Vanmali we worship him. According to Sanwata that one should go on the path of meditation - you may get everything itself. Sanwata breathed his last in Shaka Samvat 1217 on 14th Ashad Krishna.

Narhari Sunar

He was the resident of Pandharpur. How he became the follower of Vitthal while working as a Goldsmith, he has mentioned in one of his Abhangs. "O my Lord! I am your Goldsmith. I am a businessman of your kind name. This garland is a body. Its inner conscious is gold. With the help of intlects hammer I have killed my wishes and with the help of my brains scissor I stole the name of Ram, put it in my bag and completed the journey. This Narhari Sunar! O Hari! is your servant and recites your name during day and night.

Gora Kumhar

During the Gyaneshwar period Gora was eldest of all. He was born in a village named Terdhoki in Samvat 1324. He was known as chachaji. Gora was a most experienced, knowledgeable and great saint. His Abhangs are full of Vedant philosophy.

Sena Nai

He was the contemporary and disciple of Gyaneshwar. He has recorded in his Abhangs the meditation and Pooja he has inherited from his father. He has authored numberless Abhangs on the Smadhi of Namadeva. He has introduced himself that in the family of Naike Hrishikesh has gave birth to me. He has pleaded her followers and family members that follow your religion earnestly and truthfully. Since morning upto noon discharge your duty properly and after taking bath recite the name of Narayan. Follow your religious books and take shelter in the feet of Vitthal Bhagwan. In this way God will help you. He has composed a religions Abhang on shaving:

We always shave the person minutely. We show mirror of vision to the concerned person, and use sacrifices tongs and sprinkle water of peace and prosperity and tie up selflessness, clean the armpits and cut the nails of desires and anguish and thus serving all the four Varns live as a free man.

Raka Bhakat

In the area of Pandharpur a person named Raka Kumhar lived. His wife's name was Banka, and daughter's name was Vanka. His entire family was follower of Bhagvad. Raka's source of lively hood was to prepare and sell earthen pots. While reciting religious books and performing kirtan he used to perform his duty.

His meeting with Namdev is an interesting story. It is said that one day Raka's daughter Vanka went to the river Chanderbhanga for bathing. At the same time Namadeva's daughter Limbabai also reached there to wash family clothes. After taking bath Vanka came to the Ghat of the river Limbabai was busy in washing her clothes. Splashes caused by Limba fell on Vanka's clothes. Then Vanka pointing towards Lamba said, Bai, I have just taken bath and now I have to start my Pooja. Splashes caused by you are falling on me. Limbabai said in pride, Kumhar like you should not be so proudy. Vanka said, your father is great saint. He has the power to force Vitthal Bhagwan to take food? My father is a selfless devotee. After reaching home Limbabai apprised his father about the incident. Namadeva feel insulted. He immediately rushed to the temple and asked Vitthal Bhagwan, please tell me that your devotee Raka whether he is selfless or selfish devotee? Vitthal Bhagwan told Namadeva, "In these times there is no selfless devotee other than Raka Kumhar, Namadeva said, Prabhu I want to test him.

Next day, early in the morning Namadeva Vitthal Bhagwan and Rukmini started to the place where Raka, Banka and Vanka were collecting fuel woods. Namadeva said to Vitthal Bhagwan,- " Please show some miracle? Rukmini put her bangle which was made of diamond in the way and kept a peace of wood on it. Raka was leading them. As he bended himself to take that piece of wood, he notice that Bangle lying there. His wife was following him, Raka thought for a while, her wife may not dare to take it. He put some earth on it. Seeing his husband standing she saw the earth and noticed Diamond Bangle lying there. She said this would be bone of contention, after me my daughter is coming perhaps she may took it. Thinking on these lines she also poured some more earth on it. In the meantime their daughter reached the spot and she also noticed the Bangle. After removing the earth she saw the bangle lying there. Then Vanka said "O my God! you gave my birth to me from such a iliterate couple, who could not distinguish between Diamond and earth. Saying so she also proceed onwards.

Now Namadeva reached to the conclusion that really this

family is selfless devotee of God and ardent Vaishnavs. Namadeva embraced Raka with his chest.

Baba Sachidanand

He was contemporary of Gyaneshwar. He took down Gyaneshwar's Gyaneshwari. Due to this reason he became famous in Marathi literature. This work was done during Shaka Samvat 1212. This mention has been made in the end of Gyaneshwari Granth.

Banka Dhed

Was the brother of saint Chokhamal's wife. During his devotion he tried his level best for the upliftment of Harijan community. He has authored so many Abhangs in Marathi. In his Abhangs he has paid highest tribute to sant Gyaneshwar, Chokhmela, Namadeva etc.

The Marathi scholars of Maharashtra have named this glaxy of spiritual saints as Sant Mela. His poetry is in Marathi Abhangs. These saints have major contribution not only started writings but also strengthen it upto that extent that this period is called as a golden period of Abhangs.

In this group of saint consists of every type of people. They all were free thinker and caste or creed have no binding for them. They were the firm believer of meditation. Except Gyaneshwar family rest all the saints were family men. They used to discharge their professional jobs regularly. While in meditation they authored Abhangs also. They regard each other. This was the result of Gyaneshwar's contribution. Afterwards this movement became a Banyan tree now called Barkari Sampardya in Maharashtra.

Ekadashi Vrat and Namadevaji

Once on the Ekadashi day (the eleventh day of every fornight) Lord Krishna assumed the form of an old Brahman reached Namadeva's residence. He was holding a stick in his hand and bearing old clothes on His body. He said, I am dying with hunger, and have approached you for food. You are a generous man and known as Vishnu bhakta. So, you please give me some food to eat. Saying to Nama He sat down in between the door. Vishnu bhakta Nama seeing the Brahman sitting there, bowed prostrate before Him. O Swami! please tell me your wish, which have brought you here? The Lord of the world in the guise of a Brahman replied, I am in distress from lack of food. So, please give the necessary material required for the cooking and get me a meal. Hearing this answer of the Brahman, the Vishnu bhakat replied to Him, You know today is Ekadashi day (the 11th day) it will not be possible to give cooked food. If you could accept some sorts of fruits, I can give you right now. On this the Brahman said, No sorry, no I won't accept anything other than cooked food. For this reason I have come to you for charity. If you fail to oblige me, I will at once give up my life and the sin of killing a poor Brahman will fall upon you.

Namadeva replied, I have told you earlier, that I am a Vishnu bhakta. I am without good records as well as sinful deeds. I have dedicated everything at the feet of Pandurang and have become a free bird. He who cherishes in his heart no desire even for good deeds, how can then sinful deeds harm him? He who does not love intensely, seperation bring him no sorrow. If a person has discarded all love of money he will not be afraid of theives. And if one has put away all desires to be honoured, how can he feed dishonour shown him? He who feels no happiness is being praised by men, how can he feel any pain when he is reviled by men? He who feels no pleasure in mere gain can feel no sorrow when he makes no gain. So O! my dear Brahman, I have destroyed all opportunity for sin as well as good deeds. I shall never have to go to hell because of sin. The Brahman replied, You have no feelings in your heart for others, and you are going on the preach your philosophy. I am a poor Brahman in distress from lack of food. If you fail to take away my hunger, I am going to lose my life. Listen O the devotee of Vishnu take it as granted.Nama told the Brahman, if you give up your life, the same thing will happen to me, O Brahman. Hearing such words from Namadeva - Lord Krishna did a very strange and remarkable thing. He fainted there and fell on the ground. Namadeva went close to him and looked at him. The Brahman had breathed his last.

Hearing about this incident the neighbours flocked there and accused and abused Namadeva for causing a death of a Brahman on his door steps. People also said, Namadeva it is very strange that when a poor Brahman was asking from you some cooked food, you fail to oblige him and the result is before you? How could the consequences be avoided? One person remarked Namadeva always talks very high about his divine knowledge, but he never offered even a morsel of food to anyone. Every body revilled him. What Namadeva's determination was unchanged. He lifted up the dead body of the Brahman and took it to the banks of river Bhima. He prepared a funeral pyre and placed the corpse upon it. He also laid himself by the side of the corpse and set the funeral pyre on fire. Every one present there was shocked at what Namadeva did. They shouted - O Lord! The determination of Namadeva is very great. We have not seen great Vaishnav than Namadev on this earth.

The Brahman was not really a Brahman. He was Lord Krishna in the guise of a Brahman; as He died his true devotion led the Vaishnav Nama to be immolated with him in his fixed determination. Just as the fire began to blaze, the Brahman immediately got up and embraced Namadeva. Lord Krishan said to him, If I may hunt through all the three worlds, I would not find a devotee like you - O Namadeva !!! After saying so Lord Krishan became invisible. People wondered in their minds and fell at the feet of Namadeva.

Warkari Sampardaye

In the Maharashtra State there are five main sect (Sampardaye) are found. The prominent among them is Warkari Sampardaye. This sect is functioning for the last thousands years and in progress day by day. It will not be out of place to mention here that this sect is a sect of real religious movement in the Maharashtra. The followers of this sect are staunch Vaishnavs. It has been started from the pious land of Pandharpur. From this very place it has been flourished and able to set up its branches throughout India. Near about all the prominent saints of Maharashtra are the followers of this sect.

There is a magnificient statue of Vitthal Bhagwan standing on a brick. In the nearby temple there is a statue of God Almighty's wife Rukmini. Vitthal is the childhood version of Lord Krishna. Pandharpur is known as the Kashi of Maharashtra where once in a year during Asadh and Kartik's Shukal Edadeshi the devotees of Vitthal Bhagwan assembled in millions. the name of this pilgrimage is Bari and whosoever undertake it called Warkari. Wari means - Yatra (pilgrimage) and Kari means who undertake and devotees themselves in the meditation of Vitthal Bhagwan. Whosoever took this pilgrimage every year is called Warkari. Warkaries are the devotee or followers are of Shri Pandrinath, Pandurang, is Vitthal. In the temple Lord Vitthal is standing on a Vit(Brick) all alone. Rukmini's temple is in a seperate temple. The follower of this sect like the residents of Northern India have no much regards for Radhika. They preferred Rukmini instead of Radhika. In Maharashtra the Warkaries undertook pilgrimage during Asadhi Kartiki and

Maghi (Chetra) alike. Instead of these two annual pilgrimage they took yatra of Pandharpur on Ekadishi in every month. Leaving aside their caste and creed the devotees devote themselves in the service of Vitthal Bhagwan.

The childhood of Vitthal Bhagwan is fond of Tulsi. The devotees of Vitthal Bhagwan bear Tulsi mala in their necks. Bearing a Tulsi mala is an old tradition in various sects, but majority of the followers after Jap (recitation of Ram Nam) put off the mala.

On the contrary the Warkaries did not follow this tradition. They bear Tulsimala consisting of 108 Tulsi beeds. It contains Merumani in between. Whosoever bear this mala keep it till the end of ones life. As without thread one could not imagine of a Brahman similarly one Warkari without Tulsimala is incomplete. This string of beads had a great importance in Warkaries life. This beeds is supposed to be born by a warkari throughout his life. Lord Krishna has said in Shrimad Bhagvad that the devotee who offers everything to God is called Bhagvat. A Warkari always offer everything to Vitthal and is called Bhagvat. Therefore this sect is also called Bhagvat Sampardai.

About the rise of this sect one cannot say anything definitely because various scholars have different opinion about this. But Sant Gyaneshwar, Namadeva and Tukaram whatsoever have mentioned in their poetry it is assumed that in the ancient period a Mahatma named Pundlik used to meditate in Pandharpur. When owing to his meditation Lord Krishna was much pleased the God Almighty came there as a child and appeared before him, Pundlik offered a brick, which was lying near him to sit. On the very brick Lord Krishna stood up. The followers of Warkari Sampardai are of the firm opinion that the same shape of Lord Krishna has been established there, which has been preserved as it is.

The period of Sant Pandlik has not been established so far. According to famous historian V.K. Rajwade Sant Pundlik's period is about 1128 A.D. But other scholar did not agree and of the opinion that he was a saint of ancient times? But majority of the scholars of the firm opinion that rise of Pandharpur's Vitthal Bhagwan is definitely related to Sant Pundlik.

According to renewned Warkari saint Behnabai who was a disciple of saint Tukaram in one of his Abhang said:-

With the kind blessings of saints the Warkari Sects temple has been built up. Gyaneshwarji laid down its foundation. Construction work was started. Due to the preaching of Namadeva it was extended. Janardhan Swami and Eknathji hoisted the Flag of meditation on it. On the completion of the temple Tukaram presented a Klash on the temple Tower. Now the only work left out is the recitation of the name of the God. According to Sant Behnabai in thirteenth century this Sampardye (Sect) has been started. Some people are of the opinion that this Sampardye was in existence even before Gyaneshwar and Namadev came into lime light. Gyaneshwar's contribution is commendable because due to his tireless efforts he succeeded to unite all the sections of this sect under one flag. Due to his efforts in this direction he became one of the topmost Acharya of this sect. The 'Devata' of this Sampardye is Vitthal Bhagwan that is why Pandharpur area is known as 'Dakshan Dwarka'.

This Sampardye believe in "Sagun" and "Nirgun" upasana of the God Almighty.

Was Namadeva a Robber?

As recorded by Macauliffe:-

With reference to this miracle the author of the *Bhagat Mal*, in a paroxysm of devotion, remarks 'Congratulations to God who loveth His saints, and is pleased with their devotion. Thou whom the Veds call Endless and to attain whom Shiv and the other demigods performed every form of penance, art so much in the power of the saints and their love, that Thou performest everything according to their desires.

It appears that Namdev, on arriving at man's estate, for a time grew weary of saintship. He records of himself that through evil destiny he began to associate with dakaits or Indian highwaymen, and plunder travellers. He and his gang killed several Brahmans, pilgrims, and innocent men. His father and other elderly persons remonstrated with him, but he heeded not their censures. At last the Emperor dispatched a squadron of cavalry to arrest the offenders. They refused to submit and in the skirmish which ensued eighty four of the troopers were slain, whereupon the remainder decamped.

Namdev possessed a large and excellent mare on which he used to scour the country and visit distant places. Whether as the result of habit or repentance, he made a vow, which he religiously kept, to behold daily the idol of Nagnath in the village of Aundhi about sixteen miles to the east of Pandharpur.

There are different opinions about the character of Sant Namadevaji. The classification is must. It is said that during his youth times Namadev was a dacoit. Afterwards he became a sanyasi. This incident has been included by Saint poet J.R. Ajgaonkar in the biography of Namadevaji. The other authors of Maharashtra including Shri Bhave and L.R. Pangaonkar are also of the same opinion. But it did not seem an authenticated fact. Actually one Abhang which did not belong or authored by Namadeva. The so called Abhang has been interpreted as under:-

"Unfortunately due to bad company became a member of Robbers group. They killed hundreds of people. It is said while working as a robber he used to visit Abandya Nagnath temple daily without fail. One day he went to the temple. At the time of Aarti when prasad was being distributed he saw a widow with a small child in her lap. Child was weaping for prasad. Mother was beating the child. Namadev could not help asking. Namadev said, why are you beating this innocent child? She replied angrily - May I offer my bones to him? The king of the state had deputed his military to capture the gang of dacoits. His father was one of them who also had been killed by the dacoits. Listening from her Namadeva was much pained. He could hardly control her tears. He while standing in front of the statue of Nagnath, said, O Lord! what should I do now? Saying so, he came out of the temple, handed over his horse and weapons to the Brahmans and as a revenge tried to cut his neck with a knife. Brahmans rushed towards unconscious Namadeva and took him away. In the night when he gained consciousness Nagnath inspired him to go to Pandharpur. Pandurang will give forgive and purify you. Namadeva reached Pandharpur. Chanderbhanga river was flooded. People by boarding boats were going to the temple. In the meantime Lord Pandurang inspired his followers not to permit guilty Namadeva to enter area of Pandharpur. Knowing this he plunged in the sea of grief. He started weeping. Paying his obeisance from the other side of the river Namadeva said, O my Lord! Owing to my sins you have discarded me. He conveyed his feeling through a letter and sent it by a sadhu to

Pandurang. Going through his letter Pandurang purified Namadeva. Afterwards he became devotee of Vitthal Bhagwan and permanently settled at Pandharpur.

Though Macauliff by quoting Bhakat Mal's author Nabha Das in the Sikh Religion but P.N. Pataskar, Dr. Tulpute and R.H. Bhalunkar etc. intellectuals are not convinced with this narration.

This incident depends on a 56 lines Abhang. But the intellectuals of Maharashtra according to the language used in this Abhang did not agree to accept it of Namadeva's Abhang. Keeping in view the usages of Persian words in this Abhang nobody will name it as a Namadeva's Abhang.

The contemporary saints of Namadeva including Janabai, Chokhamela, Visoba Khecher, Gora Kumhar, Gyaneshwar Bandhus, Bhagni, Parisa Bhagwat have sung Namadeva's biography, but nobody have ever mentioned anything about this incident. After Namadeva numerous saints including Eknath, Narisi Mehta, Dadu Dayal, Guru Nanak, Mirabai, Ravidas, Pipa, Dhanna, Tukaram, Niloba Moropant, etc. etc. have never mentioned this incident in any place, at any time.

Moreover known authority on the biographies of Vaishnav saint was Bhakatmals Mahipati who had complied detailed and most interested and impressive biography with other saints have no mention of Namadevji's this role. This seems a coocked up and baseless story.

Two less known namesakers

Dr. Vivek Bhattacharya in his book 'The spirit of Indian Culture - Saints of India (Saint Namadeva) has recorded that this great saints name sake being very many sometimes it presents some confusion. Besides this Maharashtra Saint there was another Namadeva who founded a sect and monstery in the District of Gurdaspur in the Punjab. The last Sayyid Alam Shah built a monastery of Namadeva and made an endownment for it in 1446 A.D. There was another Namadeva in Bulandshahar who was a calico printer. Yet a fourth Namadeva was at Marward who was a carder of cotton.

Even the Gazetter of India confuses this great Saint from Maharashtra with the one from Bulandshahar who was a calico Painter. Namadev definitely did not belong to the group of cloth painter caste as mentioned there.

The saint himself has described in many abhangs that he belonged to a tailors family and that he was all the time sewing with, gold needle and silk thread the Name of the Lord.

Ironically some prejudiced people rated this one of the greatest saints of that period his family's profession as his caste. That was the period which was dominated by castes and creeds prejudices and unfortunately considered Him as low caste, which is most unfortunate and shameful. It is regretted that even after the expiry of 732 years the present day scholars, the Religious Reformers use these derogatory remarks about his caste. This attitude towards this greatest saint should be resented with full force on every platform by the followers of Maharishi Sant Namadevji Maharaj. It is to be pointed out that the regime of exploitation by Muslim rulers and British Raj in the name of religion has gone by. This most insulting and shameful attitude must end now. Moreover Tailoring is not a caste but a profession Namadev Mission Trust must play a crucial role to raise its voice against this behaviour by so called upper classes even after 55 years of the attainment of Independence.

Joti Jot Samai

According to Max Arthur Macauliffe - The Marathi Chronicles show that Namadev died on the 13th day of the dark half of the month Asuj, - A.D. 1350 at the age of eighty years and that he was burried in Pandharpur, where his head, moulded in brass on the lower step of the temple of Vishoba is now worshipped by the populace. He has left several abhangs in which he prayed Shri Vitthal to give him a last resting place at his feet. He was accordingly buried at the entrance of the temple of Vishoba under the lowest step of the stairs by which pilgrims ascend. He desired that his head should be trodden on by holy men and that he should acquire spiritual advantages from the dust of their feet. the idea is that when a man prostrates himself at the foot of a saint the dust of the saints feet purifies him. The climax of beatitude is attained when the dust of the soles of the saints feet falls on the worshippers head.

Opposite Namadeva's Samadhi was buried one Chokhya a Mahar. To the right of the visiter is seen a representation of Ganesh the elephant headed god of learning, carved in relief out of a rock and painted red. Near Ganesh is a shapeless block of stone said to represent Hanuman the monkey god and ally of Lord Ram Chander in his expedition to Ceylon.

The temple extends for inwards and contains several apartments supported by Pillars. Through these the pilgrims pass in batches controlled by police officials. Over the apartments are vent holes to prevent the pilgrims from being suffocated as they pass in large numbers. From the root of the temple is seen a chapel sacred to Rukimani the consort of Krishna at which principally women worship. The temple called Raul by Bhagata Namadeva. It now contains many and various jewels of great value, the offerings of pious pilgrims for the decoration and glory of Vishoba. In the necklaces are seen gold coins of Spain, Portugal and other European countries.

All Namadeva's compositions bear convincing testimony to the love he bore his favourite deity. Accordingly, the local traditions that he spent his old age at Pandharpur in the immediate vicinity of Vishoba's temple, and that he was buried there must be implicitly accepted.

The Sikhs and Punjabi followers of Namadeva say that he was cremated at Ghuman in the Gurdaspur district of Punjab. This belief is founded on legends current in the north of India and the records at a shrine bearing the saints name in Ghuman, but it is resolutely denied by his followers in Pandharpur.

As stated earlier that there is a Samadhi of Namadeva near the main door of Vitthal Bhawan Temple at Pandharpur. There is second Samadhi of Namadeva at village Ghumman in the district of Gurdaspur Punjab. There is an interesting story about this Samadhi. This story has been recorded first of all by Baba Purandas inNamadeva's Janamsakhi in the year 1898 (Samvat 1955 Vikrami):-

During last leg of his life Sant Namadevji was a disgusted person. No one was aware of his this type of attitude. One day a person named Bohardas who was a disciple of Namadeva asked the reason of his sadness. He said, Gurudev, you always remain quite and in gloomy face, which I could not tolerate. If you could throw some light on this issue, I would be highly obliged. Ultimately one day Namadevaji said to Bohardas, my son, I am going to disclose one secret to you, with the advice not to tell to any one. Pandharpur is my birth place, where my mother is seriously ill. She is too old. After a few days she will depart for her heavenly abode. She is remembering me a lot there. Now I will go inside the temple and go to sound sleep, and after leaving my body in the temple through yoga I will reeach Pandharpur. I would stay there for seven days and come back. You are advised not to open the doors of this room and not to disclose this secret to anybody.

Jallo, Ladha and other followers of Namadevaji used to come to temple everyday. They used to stunned not to see their Guru (Namadevaji) sitting in the temple. They fail to control their emotions. They daily used to ask Bhoardas about whereabouts of Namadeva. After all they asked Bahardas where is Gurudev? He used to get up early in the morning, but he is not seen anywhere? What is the matter? Kindly permit us to enter the temple. Bohardasji replied that Guruji has forbiden the entry on anyone in the temple. They could not acceded the request of Bohardas and forcefully break open the door. When after removing the sheet from his body they found him dead. This news broke out like jungle fire. Bohardas tried his level best to convince them but nobody paid any heed. They cremated the body.

This happened on 2 Magh, Samvat 1507 Vikarmi, it is said. On this day every year a big fair is held at Village Ghumman.

It is also said that on that day during midday the pious soul of Namadevaji reached in the temple of Ghumman to fulfill his promise. But alas!!! the body has already been cremated. The soul inquired about his body. Listening this everybody started weeping bitterly. There was voice from the sky - "Now onwards all my powers would rest in Bohardas. According to various scholars it is a misleading story and not believable. (This story has been written by Wankhede Guru in his book entitled - Sant Namadev (Hindi).

Namadeva and Bhakti Movement in Maharashtra

Sant Gyaneshwar, Namadeva, Nibritinath, Sopandev, Muktabai, Gora Kumhar, Jogi Parmanand, Narhari Sunar, Raka Kumhar, Parisa Bhagwat, Visoba Khechar, Jagmitra Naga, Janabai, Chokha Mela, Sena Nai, Banka Dhed, Soyrabai, Sanwata Mali,

Changdev, Sachdinand Baba etc. etc. Sant Mandalis effects in Maharashtra spiritual democracy was set up. The wave of Vitthal Bhakti movement started in every religion, caste and creed. It looks golden period of social awakening in Maharashtra. At that time entire Maharashtra was in the grip of Bhakti movement. Sandhya, Puja, Abhang Sankirtan and the recitation of saints literature has become the integral part of Maharashtra's religious life. Everyday at night after dinner emotional rural population and citizens of big cities used to assemble in the temple for Sankirtan and Pooja. This tradition from Gyaneshwar and Namadeva and other saints of Barkari sect have been enhanced.

History of Marathi literature

The history of the Marathi language goes back to about A.D. 1000. But the earliest writers, whose works are extant in more or less authentic forms belong to the second half of the 13th century. Marathi is a Prokritic speech standing rather by itself and the connected Konkani dialects show some special features of agreement with the North Indian Aryan speeches.

The death of Namadeva, in A.D. 1350 marks the end of a flourishing period of Marathi literature. The next two centuries a period of transition are sometimes described as the dark period of this literature. There were since A.D. 1294 almost continuous fights between the Muslims and the Marathi speaking people, leading to the gradual establishment of Muslim rule in Maharashtra. The country was suffering from war and famine, and steady literature progress was not possible. The Mahanubhava sect which at first became unpopular through some concessions granted to it by the new Muslim rulers of Maharashtra, gradually recovered some of its old prestige and as all Hindu sects were suffering from Muslim apathy and hostility, a reapproachment among them in a general adversity gradually took place. The honour paid to the mythical sage Dattatrey by the Mahanubhava sect spread also to the followers of the Varakari school. Among teachers and writers of this age of transition were Narasimha Sarasvati and Janardana Swami, the master of Eknatha, both of the Varakasi sect. Poems of a devotional nature ascribed to them are still current among the people. A disciple of Narasimha Sarasvati wrote in verse the history of the sage god Dattatrey, known as the Guru Charita, and this work is held in great esteem by both Varakaris and Mahanubhavas.

(Source: The History and Culture of Indian People—The Delhi Sultanate, General Editor, Vol. VI—R.C. Majumdar, pp. 509-510).

Vani of Sant Shiromani Namadevaji Maharaj

(Included in the Guru Granth Sahib. Rendered into English by M.A. Macauliffe and Hindi version by Late Shri. Bakhshi Ram Kainth, then President, Namadeva Mission Trust, New Delhi)

(ग्रंथसाहिब के पद प्रारंभ)

(१) राग-गौड़ीचैती

देवा पाहन तारिअलें। राम कहत जन कस न तरे। रहाउ॥
तारिले गनिका बिनुरूप कुबिजा। बिआधि अजामलु तारिअले॥
चरणा-बधिक-जन तेऊ मुकति भए। हउ बति बलि जिन राम कहे॥१॥
दासी-सुत-जनु बिदरू सुदामा। उग्रसेन कउ राज दिए॥
जपहीन तपहीन कुलहीन क्रमहीन। नामे के सुआमी ते ऊतरे॥२॥

हे देव (परमात्मा) आपने तो रामेश्वरम धाम पर पत्थरों को पानी पर तैरा दिया तो भला राम नाम लेने वाला मनुष्य क्यों नहीं तैरेगा। और फिर चरणों में (कृष्णा जी के) तीर मारने वाले मनुष्य भी मुक्त हो गए।

जिन्होंने राम नाम लिया उन पर मैं बलिहारी जाता हूं। एक दासी का पुत्र विदुर और सुदामा जैसा दरिद्र ब्राह्मण को भी तार दिया इसी प्रकार उग्रसेन को राज वापस दिलाया। ये सब लोग जपहीन, तपहीन, कुलहीन थे पर नामदेव के प्रभु ने इनको भी तार दिया।

I
GAURI

The saving influence of God's name.

O God, Thous didst cause stones to float;
Why should not man float over by repeating Thy name ?
Thou didst save the courtesan, the shapeless hunchback, the hunstman, and Ajamal.

Even the murdere *who shot Krishan* in the foot was saved—

> I am a sacrifice to those who utter God's name—
> Bidur, the son of handmaidan, Sudama and Ugrasen, who obtained regal state;
> Men without devotion, without penanace, without family and without good works, were saved by Nama's Lord.

(२) राग-आसावरी

एक अनेक विआपक पूरक जात देखउ तत सोई।
माइआ चित्र-बचित्र विमोहित, बिरला बूझै कोई॥१॥
सभु गोबिंदु है सभु गोबिंदु है, गौबिंदु बिनु नहीं कोई।
सुतु एकु मणि सम-सहस जैसे उति पोति प्रभु सोई।रहाउ॥
जल तंरग अरु फेन बुदबुदा जलने भिन्न न होई॥
इहु परपंचु पारब्रह्म की लीला विचरत आन न होई॥२॥
मिथिआ भरमु अरु सुपनु मनोरथ सति पदारथ जानिया।
सुक्रित मनसा गुरु उपदेसी, जागत ही मनु मानिया॥३॥
कहत नामदेउ हरि की रचना देखहु रिदै बीचारी।
घट घट अंतरि सरब निरंतरि केवल एक मुरारी॥४॥

एक वही परमात्मा अनके रूप में व्याप्त हो रहा है और पालन कर रहा है। जहां भी मैं देखता हूं वही नजर आता है। माया प्रकृति की यह मूर्तियां (अर्थात् संसार की रचना) आश्चर्य करने वाली है जिसके कारण वह मोह लेती है, परन्तु इस भेद को कोई नही समझता (कोई-कोई ही समझता है)। असल में सब कुछ ही परमात्मा है। केवल परमात्मा ही है। उसके बगैर और कुछ नहीं है।

जैसे एक धागे में सैंकड़ों मनके पिराये हो वैसे ही प्रभु सृष्टि के अन्दर और बाहर सभी पदार्थों में विद्यमान है।

जैसे पानी से लहर, झाग और बुलबुले अलग नहीं हो सकते वैसे ही ये रचना पाँच तत्त्वों के परमात्मा द्वारा रची हुई (इसकी) उसका खेल मात्र हैं तथा विचार करने पर और कुछ भी नहीं है।

हम झूठे भ्रम में नाश्वान पदार्थों को सदा रहने वाली वस्तु समझते हैं। परन्तु गुरु ने शुभ कर्म करने वाली बुद्धि बनाने का उपदेश दिया है और ज्ञान द्वारा जागा हुआ मन भ्रम-बुद्धि को त्याग कर अब जागरूक हो गया है।

नामदेवजी कहते हैं कि इस प्रभु की रचना को अपने हृदय द्वारा विचार कर देखो। हर एक हृदय में अथवा में केवल एक रस प्रभु ही रम रहा है।

2
ASA

The omnipresence of God. In the Hindu system there is no teleological purpose assigned for the creation of the world. It is the sport of Maya who proceeded from God. Maya still practises every art to bewitch and deceive mankind. Namdev's creed is the unity of God, who is contained in everything and fills all creation.

There is one God of various *manifestations* contained in and filling everything; whithersoever I look there is He.
Maya's variegated picture hath so bewitched *the world*, that few know *God*.
Everything is God, everything is God, there is nothing but God.
One string holdeth hundreds and thousands of beads; God is the warp and woof.
Waves and foam and bubbles cannot be distinct from water.
This illusion, *the world*, is the play of the Supreme God; on reflection *thou shall* not *find it* different from Him.
Fleeting phantoms, illusions of dreams man deemeth real advantages.
My guru instilled into me right ideas, and when I awoke *to reason* my mind accepted them.
Saith Namdev, behold the creation of God, and reflect on it in thy mind;
In every heart and in all things uninterruptedly there is only the one God.

(३) राग-प्रासावरी

आनीले कुंभ भराइले उदक ठाकुर कउ इसनानु करऊ।
बहआलिस लख जी जलमहि होते, बीठलु भैला काइ करऊ॥१॥
जत जाउ तत बीठलु भैला महा आनन्द करे सद केला।रहाउ॥
आनीले फूल परोइले माता ठाकुर की हद पूज करऊ।
पहिले बासु लई है भवरह, बीठल भैला काइ करऊ॥२॥
आनीले दूधु रींधाइले खीर, ठाकुर कउ काइ करऊ।
पहिले दूधु बिटारिउ बछरे, बीठलु भैला काइ करऊ॥३॥
इभै बीठुल उभै बीठलु, बीठल बिनु संसारु नहीं।
थान-थनंतरी नामा प्रणावै, पूरि रहिउ तूं सरब मही॥४॥

मन में यह विचार हुआ हि घड़ा लाऊ और पानी से भर कर ठाकुरजी को स्नान कराऊँ। फिर विचार आया कि जल में तो ४२ लाख (अनेक) जीव होते है जिसके कारण जल शुद्ध नहीं रहता। ठाकुर जी को कैसे स्नान कराऊँ क्योंकि परमात्मा सब में मौजूद है और जल अपवित्र है।

वह परम आनन्द स्वरूप निरंतर खेल कर रहा है। और जहां भी जाऊ वहीं पर वह पहले से ही विद्यमान है। फिर विचार किया कि फूल ला कर माला पिरोऊँ और परमात्मा की पूजा करूँ। परन्तु विचार आया कि सबसे प्रथम भवरों ने फूलों को सूंघ लिया है जिससे वह जूठे हो गये हैं तो परमात्मा को वह जूठे फूल कैसे अर्पण करूँ।

फिर विचार आया कि दूध ला कर खीर बनाऊँ और उसे परमात्मा के अर्पण करूँ। परन्तु विचार आया कि दूध तो पहले ही बछड़े ने झूठा कर दिया है। तब परमात्मा को कैसे भेंट करूँ। परमात्मा तो सभी स्थानों पर इधर-उधर, ऊपर-नीचे विराज रहा है। उस से खाली कोई स्थान है ही नहीं नामदेवजी कहते है कि हे प्रभु! तू सारे संसार में भरा हुआ है।

3

The futility of idolatry

If I bring a pitcher and fill it with water to bathe the idol,
Forty-two lakhs of animal species are in the water; God is contained *in them*; why should I bathe Him ?
Wherever I *go* there God is contained;
God superemely happy ever sporteth.
If I bring flowers and weave a garland to worship the idol,
The bee hath first smelled the flowers; God is contained *in the bee*; why should I weave Him a *garland* ?
If I bring milk and cook it with khir to feed the idol,
The calf hath first defiled the milk *by tasting it*; God is contained *in the calf*; why should I feed Him ?
In this world is God; in the next world is God; *there* is no *part of the* world without Him.
Thou art, O God, in every place; Nama representeth, Thou fillest the whole earth.

Namdev had renounced his secular duties, and it was represented to him that he ought to embrace them again. He here gives substitutes for the tools of his trade.

(४) राग-आसा

मन मेरे गजु जिहवा मेरी काती।
मपि मपि काटउ जम की फांसी॥१॥
कहा करउ जाती कहा करउ पाती।
राम को नामु जपउ दिन राती॥रहाउ॥
रांगति रांगउ सीवनि सीवउ।
राम नाम बिनु धरीअ न जीवउ॥२॥
भगति करउ हरि के गुन गावउ।
आठ पहर अपना खसमु धिआवउ॥३॥
सुइने की सुई रूपे का धागा।
नामे का चितु हरि सउ लागा॥४॥

मेरा मन गज की तरह है और मेरी जिह्वा कैंची की तरह है। मैं इनसे माप-माप कर यम के फन्दे काट रहा हूं। वहां जाति-पाति, धर्म, सम्प्रदाय आदि का कोई भेद नहीं है इसलिए मैं तो प्रभु का नाम दिन-रात जपता हूं।

प्रभु प्रेम के रंग में रंगने योग्य मन को रंगता हूं और सोने योग्य प्रभु की याद को अपने हृदय में चिन्तन द्वारा सीता और पिरोता रहता हूं।

इस तरह प्रभु नाम के बगैर मैं एक घड़ी भी नहीं रहता। मैं प्रभु के गुण गाकर उसकी भक्ति करता हूं और आठों पहर अपने मालिक का ध्यान करता हूं।

मेरी चित रूपी सुई सोने की है और प्रभु भक्ति रूपी धागा चांदी का है जिससे यह दोनों मूल्यवान हैं।

नामदेवजी कहते हैं कि इनके सहारे प्रभु से जुड़ा रहता हूं।

4

My heart is a yard measure; my tongue a shears.
With it I measure and cut off Death's noose.
What care I for caste ? What care I for lineage ?
I repeat the name of God day and night;
I dye what ought to by dyed, and I sew what ought to be sewe.
I can not live for a ghari without God's name;
I perform worship and sing God's praises;
During the eight watches of the day I meditate on my Lord.
My needle is of gold, my thread of silver—
Nama's soul is attached to God.

(५) राग-आसा

सांपु कुंच छोडै बिखु नहि छाड़ै।
उदक माहि जैसे बगु धिआनु मांडै॥१॥
काहेकउ कीजै धिआन जपना।
जब ते सुधु नाही मनु अपना।रहाउ॥
सिंधव भोजन जो नरु जाने।
जैसे ही ठग देउ बखाने॥२॥
नामे के सुआमी लाहिले झगरा।
राम रसाइन पीउ रे दगरा॥३॥

सांप अपनी केंचुली तो उतार देता है परन्तु विष नहीं त्यागता। अर्थात् भले ही चमड़ी उतर जावे परन्तु स्वभाव का परित्याग नहीं करता। बगुला पानी में एक टांग के सहारे तपस्वी की भांति खडा रहता है परन्तु अपना ध्यान मछली को पकड़ने में रखता है। इसी प्रकार प्रभु का ध्यान लगाने से और उसका नाम जपने का कोई लाभ नहीं जब तक कि अपना मन शुद्ध नहीं होता तथा माया का त्याग नहीं करता।

भुलिंग नाम का एक पक्षी होता है जो स्वयं तो यह कहता है कि "साहस मत कर" परन्तु करता यह है कि जब शेर जम्हाई लेता है तो अपनी दाढ़ों में फंसे मांस को निकार कर रख देता है अर्थात् कहता कुछ और है करता उसके विपरीत है। ऐसा मनुष्य भी प्रभु भक्ति करने के योग्य नहीं है।

नामदेवजी फरमाते हैं कि मेरे स्वामी ने यह कह कर झगड़ा ही निवेड़ दिया है कि दगाबाज मनुष्य तू राम के नाम रूपी अमृत को पी।

The following hymn was addressed to a reputed holy man who had stolen a merchant's money, and falsely imputed the offence to Namdev. The merchant had gone to bathe, and while doing so the hypocrite seated in a religious attitude stole his purse. The merchant missed it on returning. He could not think of attributing the theft to the man in the religious garb, so he charged Namdev with it. The merchant would not accept Namdev's denial, and had him flogged. While Namdev was being punished a storm arose which lifted the cloth on which the reputed holy man sat. The missing purse was then found under the cloth. Upon that Namdev addressed the following verses to the hypocrite :

5

The serpent casteth its slough, but not its poison:
Since thy heart is not pure,
Why perform *mock* meditation and repetition of God's name ?
Thou art as the crane watching *for fish* in the water,
The man who eateth the food of lions,
Is called the god of thieves.
Nama's Lord hath settled the quarrel;
Drink God's elixir, O double-faced one.

(६) राग-आसा

पारब्रह्मु जि चीनसी आसा ते न भावसी।
रामा भगतह चेती-अले अचिंत मनु राखसी॥१॥
कैसे मन तरहिगा रे संसार-सागरु बिखे को बना।
झूठी माइया देखिकै भूला रे मना॥रहाउ॥
छीपे के घरि जनमु दैला गुर उपदेसु भैला।
संतहुं के परसादि नामा हरि भेटुला॥

जो परमात्मा को पहचान लेता है उसको और इच्छाएँ अच्छी नहीं लगती।

इसी प्रकार जो प्रभु की भक्ति चित में रखता है उसकी मन किसी चिन्ता की तरफ नहीं जाता। हे मेरे प्रभु! "तू विषय रूपी संसार समुद्र कैसे पार करेगा?" फिर तू माया रूपी झूठे पदार्थों को देख कर प्रभु को ही भुला बैठा है। प्रभु ने मुझे शिल्पी के घर जन्म दिया परन्तु मुझे गुरु उपदेश मिल गया। और संतों की कृपा से नामदेव अपने प्रभु को मिल पाया।

6

Devotion to God is sufficient for human happiness

If thou see the Supreme God, thou shalt have no other desire;
If thou think of the worship of God, thou shalt keep thy mind free from care.
O my soul, how shalt thou cross over the world's ocean *filled with* the water of evil passions ?
O my soul, thou hast been led astray on seeing the deceitful world.
A calico-printer's house gave me birth, yet I became saturated with the guru's instruction.
Through the favour of holy men Nama hath met God.

(७) राग-गुजरी

जौ राजु देहि त कवन बढ़ाई।
जौर भीख मंगावहि त किआ घटि जाई।।१।।
तूं हरि भजु मन मेरे पदु निरबानु।
बहुरी न होइ तेरा आवन-जानु।।रहाउ।।
सभ ते उपाई भरम भुलाई।
जिस तूं देवहि तिसहि बुझाई।।२।।
सतिगुरु मिलै त सहसा जाई।
किस हऊ पूजुऊ दूजा नदरि न आई।।३।।
एक पाथर कजै भाऊ। दूजै पाथर धरिए पाऊ।।
जे वह देउ त उहु भी देवा।
कहि नामदेउ हम हरि की सेवा।।४।।

यदि परमात्मा राज्य दे देवें तो इसमें भी कोई बढ़ाई नहीं है। और यदि वह गरीब बना कर भिक्षा मांगने पर लगा दे तो भी कुछ नहीं घटता।

हे मेरे मन! तू अपने सदामुक्त प्रभु की भक्ति ही कर, जिससे माया के प्रभाव से ऊँचा मुक्ति-पद मिलता है और जन्म मरण में नहीं आता।।रहाउ।।

हे प्रभु तूने यह सारी रचना आप उत्पन्न की है। जिसने सबको भ्रम में डाल रखा है! जिसको तू अपनी भक्ति देता है उसे ही असलीयत की कुछ समझ आती है।

परन्तु सच्चे गुरु के मिलने से ही यह संशय रूपी भ्रम दूर होता है। फिर सब जगह प्रभु ही दिखाई पड़ता है तो किसी एक को कैसे पूजूं ?

एक पत्थर से तो प्यार करते हैं पर दूसरे पर तो पैर रखते है। नामदेव कहते हैं कि हम तो केवल एक प्रभु को ही सर्व व्यापक जानकर उसी की सेवा करते है। अर्थात् मन में यदि द्वैत भाव है तो दोनों पत्थर (पांव रखने वाला, तथा पूजा के योग्य) भिन्न-2 दिखाई पड़ते हैं और जब समभाव अद्वैत पद को प्राप्त कर लें तो दोनों की प्रभु का सर्व व्यापक जान लेने पर समान ही जाने जाते हैं।

7
GUJARI

Namdev worships the true God and is prepared to accept whatever He sands.

If Thou give me an empire, what glory shall it be to me ?
If Thou cause me to beg, how shall it degrade me ?

Worship God, O my soul, *and thou shalt obtain* the dignity of salvation.
And no more transmigration shall await thee.
O God, Thou didst create all men and lead them astray in error:
He to whom Thou givest *understanding* knoweth Thee.
When I meet the true guru, my doubts shall depart.
Whom shall I then worship ? none other would be seen *but Thee.*
One stone is adored.
Another is trodden under foot:
If one is a god, the other is also a god—
Saith Namdev, I worship the *true* God.

(८) राग-गुजरी

मलै न लाछै पार मलो परमजीउ बैठो री आई।
आवत किनै न पेखिउ कवनै जणौ री बाई॥१॥
कवण कहै किणि बूझिऐ, रमइआ आकुलु री बाई॥रहाउ॥
जिऊ आकासै पंखिअलो खोज निरखिउ न जाई।
जिऊ जलमाझै माछली मारगु पेवणो न जाई॥२॥
जिऊ आकासै घडुअलो मृग-त्रिसना भरिआ।
नामे के सुआमी बीठलो जिन तीनै जरिआ॥३॥

जिस परमात्मा का कोई मलीन माया रूपी चिह्न नहीं है और उससे वह बहुत दूर है, फिर उसकी चन्दन रूपी सुगंधि मेरे में प्रकट हो गई है, उसे किसी ने आते नहीं देखा इसलिए है भाई! उस देव-शक्ति को कोई नहीं जान सकता।

हे भाई, उसका कोन वर्णन कर सकता है? उसे किसने समझा है? वह तो सर्व व्यापक है। [रहाउ] जैस आसमान में पक्षी उड़ता है, परन्तु उसके पद चिह्न देखे नहीं जा सकते। अथवा पानी में मछली तैरती है, उसका रास्ता देखा नहीं जा सकता, इसी प्रकार परमात्मा कब और कहां से आया कहा नहीं जा सकता। आकाश में भ्रमजाल द्वारा नीलेपन के कारण पड़े हुए भ्रम की कोई हद नहीं होती, वैसे ही नामदेव के स्वामी तीनों लोकों में विस्तृत रूप से व्यापक हैं।

8

God's presence is felt though he cannot be discribed.

He who hath no trace of impurity, who is beyond impurity, and who is perfumed as with sandal hath taken His seat *in my heart.*

No one saw Him coming; who knoweth *Him*, O sister?
Who can describe, who can understand the All-prevading and unknowable?
As the trace of a bird is not perceived in the sky,
As the path of a fish is not seen in the water,
As a vessel is not filled with the mirage-water of the sky,
Such is God, Nama's Lord, in whom these three *qualities* are blended; *His coming or going is not seen.*

(९) राग-सोरठ

जब देखा तब गावा तउ जन धीरजु पावा।
नादि समाइलो रे सतिगुरु भेटिले देवा।।रहाउ।।
जह झिलिमिलिकरि दिंसता तह अनाहद सबद बंजता।
जोती जोति समानी मैं गुरु परसादी जानी।।१।।
रतन कमल कोठरी चमकार बीजुलत ही।
नेरै नाही दूरी निज आतमै रहिआ भरपूरि।।२।।
जह अनाहत सूर उजारा तह दीपक जलै छछांरा।
गुर परसादी जानिआ जनु नामा सहज समानिया।।३।।

जिस समय मैं तुझे देखता हूं तेरे गुण गाता हूं। इससे मुझे तेरे दास को धीरज और शांति मिलती है। सतगुरु के उपदेश मानने से शब्द-ब्रह्म-ज्योति में लीन हो गया हूं। [रहाउ]

यहां तेज रोशनी की चमक है तथा अनाहद शब्द बज रहा है। मेरी ज्योति भी ब्रह्म-ज्योति में समा रही है। मैंने गुरु कृपा से ही प्रभु-ज्योति को जाना है। हृदय-कंवल रूपी कोठड़ी में गुण रूपी रत्न पड़े हैं, जिनका बिजली जैसा प्रकाश है। यह प्रभु अति समीप रहता है तथा दूर नहीं होता क्योंकि अपनी आत्मा में रमा होता है।

ज्ञान रूपी प्रभु सूर्य के प्रकाश जैसा होने से अन्य दिये, चांद आदि का प्रकाश मध्यम पड़ जाता है। यह सब गुरु कृपा से ही पाया है तथा मैनें सहज अवस्था प्राप्त कर ली है।

9
SORATH

Namdev advises to accept divine instruction so that man may be contented and happy.

When I sing of God, then I behold Him;
Then I, His slave, obtain contentment.

Accept divine instruction, O man; the true guru shall cause thee to meet God.

Where the heavenly light shineth,
There playeth spontaneous music.
'God's light is all-pervading'—
By the guru's favour I know that.
In the chamber of the heart are jewels
Which glitter there like lightning.
God is near, not distant,
And *His Spirit* completely filleth mine.
Where the inextinguishable sun of *God's word* shineth,
There *carthly* lamps grow pale:
Through the guru's favour I have know this.
God's slave Nama hath been easily absorbed in Him.

(१०) राग-सोरठ

पाड़ पड़ोसणि पुछिलै नामा कापहि छानि छवाई हो।
तोपहि दुगणी मजूरी दैहउ मोकउ बेड़ी देहू बताई हो॥१॥
री बाई देनु न जाई देखु बेड़ी रहिउ समाई हमारै बेड़ी प्राण अधारा॥रहाउ॥
बेड़ी प्रीति मजूरी मांग जऊ कोऊ छानि छबावें हो।
लोग कुटंब समहु ते तारै तउ आपन बेड़ी आवै हो॥२॥
ऐसो बेड़ी बरनि न साकउ सभ अंतर सभ ठाई हो।
गुंगे महा अम्रित-रस चाखिआ पूछे कहनुन जाई हो॥३॥
बेड़ी के गुन सुनि री बाई जलधि बांधि ध्रु थापिउ हो।
नामे के सुआमी सीअ बहोरी लंक भभीखण आपिउ हो॥४॥

साथ की एक पड़ोसन नामदेवजी को पूछने लगी कि आपने ये छप्पर किससे बनवाया? मैं उसको तुम्हारे से दुगनी मजदूरी दूंगी मुझे वह कारीगर बता दें।

हे बहन वह कारीगर किसो को बताया नहीं जा सकता वो तो सभी में समाया है। वह कारीगर हमारे प्राणों का आधार है। जो भी उस कारीगर से छप्पर बनवाता है उससे वह प्रीत रूपी मजदूरी मांगता है।

जी संसार और परिवार से मोह तोड़ कर उसके साथ प्रीत करता है तो वह कारीगर स्वयं आ जाता है। वह ऐसा कारीगर है जिसका मैं वर्णन भी नहीं कर सकता क्योंकि वह सर्व व्यापक है। जैसे एक गूँगा प्राणी महाअमृत रस पीकर उसके स्वाद का वर्णन नहीं कर सकता वैसे ही उस प्रभु का आन्नद है।

हे बहन तू उस कारीगर के गुण सुन। उसने समुद्र पर पुल बनाया और ध्रुव को अटल पदवी प्रदान की नामदेव के स्वामी तो सीता को वापस लाए थे और लंका विभीषण को सौंप दी थी।

10

The roof of Namdev's hut was blown away by a storm while the inmates were asleep. A devout friend whom Namdev recognized as God incarnate at once procceded to re-roof the building. This incident was versified by Namdev in the Sorath measure as follows:—

> A near neighbour asked Nama, 'By whom didst thou have this hut rebuilt'?
> 'If thou show me the carpentei, I will pay him twice the wages thou didst'.
> 'O my sister, my Carpenter cannot be given thee;
> Lo! my Carpenter pervadeth all things;
> My Carpenter is the Support of the soul.
> If any one want such a hut to be built, the Carpenter will require love for His wages.
> When man breaketh with his family and all his friends, then the Carpenter of His own accord cometh to him.
> I cannot describe such a Carpenter; He is contained in everything and in every place.
> As when a dumb man tasteth the great flavour of nectar, if thou ask him, he cannot describe it.
> Hear the praises of the Carpenter, my sister—He restrained the ocean and fixed Dhru *as the polar star.*
> Nama's Lord recovered Sita, and bestowed Lanka on Babhikhan.

(११) राग-सोरठ

अण मडिआ मंदलु बाजै। बिनु सावन घन हरु गाजै।
बादल बिनु बरखा होई। जउ ततु बिचारे कोई॥१॥
मोउ मिलिउ रामु सनेही। जिह मिलिए देहसु देही॥रहाउ॥
मिलि पारस कंचनु होइआ। मुख मनसा रतनु परोइआ।
जिन भाऊ भइआ भ्रमु भागा। गुरु पूछे मनु पति आइगा॥२॥
जल भीतरि कुंभ समानिआ। सभ रामु एकु करि जानिआ।
गुरु चेले है मनु मानिआ। जनु नामा ततु पछानिआ॥३॥

प्रभु मिलाप की खुशी के कारण मन रूपी अनमड़्या (बगैर मड़ा) ढोल बजता है। इस प्रभु नाम की गर्जना सावन महीने की गर्जना के तुल्य हर समय होती है।

यह नाम रूपी अमृत की वर्षा बिना बादलों के होती है। परन्तु यह प्राप्ति तब होती है यदि कोई व्यापक परम तत्व पर विचार करता रहे। मुझे मित्र रूप में प्रभु मिला है जिसके मिलने से मेरी काया पुनीत हो गई है। गुरु रूपी पारस से मिल कर मेरा लोह रूप जीव आत्मा सोना बन गया है। मन और मुख में नाम रूपी रत्न पिरोया गया है। जब अपने असली स्वरूप से प्रेम हो गया तो भ्रम नाश हो गया है। गुरु के उपदेश लेने के कारण इस प्रकार मन को तसल्ली हुई। अब जीव आत्मा रूपी घड़ा समुद्र रूप परमात्मा में समा गया है। हर स्थान में व्यापक प्रभु को ही देखता हूं जब गुरु और चेले का मन एक हो गया तो प्रभु के दास नामदेव ने परम तत्व को पहचान लिया।

11

The whole of the following hymn relates to the Jog philosophy and the exaltation of mind produced by its practice:—

Without covering it with leather the drum of *the brain* playeth;
Without *waiting for the month of* Sawan the thunder roreth,
And it raineth without clouds,
If any one consider the real state of things,
I have met my dear Lord.
By meeting Him my body hath become perfect;
Having touched the philosopher's stone I have become gold.
In word and thought I have strung the gems of *God's name.*
I feel real love *for God,* my doubts are dispelled:
On questioning the guru my mind is satisfied.
As the pitcher is filled with water,
I know that the world is filled with the one God.
When the disciple's mind accepted the guru,
The slave Nama recognized God.

However great man may be, he should reflect that death is his fate at last.

(१२) राग-धनासरी

गहरी करिके नीव खुदाई, उपरि मंडप छाए।
मारकंडे ते कोअधिकाई, जिनि त्रिण धरि मूंड बलाएं॥१॥
हमरो करता रामु सनेही।
कहि रे नर गरबु करतउ बिनसि जाई झूठी देही॥रहाउ॥

मेरी मेरी कौरउ करते दुरजोधन सौ भाई।
बारह जोजन छत्र चले था, देही गिरझन खाई॥२॥
सरब सोइन की लंका होती, रावन ते अधिकाई।
कहां भइउ दरि बांधै हाथी, खिन महि भई पराई॥३॥
दुरवासा सिऊ करत ठगऊरी, जादब ए फल पाए।
कृपा करी जन अपने ऊपर, नामदेउ हरि गुण गाए॥४॥

जीवन को चिरस्थायी समझ कर तुमने गहरी नींव खुदवा कर उस पर महल-माडी बनाए। परंतु सबसे लम्बी आयु वाले मारकंड़े ऋषि ने अपने दिन सिर पर घास फूल रख कर बिता लिये।

हमारा रचने वाला प्रभु सबसे स्नेह करता है। हे जीव! क्यों अहंकार करता है। इस नाशवान शरीर ने तो समाप्त ही होना है। कौरव, जिनके दुर्योधन जैसे सौ भाई थे वो कहते थे कि सब कुछ हमारा है उनका छत्र बारह योजन तक चलता था। परन्तु उनके शरीर को अन्त समय गिदों ने ही खाया।

रावण जैसे बड़े बलि राजे हुए हैं जिनकी लंका सोने की बनी हुई थी और जिसके दरवाजे पर हाथी झूलते थे वह भी नाश हो गए और उनकी सारी दौलत पराई हो गई। यादवों ने भी दुर्वासा ऋषि से अहंकार में आकर हंसी ठठोल की थी जिसके कारण उनका सारा वंश नाश हो गया। परन्तु सतगुरु ने अपने दास नामदेव पर कृपा की है जिसके कारण प्रभु के गुण गाने के योग्य हो पाया।

12
DHANASARI

Men dig deep foundations and build palaces thereon.
Was any one longer lived than Markand's who *put* grass on his hea and *thus* whiled away *his days* ?
Only God the Creator is dear to me;
O man, why art thou proud ? this unsubstantial body shall be destroyed.
The Kauravs, Duryodhan and his brothers, used to say, 'Everything is ours'.
Their umbrellas extended over a space of twelve jojans, *yet* the vultures devoured their bodies.
Lanka was all gold; was any one greater than Rawan ?
What availed him the elephants tethered at his gate ? In a moment they become the property of others.
The Yadavs practised deception on Durbasa, and obtained the fruit thereof.

God showed merey to His slave; Namdev singeth His praises.

The following hymn was addressed to a Jogi who endeavoured to induce Namdev to embrace his religion.

(१३) राग-धनासरी

दस बैरागनि मोहि बसि कीनि पचहु का मिट नावऊ।
सत्तरि-दोड़ भरे अम्रित-सरी विखु कउ मारि कढ़ावऊ॥१॥
पाछे बहुरि न आवनु पावउ।
अम्रित वाणी घट ते उचरऊ आतम कउ समझावऊ॥रहाउ॥
बजर कुठारु मोहि है छीना, करि बिनति लगि पावऊ।
संतन के हम उलटे सेवक, भगतन ते डर पावऊ॥२॥
इस संसार ते तब ही छू टऊ जऊ माइआ नह लपटावऊ।
माइआ नाम गरभ जोनि का, तिह तजि दरसनु पावऊ॥३॥
इतुकरि भगति कराहि जो जन तिन भउ सगल चुकाइए।
कहत नामदेऊ बाहरि किआ भरमहु इह संजम हरि पाइए॥४॥

मैंने पदार्थों के पीछे भागने वाली दस चंचल इन्द्रियों को वश में कर लिया है और पांचों विकार (काम, क्रोध, लोभ, मोह, अहंकार) को मूलतः खत्म कर दिया है शरीर में बहत्तर मुख्य नाड़ियों को नाम रूपी अमृत सरोवर से भर लिया है। अथवा विषय रूपी जहर को नष्ट कर दिया है।

जब में संसार में वापस नहीं आऊँगा। इसलिए मैं अमृत रूपी वाणी अपने हृदय द्वार से उच्चारण करता हूं ओर अपनी जीव आत्मा को समझता हूं। गुरु की कृपा से शब्द रूप कुल्हाड़ी ले कर मैंने मोह को काट दिया है। अब संसार से परे होकर हमने संत सेवा और भक्तों का आसरा लिया है।

इस संसार से तो तब छुटकारा होता है जब माया से निर्लेप रहे क्योंकि उसके असर से गर्भ (योनि) में पड़ना पड़ता है, ओर इसके त्याग से प्रभु दर्शन प्राप्त होता है। इस प्रकार जो भी प्राणि भक्ति करते हैं उनका सारा डर दूर हो जाता है।

नामदेवजी कहते हैं कि बाहर ढूंढने की बजाय आत्मिक साधना ही प्रभु प्राप्ति का साधन है।

13

I have restrained the ten organs of sense; the *very* name of the five evil passions I have erased.
Having extracted the poison from the seventy-two tanks of the heart, I have filled them with ambrosia;

I shall not allow the poison to return again.
The ambrosia word I utter from my heart; my spirit I instruct *not to attach itself* to worldly things.
I have destroyed worldly love with an axe of adamant: I touch the guri's feet and implore him.
Turning away *from the world,* I have become a servant of the saints and I fear them.
I shall be saved from this world the moment I cease to be entangled by Maya.
Maya is the name of the power which placeth man in the womb; abandoning it I shall obtain a sight of God.
The man who worshippeth in this way shall be freed from all fear.
Saith Namdev, O man, why wander abroad? obtain God in the way *I have told thee.*

Namdev tells by familiar examples how dear God is to him.

(१४) राग-धनासरी

मारवाड़ी जैसे नीरु बालहा, बेलि आलहा कराहला।
जउ कुरंगनिसि नादु बालहा, तिउ मेरै मनि रमाइआ॥१॥
तेरा नाम रुडो, रूप रुडो अति रंग रुडो, मेरो रमाइआ।रहाउ॥
जिउ धरणी कड इंद्र बालहा, कुसम बासु जैसे भवरला।
जिउ कोकिल कउ अंबु बालहा, तिउ मेरै मनी रामइआ॥२॥
चकवी कउ जैसे सूरू बालहा, मान सरोवर हंसुला।
जिउ तरुणी कउ कंतु बालहा, तिउ मेरै मनी रामइआ॥३॥
बारिक कउ जैसे खीरु बालहा, चात्रिक मुख जैसे जलधरा।
मछली कउ जैसे नीरु बालहा, तिउ मेरै मनि रामइआ॥४॥
साधिक, सिध सगल मुनि चाहहि, बिरलो काहु डीठुला।
सगल भवल तेरे नामु बालहा, तिउ नामें मनि बीठुला॥५॥

जैसे मारवाड़ में पानी प्यारा लगता है, ऊँट को बेल से प्यार होता है और हिरन को राम समय घंटी की आवाज प्यारी लगती है वैसे ही मेरे मन को राम प्यारा लगता है।

हे मेरे प्रभु! तेरा नाम और स्वरूप सुन्दर है और तेरा प्रेम भी अति उत्तम है। जैसे धरती को बादल, भंवरे को फूल की सुगंध और कोयल को आम प्यारा होता है वैसे ही मेरे मन को राम प्यारा लगता है। जैसे चकवी को सूर्य प्यारा है, हंस को मानसरोवर, स्त्री

को पति प्यारा होता है, वैसे ही मेरे मन को राम प्यारा लगता है। जैसे बच्चे को दूध, चांत्रिक को स्वाति बूंद और मछली को नीर प्यारा होता है, वैसे ही मेरे मन को राम प्यारा लगता है। साधना करने वाले सिद्ध पुरुष और ऋषि मुनि सारे ही चाहते हैं कि तेरे दर्शन हों पर किसी को ही तेरे दर्शन होते हैं जैसे सारे ब्रह्मांड को तेरा नाम प्यारा है, वैसे ही नामदेव के मन को प्रभु विठ्ठल प्यारा है।

14

A water is dear *to the traveller* in Marwar, and the creeper to the camel:
As the huntsman's bell at night is dear to the hind, so is God to my soul—
Thy name is beautiful, Thy form is beautiful, very beautiful Thy colour, O my God—
As rain is dear to the earth, as the odour of flowers is dear to the bumble-bee;
As the mango is dear to the kokil, so is God to my soul.
As the sun is dear to the sheldrake, as the lake of Mansarowar is dear to the swan;
As the husband is dear to the wife, so is God to my soul.
As milk is dear to the child, as a torrent of rain to the mouth of the chatrik;
As water is dear to the fish, so is God to my soul.
All penitents, sidhs, and munis seek God, but few have seen Him.
As Thy name is dear to all creation, so is Vitthal to Nama's heart.

(१५) राग-धनासरी

पहिले पुरिए पुंडरक बना। ताचे हंसा सगले जना।
कृसनाते जानऊ, हरि नाचंती नाचना॥१॥
पहिले पुरसा बिरा। अयोंन पुरसा दमरा॥
अस गा उस उसगा। हरि का बागरा नाचै पिंघी पहि सागरा॥रहाउ॥
नाचंती गोपी जना। नइप्रा ते वैरे कंना।
तरकु न चा। भ्रमीअचा॥
केसवा बचवुनी अइए मइए, एक आनै जीऊ।
पिंघी उभकले संसारा॥२॥
भ्रमि-भ्रमि आए तुमचे दुआरा। तूं कुनु रे। मैं जी नामा॥
हो जी आला। ते निवारण जब कारणा॥३॥

संसार रचना से पहले कमल बना। उस कमल से ब्रह्मा तथा सारे जीव पैदा हुए।

यह हर प्रकार की सृष्टि, माया सबल, भ्रम, कृष्ण के अनुसार ही नाच रही है। प्रथम अकाल पुरुष से वाणी बनी, फिर माया बनी और उसके मेल से सब कुछ उत्पन्न हुआ यह सारा संसार प्रभु का एक बगीजा है जिसमें प्रभु आप नाच रहा है। [रहाउ]

स्त्री-पुरुष प्रभु की गोपी रूप होकर नाच रहे हैं परमात्मा से अलग कोई भी नहीं। इस पर कोई तर्क न करे क्यों वह एक भ्रम है। यह परमात्मा के वचन है कि ये संसार और मैं एक हैं। इस संसार रूपी कुँए में रहट की तरह ऊपर नीचे अर्थात् जन्म-मरण के चक्कर में पड़ा हूं।

अथवा अब मैं कई योनि से होकर तेरे द्वारे पर पहुंचा हूं। ओर अब परमात्मा पूछता है कि तू कौन है क्या चाहता है? और नम्रता से नामदेवजी कहते हैं कि मैं नामदेव हूं मुझे यम के हाथों से बचाना।

15

Namdev asked his guru how the world had been created-The guru replied

Before the world a lotus was formed;
From it proceeded Brahma, and from Brahma all men. Know that everything else teas *produced* from Maya, who leadeth the world a dance.
Namdev then inquired how Maya was produced. The guru replied:—
First a voice proceeded from God;
Afterwards Maya proceeded from God
Through that voice the parts of this *Maya* and of that *God* blended, *and the world was produce.*
In this garden of God *men dance* like water in the pots of a well;
Women and men dance.
There is no god but God—
Argue not on this point.
If thou have doubts
God saith, 'Consider in thy heart that this world and I are one.
The world is like water-pots, sometimes above, sometimes below.
Wandering about I have come to Thy gate.
God—Who art Thou?
Nanet—I am Nama, Sire—
O Lord, save me from the world which bringeth death.

(१६) राग-धनासरी

पतित पावन माधऊ बिरदु तेरा।
धंनि ते वै मुनि जन, जिन धिआइउ हरि प्रभु मेरा॥१॥
मेरै माथै लागीलै धूरि गोविंद चरणन की।
सुर नर मुनि जन तिनहु ते दूरि।रहाउ॥
दीन का दइआलु माधौ गरब परिहारी।
चरण सरन नामा बति तिहारी॥२॥

हे माधव जी! मुझे माया रूपी संसार से, जो मौत का मूल है बचा लीजिए। हे माया पति, आप विकारों में लगे पापियों को पवित्र कर दें।

वे मुनि लोग धन्य हैं जिन्होंने मेरे प्रभु का सिमरन किया है।

मेरे माथे पर प्रभु के चरणों की धूल लगी है जो कि देवता और मनुष्य प्राप्त नहीं कर सकते। [रहाउ]

हे माधव आप गरीबों पर दया करने वाले हैं और अहंकारियों के गर्व को नीचा दिखाते है। मैं नामदेव आपके शरण आया हूं और आप पर बलिहारी जाता हूं।

16

O Lord, the purification of sinners is Thy daily work;
Hail to those saints who have mediated on my God.
On my forehead is the dust of God's feet,
Which is far from even demigods, worldly men, munis, and saints.
Compassionate to the poor, O God, destroyer of pride,
Nama hath found the asylum of Thy feet, and is a sacrifice unto Thee

(१७) राग-तोड़ी

कोई बोलै नीरवा कोई बोलै दूरि।
जल की मछली चरै खजूरी॥१॥
कांइ रे बक-वादु लाइउ।
जिन हरि पाइउ तिनहि छपाइउ।रहाउ॥
पंडित होइकै बेदु बखानै।
मूरख नामदेउ रामहि जानै॥२॥

कोई परमात्मा को निकट भाव से अपने अन्दर देखता है और कोई दूर भाव से बाहर देखता है। ये बात ऐसी है जैसे की कोई मछली अपने जीवन आधार जल को छोड़ कर किसी खजूर के वृक्ष पर चढ़ने का यत्न करे।

हे भाई व्यर्थ बहस क्यों करते हो। जिन्होंने प्रभु को पाया है वो उसे प्रकट नहीं करता।

आप वेद शास्त्रों के ज्ञाता होकर केवल वेद ही उच्चारण करते हो और मूर्ख नामदेव इनके व्यापक तत्व (को) प्रभु पहचानता है।

17

It is said that Namdev composed the following on hearing two pandits disputing whether God was far or near:—

TODI

Some say God is near, others that He is far away.
To say He is near or far is, as it were, to say that a fish could climb a date-tree.
Why, Sir, talkest thou nonsense?
They who have found God have concealed *the fact.*
Men who are pandits shout the Veds,
But the ignorant Namdev *only* knoweth God.

On the eleventh day of every half lunar month the Hindus fast. Namdev relinquished the practice, and also ceased to go on pilgrimages. A visitor to his house reproached him with his neglect of both these religious duties. The following is his reply.

(१८) राग-तोड़ी

कउन को कलंकु रहिउ, रामु नामु लेतही।
पतित पवित भये रामु कहत ही॥१॥
राम संगि नाम देउ, जन कऊ प्रतिगिआ आई।
एकादशी व्रतु रहै काहे कउ तीरथ जाई॥२॥
भनति नामदेऊ सुक्रित सुमति भए।
गुर मति राम कहि, को कोन बैकुंठी गए॥३॥

प्रभु का नाम जपने से किसी का कलंक नहीं रहा। विकारों में पड़े हुए पापी भी प्रभु का नाम लेने से पवित्र हो गए हैं।

प्रभु के साथ जुड़ने से ही नामदेव को यह दृढ़ विश्वास हुआ।

एकादशी का व्रत रखने वाले को तो तीर्थदिकों की यात्रा करने से क्या काम?

नामदेवजी कहते हैं कि हमें पुण्य रूप श्रेष्ठ मति मिली है कि गुरु की शिक्षा के अनुसार नाम जपने से सारे ही बैकुंठ तक पहुंच जाते हैं।

18

Who that uttereth God's name retaineth the stain of sin?
Sinners have become pure by uttering His name.
In the company of God His slave Namdev hath acquired ocular evidence.
He hath ceased to fast on the eleventh day, and why should he go on pilgrimages?
Saith Namdev, my acts and thoughts have become good.
Who hath not gone to heaven by uttering the name of God under the guru's instruction?

Namdev is satisfied with God as his portion.

(१९) राग-तोड़ी

तीनि छंदे खेलु आछै।
तीनि छंदे खेलु आछै।रहाउ॥
कुंभार के घर हांडी आछै।
राजा के घर सांडी गो॥
बामन के घर रांडी आछै।
रांडी सांडी हांडी गो॥१॥
बाणी के घर हींगु आछै।
भेसर माथै सींगुगो॥
देवल मघे लींगु आछै।
लींगु सींगु हींगु गो॥२॥
तेली के घर तेलु आछै।
जंगल मघे बेलगो॥
माली के घर केल आछै।
केल, बेल, तेल गो॥३॥
संतामघें गोबिंदु आछै।
गोकल मघे सिआम गो॥

नामे मघे रामु आछै।
राम सिआम गोबिंदु गो॥४॥

इस शब्द से त्रिगुणी खेल प्रधान है। जैसे कुम्हार के घर मिट्टी के बर्तन, राजा के घर हाथी ऊँट आदि, ब्राह्मण के घर वेद, शास्त्र आदि ग्रन्थ हों तो यह तीनों पदार्थ अपने अपने स्थानों पर अच्छे लगते हैं। जैसे बनिये के घर हींग आदि सौदे, भैंस के सर पर सींग और शिवालय में शिवलिंग ही उत्तम हैं, यहां वैसे ही शिवलिंग, सींग ही प्रधान हैं।

जैसे तेली के घर तेल, जंगल में बेल और माली के घर केले ही शोभा देते हैं यहां केले, बेल और तेल ही प्रधान हैं।

जैसे संतों के हृदय में गोबिंद, गोकुल में कृष्ण जी शोभायमान हैं वैसे नामदेवजी कहते हैं मेरे हृदय में राम ही शोभायमान हैं और यहां राम, कृष्ण और गोबिंद ही प्रधान हैं।

19

There is a play on three sets of words.
There is a pot in a potter's house, an elephant in a king's house,
A widow in a Brahman's house—sing randi, sandi, handi O!
Asafoetida in a baniya's house, horns on a buffalo's forehead,
A lingam in a temple of Shiv—sing ling, sing, hing O!
Oil in an oilman's house, creepers in a forest,
Plantains in a gardener's house—sing kel, bel, tel O!
Gobind in the company of the saints, Krishan in Gokal,
And God in Nama—sing Ram, Siyam, Gobind O!

(२०) राग-तिलंग

मैं अंधुले की टेक, तेरा रामु खुंदकारा।
मैं गरीब मैं मसकीन, तेरा नामु है अधारा।रहाउ॥
करीमां रहीमां अलाह तूं गनी।
हाजरा हजीर दरि पेसि तूं मनी॥१॥
दरिआऊ तूं दिहंद तूं बिसिआर तूं धनी।
देहि लेहि एकु तूं दिगर को नहीं॥२॥
तूं दाना तूं बीना मैं बिचारू किया करी।
नामेचे सुआमी बखसंद तूं हरी॥३॥

हे सर्व के मालिक! मुझ अन्धे का सहारा तेरा नाम है मैं गरीब और (निर्माण) बेसहारा हूं तेरा नाम ही एक सहारा है। हे अल्लाह! तू ही दयालु और रहम करने वाला मेरा धनी है।

तू मेरे अन्दर बाहर सब जगह मौजूद है। सब कुछ तेरे ऊपर है, तू दाता और बड़ा धनी है। देने और लेने वाला दाता एक तू ही है और कोई दूसरा नहीं। तू सब कुछ जानने वाला और सब कुछ देखने वाला है, मैं तेरा वर्णन क्या करूँ।

नामदेव जी कहते हैं मेरे स्वामी प्रभु तू दया करनो वाला तथा क्षमा करने वाला है।

20
TILANG

Namdev feels his dependence on God whom he magnifies.

Of me who am blind Thy name, O King, is the prop.
I am poor, I am miserable. Thy name is my support.
Bounteous and merciful Allah. Thou art generous;
I believe that Thou art present before me;
Thou art a river of *bounty*, Thou art the Giver, Thou art exceeding wealthy;
Thou alone givest and takest, there is none other;
Thou art wise, Thou art far-sighted; what conception can I form of Thee?
O Nama's Lord. Thou art the Pardoner, O God.
Namdev on the way to Dwaraka was seized by a Mughal official and made a forced labourer.

In his devotion he appears to have recognized the Mughal as God, and to have believed that his degradation was God's will. He composed the following on the occasion:—

(२१) राग-तिलंग

हले यारां हले यारां खुसि खबरी।
बलि बलि जाऊँ हउ बलि बलि जाऊँ॥
नीकी तेरी बिगारी आले तेरा नाऊ।रहाउ॥
कुजा आमद, कुजा रफती, कुला मेरवी।
द्वारिका नगरी रासि बुगोई॥१॥
खूबु तेरी पगरी मीठे तेरे बोल।
द्वारिका नगरी काहे के मगोल॥२॥
चंदी हजार आलम एक लखाना।
हम चिंनी पातिसाह सांवले बरना॥३॥
असपति गजपति नरह नरिंद।
नामेके स्वामी मीर मुकुदं॥४॥

पठान के रूप में घोड़े पर सवार वेष में (प्रभु से) सम्बोधन करते हुए: हे मित्र! हे सज्जन! सुख आनन्द तो है। मैं तुझ पर बलिहारी जाता हूं, कुर्बान जाता हूं तेरी बेगार भी अच्छी है (घोड़े के बच्चे को उठाना) और तेरा नाम भी बड़ा है। [रहाउ]

तू कहां से आया है और किधर जाना है (भाव तू तो सर्व व्यापक है) यह द्वारिका नगरी है, अत: सच बताओ तेरी पगड़ी सुन्दर है, अत: तेरे शब्द मीठे हैं। इस द्वारिका नगरी में भला मुगल कहां से आ गए (भाव तू तो हरी का रूप है) यहां हजारों लोगों में केवल तुझे ही अलग सा (मुगल) देखता हूं।

परन्तु हमें ए, बादशाह! ऐसा जान पड़ता है कि आप सांवले रंग वाले कण हैं। आप ही सूर्य देवता, इन्द्र देवता और नरों मे राजा ब्रह्मा हैं।

नामदेव जी कहते हैं, कि हे मेरे स्वामी आप सब को बादशाह और मुक्ति दाता हैं।

21

Hallo! my Friend, hallo my Friend, how art Thou!
I am a sacrifice unto Thee, I am a sacrifice unto Thee.
Good is Thy forced labour, exalted Thy name;
Whence hast Thou come? where hast Thou been? and whitherart Thou going?
This is the city of Dwaraka; tell the truth.
Handsome is Thy turban, sweet Thy discourse;
But why should there be a Mughal in the city of Dwaraka?
Among several thousands of people *Thou art* the only *Mughal* seen;
Thou art the very picture of the king of sable hue;
Thou art the Lord of the horse, the Lord of the elephant, and the Ruler of men.
Thou art Nama's Lord, the King of *all,* and the Giver of salvation.

(२२) राग-बिलावल

सफल जनम मोकउ गुरु कीना।
दुख विसारि सुख अंतरि लीना॥१॥
गिआन अंजनु मोउ गुरु दीना।
राम नाम बिनु जीवनु मन हीना।रहाउ॥
नामदेव सिमरनु करि जानां।
जग जीवन सिऊ जीऊ समानां॥२॥

गुरु ने नाम देकर जन्म सफल कर दिया है। दुख दूर हो गए हैं और अन्तर आत्मा सुखी हो गई है। गुरु ने मुझे ज्ञान रूपी सुरमा दिया है जिस के कारण मुझे राम-नाम के बगैर जीवन आत्मा रहित लगता है।

नामदेव ने समर्ण द्वारा ही प्रभु को पाया है और मेरा मन जगत के प्राणाधार में समा गया है।

22
BILAWAL

Through his guru Namdev has obtained discernment and rendered his life profitable.

The guru hath made my life profitable—
I have forgotten sorry and obtained joy within me.
The guru hath granted me the eye-slave of divine knowledge.
O my soul, without God's name man's life is vain.
Namdev knoweth God by keeping Him in mind;
My soul is absorbed in Him who giveth life to the world.

To sing God's praises and remember Him is infinitely superior to all Hindu forms of devotion.

(२३) राग-गौड़

असु-मेघ जगने, तुला पुरख दाने प्राग इसनाने॥१॥
तउ न पुजहि हरि कीरति नामा॥
अधुने रामहि भजु, रे मन, आलसीआ॥रहाउ॥
गइआ पिंडु भरता, बनारसि असि बसता।
मुखि बेदु चतुर पड़ता॥२॥
सगल धरम अधिता। गुर गिआन इंद्रो द्रिड़ता।
खटु करम सहित रहता॥३॥
सिवा सकति संवादं। मन छोड़ि छोड़ि सगल भेदं।
सिमरि सिमरि गोविंद। भजु नामा तरसि भवसिंधं॥४॥

यदि कोई अश्व-मेघ यज्ञ करे अथवा अपने बराबर सोना तोल कर दे (तुलादान) और प्रयाग तीर्थ का स्नान करे तब भी वह कर्म प्रभु नाम कीर्तन के बराबर नहीं हो सकते। इसलिए मेरे आलसी मन, अपने प्रभु का भजन कर।

गया तीर्थ पर पित्रों के पिंड़ भराना, काशी जी में नदी के किनारे बसेरा करना, मुख से चारों वेदों का उच्चारण करना अन्य सारे कर्म धर्म संयुक्त होना, गुरु के उपदेश अनुसार इन्द्रियों को वश में रखना।

जप, हवन, संध्या, स्नान, पूजा, देव अर्चना, शिव-पार्वती सेवा और रामायण आदि सभी छ: कर्म करने यह सब दिखावा है। अत: मेरे मन! इन सब को त्याग दे। ए नामेदव! तू प्रभु का स्मरण कर, प्रभु के भजन द्वारा ही संसार समुद्र को पार करेगा।

23
GAUND

Were I to perform the horse-sacrifice.
Give my weight *in gold* as alms
Bathe at Pryag,
It would not be equal, O Nama, to singing God's praises. O listless man, worship thy God.
Were I to offer rice-balls at Gaya.
Dwell at Banaras.
Recite the four Veds,
Fulfil all religious offices,
Resstrain my senses under the guru's instruction,
Perform the six duties of Brahmans,
Read the conversations between Shiv and his consort—
All these different *occupations would be useless*; O my soul, lay them aside,
And remember, remember God's name.
Worship Him, Nama, and thou shalt swim across the world's ocean.

Namdev by familiar examples describes his love for God.

(२४) राग-गौड़

नाद भ्रमे जैसे मिरगाए। प्रान तजे वाको धिआनु न जाए।।१।।
ऐसे राम ऐसे हेरऊ। राम छोड़ि चितु अनत न फेरउ।।रहाउ।।
जिऊ मीना हेरै पसुआरा। सोना गड़ते हिरै सुनारा।।२।।
जिऊ बिखई हेरै परनारी। कउड़ा डारत हिरै जुआर।।३।।
ज़ह जह देखऊ तह तह रामा। हरिके चरन नित धिआवै नामा।।४।।

जैसे हिरन (घंटाहेड़े) की आवाज सुन कर उधर दौड़ता है और प्राण तक देकर भी उसका ध्यान नहीं हटता, मैं भी ऐसे ही राम जी को देखता हूं अपने चित्त को अन्य दिशा में जाने नहीं देता।

ऐ मित्र! प्रभु नाम ही ग्रहण कर, जैसे बगला मछली को देखता है, सुनार सोना घड़ते समय उस पर ध्यान रखता है। जैसे विषयी पुरष पराई स्त्री को ताकता है। जैसे जुआरी कोड़ी फैंक कर उन्हें रीझ कर देखता है। तैसे नामदेव प्रभु को सर्वत्र देखता है और प्रभु चरणों मे ही ध्यान रखता है।

24

As the deer followeth the *huntsman's* bell,
And giveth up its own life rather than cease its attention,
In the same way I gaze on God
I do not leave Him to turn my mind in another direction.
As the kingfisher gazeth on the fish,
As the goldsmith *meditateth* stealing gold while fashioning it,
As the lustful man gazeth on the wife of another,
As the gambler meditateth cheating while playing kauris,
So Nama ever meditateth on God's feet—
Wherever I gaze there is God.

(२५) राग-गौड़

मोकउं तारिले रामा तारिले।
मैं अजानु जनु तरिबे न जानऊं बाप बीठुला बाह दे।रहाउ॥
नर ते सुर होइ जात निमखमै सतिगुरु बुधि सिखलाई।
नर ते उपजि सुरग कउ जीतिओ सो अवखद मैं पाई॥१॥
जहां जहां धुआ नारदु टेके नैकु टिकावहु मोहि।
तेरे नाम अवलंबि बहुतु जन उधरे, नाम की निजमति एहि॥२॥

हे मेरे राम! मुझे संसार सागर से तार ले, बचा ले, हे मेरे पिता प्रभु! मुझे अपनी भुजा पकड़ा।

मैं तेरा अन्जान सेवक हूं। तैरना नहीं जानता सतगुरु ने जिसको शिक्षा दी है वह आंख के फड़कने में ही मनुष्य से देवता हो गये। और उस ने मनुष्य जन्म लेकर स्वर्ग प्राप्त कर लिया। यही द्वाई (उपदेश) गुरु ने मुझे भी बखशी है। हे प्रभु! जिस अवस्था में ध्रुव और नारद को तूने टिकाया अब मुझे भी थोड़ा से वैसे ही टिका दे।

आपके नाम के आसरे बहुत भक्त पार हो गए हैं। और नामदेव का यह विश्वास है कि केवल नाम द्वारा ही बेड़ा पार हो सकता है।

A prayer for salvation:—

25

Float me over, O God, float me over!
I am unskilful and know not how to swim; O God, my Father, give me Thine arm.
He to whom the true guru hath taught knowledge, is changed in a moment from a man into a demigod.
I have obtained the medicine by which, though begotten by man, I have conquered heaven.
Place me even for a short time where Thou hast placed Dhru and Narad.
By the support of Thy name many have been saved: this is Nama's private opinion.

By other familiar examples Namdev describes his ardent longing for God.

(२६) राग-गौड़

मोहि लागती तालबेली। बेछरे बिनु गाइ अकेली।।१।।
पानीया बिनु मीनु तलफै ऐसे। राम नामा बिनु बापरो नामा।।रहाउ।।
जैसे गाइका बाछा छटुला। थन चीखता माखुन घुटता।।२।।
नामदेउ नाराइणु पाइआ। गुरु भेटत अलखु लखइआ।।३।।
जैसे बिखै हेत परनारी। ऐसे नामें प्रीति मुरारी।।४।।
जैसे तापते निरमल घामा। तैसे रामनामा बिनु बापुरो नामा।।५।।

प्रभु से बिछुड़ने पर मुझे तड़पन सी लगती है। जैसे बछड़े से बिछुड कर गऊ तड़पती है। जैसे पानी के बगैर मछली तड़पती है। इसी प्रकार नामदेव भी राम नाम के बगैर तड़पता है।

जैसे गऊ का बछड़ा छूटने पर झट अपनी माँ का दुग्ध पीने लगता है। इसी प्रकार नामदेव ने भी अपने अन्तर स्वरूप प्रभु को पाया है। परन्तु गुरु कृपा से ही अदृष्य वस्तु को देखा है। जैसे विषयी पुरुष को पर स्त्री से प्यार होता है वैसे ही नामदेव को प्रभु से प्यार है। जैसे चमकती धूप में जीव तपते हैं वैसे प्रभु नाम बिना नामा तपता है।

26

I am ardently longing for the Friend—
Without her calf a cow is lonely,
Without water a fish writheth,
So without God's name doth poor Nama.
As the calf, when let loose,

Suketh his dam's teats and swalloweth her milk,
So Namdev hath obtained God—
When man meeteth the guru he showeth the Unseen—
As the wicked man loveth another man's wife,
So Nama loveth God
As man's body burneth in the bright sunshine,
So dpth poor Nama without the name of God.

The advantages of repeating God's name.

(२७) राग-गौड़

हरि हरि करत मिटे सभि भरमा। हरि को नाम लै उत्तम धरमा॥
हरि हरि करत जाति कुल हरी। सो हरि अंधुले की लाकरी॥१॥
हरए नमसते हरएनमह। हरि हरि करत नहीं दुख जमह।।रहाउ॥
हरि हरनाखस हरे परान। अजैमल कीऊ बैकुंठ हि थान॥
सुआ पड़ावत गाणिका तरी। सो हरि नैनहु की पूतरी॥२॥
हरि हरि करत पूतना तरी। बाल घातनी कपट हि भरी॥
सिमरत द्रोपत-सुता ऊधरी। गऊतम सती सिला निसतरो॥३॥
केसी कंस माथुन जिनि कीआ। जीअ दानु काली कउ दीआ॥
प्रणावै नामा ऐसो हरि। जासु जपद भै अपदा टरी॥४॥

प्रभु-नाम जपने से सारे भ्रम दूर हो जाते हैं। ऐ जीव! प्रभु का नाम जपना एक उत्तम धर्म है। प्रभु के जपने से कुल और जाति का अभिमान दूर होते हैं। यह प्रभु-नाम के जाप अन्धे को लाठी का सहारा है। मेरा उस परमात्मा को बार-बार नमस्कार है। नाम स्मरण से यह (मृत्यु) का दुख नहीं रहता (रहाउ) प्रभु ने ही हर्णाकुश के प्राण लिए थे। अजामिल पापी को बैकुंठ में स्थान दिया था। तोते को प्रभु-नाम जपाने पर गणिका तर गई थी वही प्रभु मेरे आँखों की पुतली है। प्रभु नाम जपने से पूतना दाई भी तर गई जो बच्चों को मारने वाली थी और कपटी थी। नाम स्मृण से ही द्रुपद-सुता का उद्धार हुआ (अपमान से बची) सत्ववती अहल्या जो पति (गौतम) के श्राप से शिला बन गई थी वह भी तर गई।

केसी राक्षस और राजा कंस को भी मारा। काली नाग को जीवन दान दिया।

नामदेव जी नम्रता सहित कहते हैं कि मेरे प्रभु का नाम जपने से दुख तकलीफ नष्ट हो जाते है।

27

By repeating the name of God all doubts are dispeled—
Repeating the name of God is the highest religious *exercise*—
By repeating the name of God caste and lineage are effaced.
That God is the staff of the blind man.

I bow before God! I bow before God!
By repeating God's name Death tortureth not,
God took the life of Harnakhas
And made for Ajamal a dwelling in heaven
The courtesan who taught her parrot *to repeal God's name* was saved—
That God is the apple of mine eye—
By repeating the name of God, Putana[1] full of deceit.
The destroyer of children was saved;
By remembering the name of God the daughter of Drupad was saved;
Gautam's wife[2] *though turned* into a stone, was saved.
God destroyed Kesi and Kans,
And conferred the gift of life on Kalinag.
Nama representeth, by repeating the name of such a God fear and trouble depart.

(२८) राग-गौड़

भैरउ भूत सीतला धावै। खर बाहन उडु छार उड़ावै॥१॥
हउ तउ एक रमइआ लैहउ। आन देव बदलावनि दैहउ।रहाउ॥
सिव सिव करते जो नरु धिआवै। वरद चढ़ै डउरू ढमकावै॥२॥
महामाई की पूजा करै। नरसै नारि होइ अउतरै॥३॥
तू कहीअत हो आदि भवनी। मुकति की बरीआ कहां छपानी॥४॥
गुरमति राम नाम महु मीता। प्रणवै नामा इऊ कहे गीता॥५॥

जो भैरव, भूत या शीतला का ध्यान करता है वह उन्ही का रूप बन जाता है अथवा उन की सवारी बन जाता है (जैसे भैरव का वाहन कुत्ता, भूत का आंधी और शीतला का गधा आदि) और राख उड़ाते हैं।

मैं तो एक व्यापक प्रभु का नाम लेता हूं। और सारे देवताओं के नाम उसी के बदले मे देता हूं।

जो शिवजी का नाम लेते हैं, वह सब बैल पर सवार होकर डमरू बजाते हैं। जो यदि कोई महामाई (देवी) की पूजा करता है वह मनुष्य की बजाय स्त्री का जन्म लेता है। हे भवानी माई तुझे आदि शक्ति कहा जाता है परन्तु मुक्ति के समय तू कहां चली जाती है।

नामदेव जी कहते है कि ऐ मित्र! तू केवल प्रभु का नाम ही ग्रहन कर यही उपदेश गीता भी देती है। यथा गीता 9/25

The fate of worshippers of false gods.

28

They who worship Bhairav shall become sprites;
They who worship Sitala shall ride on donkeys and scatter dust—
For myself I take *the name* of the one God;
I would give all other gods in exchange for it.
They who repeat the name of Shiv and worship him,
Shall ride on an ox and play the drum;
They who worship the great mother *Durga,*
Shall be born as women instead of men.
Thou callest thyself, *O Durga,* the primal Bhawani,
When it came to my turn to be saved, where didst thou hide thyself?
Under the instruction of the guru, O my friend, cling to God's name—
Nama representh,, thus saith the Gita.

(२९) राग-बिलावल गौड़

आजु नामे बीठलु देखिआ, मूरख को समझाऊ रे॥रहाउ॥
पांडे तुमरी गाइत्री लोधेका खेतु खाती थी॥
लैकरि ठेंगा टंगरी तोरी लांगत लांगत जाती थी॥१॥
पांडे तुमरा महादेउ धउले बलद चड़िआ आवत देखिआ था।
मोदी के घर खाणा पाका, वाका लड़का मारिआ था॥२॥
पांडे तुमरा रामचंदु सो भी आवत देखिआ था॥
रावनसे ती सरबर होई घर की जोइ गवाइ थी॥३॥
हिंदु अंना तुरकू काणा, दुहांते गिआनी सिआणा॥
हिंदु पूजै देहुरा, मुसलमाणु भसीत॥
नामें सोई सेविआ जह देहुरा न समीत॥४॥

नामदेव जी ने इस पनुष्य जन्म मे ही परमात्मा के दर्शन कर लिए हैं ऐ मूर्ख पंडित अब मैं तुझे समझाता हूं। (उहाऊ)

तेरी गायत्री पहले पापों का खेत खाती थी (अर्थात् ब्रह्म हत्या का दोष दूर करती थी) परन्तु वशिष्ट जी ने तप रूपी डंडा लेकर गायत्री की टांग तोड़ दी (अर्थात् 32 मे से 8 अक्षर निकाल दिये) ओर अब वह लंगडी-लंगडी चलती है (अर्थात् उसमें पाप निवारण की क्षमता नहीं रही) ऐ पांडे तेरे शिवजी को भी सफेद बैल पर सवार होकर जाते देखा था। कृपालु पार्वती के घर जब प्रसाद तैयार था तो (क्रोध में आकर) उसके पुत्र को ही

मार डाला था। ऐ पांडे! तेरा रामचन्द्र (उपासना) भी हमने देखा है उसने अपने घर की स्त्री ही गंवा दी थी और रावण से लड़ाई हुई थी।

ईश्वर के पूर्णा व्यापक रूप के दर्शन करने के लिये हिन्दु अन्धा है (और बहुत से देवताओं का पूजन करता है) और मुसलमान काना है (क्योंकि वह कावे की दिशा ढूंड़ता है) इन दोनों से आत्म ज्ञानी स्याना है।

हिन्दु उस को मंदिरों में और मुसलमान मसजिदों में पूजते हैं। परन्तु मैं नामदेव ने उस परमात्मा को पूजा है जो न मंदिरों में है और न मसजिदों में है (अर्थात् सर्वव्यापक प्रभु जो घट-घट में निवास करता है।)

Namdev admonishes an idolatrous Brahman

29

To-day I Nama saw God, I *now* admonish the fool—
O pandit, thy gayatri used to graze on the boor's field.He took a stick and broke her leg; *since then* she hath walked lame.[1]
O pandit, I have seen thy great good Shiv going along on a white bullock.
In his consort *Parbati's* house a banquet for him was prepared; he killed her son.[2]
O pandit, thy Ram Chandar—I have seen him too going along;
Having lost his wife he fought with Rawan.
The Hindus are blind, the Musalmans purblind;
The man who knoweth God is wiser than either.
The Hindus worship their temple, the Musalmans their mosque.
Nama worshippeth Him who hath neither temple nor mosque.

The saint Trilochan once twitted Namdev with being always engaged in his trade. Namdev made him the following reply:—

(३०) राग-रामकली

आनीले कागदु काटीले गूड़ी अकासामधे भरमीअले।
पंच जना सिउ बात बताऊआ, चीतु सु डोरी राखीअले॥१॥
मनु राम नामा बेधीअले। जैसे कनिक कला चितु मांडीअले॥रहाउ॥
आनीले कुंभु भराइले ऊदक, राजकुआरि पुंरदरीए॥
हसत बिनोद बीचार करती है, चीतुसु गागरि राखीअले॥२॥
मंदरू एकु दुआर दस जाके, गऊ चरावन छाडीअले॥

पांच कोस पर गऊ चरावत चीतुसु बछरा राखीअले॥३॥
कहत नामदेउ सुनहु तिलोचन बालकु पालन पउडीअले॥
अंतरि बाहरि काज विरुधी चीतुसु बारिक राखीअले॥४॥

देखिये लड़का कागज लाता है, उसे पतंग बनाता है जो आसमान में उड़ती है वह अपने साथियों से बात चीत भी करता जाता है, पर अपना मन वह पतंग की डोरी में ही टिकाए रहता है। हे लोगो अपने मन को राम के नाम से बीघ डालो। जैसे सुनार अपना मन दूसरों के साथ बात चीत करते हुए भी सोने में ही जोड़े रखता है (रहाऊ) जैसे गऊयें चार-चार कोस तक चरती हुइ निकल जाती है पर अपना ध्यान सदा बछड़े में रखती है उसी प्रकार इस दस द्वारों वाले घर से इन्द्रिया रूपी गऊए अपना अपना कार्य करती रहें पर मन अपना ध्यान सदा प्रभु में ही लगाये रखें। जवान लड़कियां, घड़ों में पानी भर कर सिर पर रख लेती हैं और हंसती खेलती बातें करती हुई भी अपना मन घड़े में ही रखती हैं।

नामदेव जी कहते हैं कि त्रिलोचन! सुन! माता अपने बालक को पंगूडे में डाल कर घर का काम काज करती रहती हैं, परन्तु मन उसका बच्चे में ही रहता है। इसी प्रकार मनुष्यों का उपासना करनी चाहिए। यथा बुल्लेशाह (हत्यकार वल्ल चित्त यार वल्ल)

30
RAMKALI

A boy taketh paper, cutteth it into a kite, and flyeth it in the sky.
While conversing with his companions, he keepeth his attention on the string.
I have pierced my soul with God's name.
As the goldsmith's attention is engrossed *in his work*.
The queen's female servant taketh her pitcher, filleth it with water.
Converseth laughingly and pleasantly, yet keepeth her attention on the pitcher.
If the cows of a city with ten gates be let loose to graze.
And they go grazing for even five miles, they will remember their young *and return each by her own gate.*
Saith Namdev, hear, O Trilochan, when a child is laid in its cradle.
Its mother, whether engaged at home or abroad, keepeth her thoughts on her child.

The following hymn embodying Namdev's resolutions is also believed to have been addressed to Trilochan:—

(३१) राग-रामकली

वेद पुरान सासत्र आनंता, गीत कवित न गावउ गो ॥
अखंड मंडल निराकार महि, अनहद बेनु बजावउ गो ॥ १ ॥
बैरागी रामहि गावउ गौ ॥
सबिद अतीत अनाहदि राता, आकुल कै घरि जाउ गो ॥ रहाउ ॥
इदा पिंगुला अउरू सुखमना, पउने बंधि रहाउ गो ॥
चंदु सूरजु दुह समकरि राखउ, ब्रह्म जोति मिलि आउगी ॥ २ ॥
तीरथ देखि न जलमहि पैसउ जीउ जंत न सतावउ गो ॥
अठसठि तीरथ गुरु दिखाए घटटी भीतरि नहाउ गो ॥ ३ ॥
पंच सहाई जनकी शोभा भलो भलो न कहा वउ गो ॥
नामा काहै चितु हरिसिउ राता सुंन समधि समाउ गो ॥ ४ ॥

वेद पुरान और शास्त्र अनेक है परंतु मुझे उनके छंद गाने की जरूरत नहीं। हैं तो निराकार के एक रस मंडल, में परम आत्मा, के उस प्रेम रूपी नाम की एक-रस ध्वनि रूपी बांसुरी बजाऊंगा । मैं तो निर्लेप प्रभु के गुण गाँऊगा निर्लेप और एक रस शब्द ब्रह्म में लीन ही एक मैं संपूर्ण व्यापक रूप में टिक जाऊँगा।

पिंगल और सुष्मना में प्राणवायु को बाधूंगा अर्थात् वहाँ प्राण स्थित करके प्रभु का ध्यान करूंगा । दायीं और बायीं नास्का से विचरने वाले प्राणों को समान रूप में कर लूंगा और इस प्रकार में ब्रह्म जोत में समा जाऊँगा ।

तीर्थी पर जाकर स्नान करके मछली आदि जीव जंतु को सताने की आवश्यकता नहीं रहेगी । मैंने तो अपने गुरु के दिए असली 68 (अडसठ) तीर्थ अपने ही भीतर रख लिए है और अपनी स्तुति सुनना पाचों विकारों की सहायक है अत: अपनी स्तुति मनने की कामना का मैं परित्याग कर दूगां वहीं घट में ही स्नान करता हूं ।

नामदेव जी कहते है कि मेरा मन तो प्रभु में लीन हो गया है मैं तो (अपूर्व) अन्न समाधि में समाऊंगा ।

31

The endless songs and poetry of the Veds, Purans, and Shastars
I will not sing;
I will play unbeaten music in the imperishable region of God
Censing to love the world I will sing of God.
Imbued with Him who is beyond expression and indestructible,
I shall go to the abode of the Inscrutable One.

I will cease to hold my breath in the right or left nostril or between them both.
I deem the left and right nostril the same; I shall be blended with the light of God.
I will not go to see places of pilgrimages nor enter their waters; I will not annoy men or lower animals.
The guru showed me the sixty-eight places of pilgrimatge in my heart where I will bathe.
I will not have myself glorified and congratulated by my select friends.
Nama saith, my heart is dyed with God, and I shall be absorbed in Him.

God preceded all creation, all religious books, and all karma.

(३२) राग-रामकली

माई न होती, बापु न होता, करमु न होती काइला ॥
हम नहीं होते, तुम नहीं होते, कवनु कहांते आइआ ॥ १ ॥
राम कोइ न किस ही केरा जैसे तरवर पंखि बसेरा ॥ रहाउ ॥
चंदु न होता, सुरु न होता, पानी पवन मिलाइआ ॥
सासतु न होता, वेदु न होता, करमु कहाते आइआ ॥ २ ॥
खेचर भूचर तुलसी-माला, गुरपरसादी पाइआ ॥
नामा प्रणवै परम ततु है सति गुर होई लखाइआ ॥ ३ ॥

जगत रचना से पहले जब न माता थी न पिता न कोई मनुष्य शरीर था तो न ही उसका क्रिया कर्म था न हम थे और न तुम थे, उस समय कौन किस जगत से आया था हे राम तू ही आप (सब को भेजने वाला हैं) तेरे बिना कोई किसी का सहायक नहीं है।

यह संसार तो वृक्ष की भांति है जिस पर पंछी केवल रात को निवास करते है और दिन चढ़ते उड़ जाते हैं । जिस समय चंद्रमा नहीं था सूरज भी नहीं था और पाँचों तत्व (पानी, पवन आदि स्थूल मूल) भी नहीं थे ना शास्त्र थे ना ही वेद था जो का कमा विचार देते है तो फिर कर्म पहले कैसे हो सकता है ।

मेरे लिए तो सांस के उतारने और चढ़ाने का साधन और तुलसी माला आदि गुरु की कृपा से प्राप्त किये हैं । नामदेव जी कहते है कि यह रहस्य की बातों को सतगुरु ही समझा सकता हैं ।

32

When there was no mother, no father, no karma, and nobody;
When we were not and you were not, who was there and whence did he come?
O God, no one hath any relation;
Man's dwelling *in this world is like the perching* of a bird on a tree.
When there was no moon, no sun, *when there was only* water and air blended together.
When there were no Shastars and no Veds, whence did karma come?
I have by the favour of the guru obtained *God, for whom* the Jogis suspend their breath, and fix their attention on the bridges of their noses, and the *Bairagis* wear necklaces of sweet basil.
Nama representeth, God is the Primal Essence; when there is a true guru he showeth Him.

The repetition of God's name is superior to all other forms of worship.

(३३) राग-रामकली

बानारसी तपु करै, उलटि तीरथ मरै ॥
अगानि दहै, काइआ कलपु कीजै ॥
असुसेध जगु कीजै, सोना गरभ दानु दीजै ॥
राम नाम सरि तऊ न पूजै ॥ १ ॥
छोड़ि छोड़ि रे पाखंडी, मन कपटु न कीजै ॥
हरिका नामु नित नितही जीजै ॥ रहाउ ॥
गंगा जउ गोदावरी जाइए कुंभि जउ केदार नाहए ॥
गोमति सहस गाऊ गाऊ हिवालै गारै ॥
राम नाम सरि तउ न पूजै ॥ २ ॥
असुदान गजदान सिहजा नारी भूमिदान ॥
ऐसो दान नित नितहि कीजै ॥
आतम जउ निरमाइलु कीजै, आप बराबरी कंचनु दीजै ॥
राम नाम सरि तउ न पूजै ॥ ३ ॥
मन ही न कीजै रोसु जमहि न दीजै दोसु ॥
निरमल निरबाणु पटु चीनि लीजै ॥
जसरथ राइ नंदु, राजा मेरा रामचंदु ॥
प्रणावै नामा ततु रसु अंम्रितु पीजै ॥

कोई काशी में उल्टा लटक के तप करे तीर्थों पर शरीर त्यागे अपने आपको अग्नि में जलादे अथवा काया कल्प द्वारा शरीर को चिरंजीवी बना दें ।

अश्वमेघ यज्ञ करे, सोना गुप्त दान करे, फिर भी वह राम नाम के तुलना में नहीं हो सकता ।

हे पाखंड़ी मन कपट करना छोड़ दे और नित्य प्रति प्रभु का नाम ले ।

यदि कोई हर बारवें साल कुँभ पर गंगा और गोदावरी जाएं केदार तीर्थ स्नान करें ओर गोमी नदी पर हजार गऊ का दान दे, करोड़ों तीर्थ यात्रा करे पा अपना शरीर हिमालय पर्वत में गला दे, तो भी राम नाम की तुलना नहीं कर सकता ।

अश्व और हाथियों का दान सेजा समेत स्त्री दान, भूमि दान, नित्य प्रति करता रहे, अपना आप भी भेंट कर दें अथवा अपने बराबर सोना दे दें फिरी भी राम नाम की तुलना में नहीं पहुंच सकता है ।

इस कथन पर रोष न करना और ना ही यम को दोष देना यदि वो यह सभी साध न करते हुए आ जाए, यम से बचना है तो बंधनों से रहित निर्मल आत्म पद की पहचान कर लो ।

नामदेव कहता है दशरथ राजा के पुत्र (रामचन्द्र) सब रसों का मूल रस है उसका नाम अमृत ही पियो ।

33

If one perform penance with body reversed at Banaras,
and die at a place of pilgrimage; if one burn one's body with fire,
or strive to make it survive for a kalpa;
If one perform the horse sacrifice or offer secret presents of gold, all that would not be equal to the name of God.
O hypocritical man, renounce deception; practise it not;
Ever and ever take God's name.
Wert thou to go to the Ganges and the Godavari every twelfth year, bathe at Kedarnath,
And make offerings of thousands of cows at the Gomti;
Wert thou to perform millions of pilgrimages, freeze thy body in the Himalayas, all would not be equal to the name of God;
Wert thou to offer horses, elephants, women with their couches, lands, and make such gifts continually *to Brahmans;*
Wsert thou to purify thy body and offer its weight in gold, all would not be equal to the name of God.
Look for the pure dignity of Nirvan, and be not *afterwards* angry with thyself, or attribute blame to the god of death.
Nama representh, drink the real nectareous elixir of my king Ram Chandar, the son of Jasarath Rai.

(३४) राग-माली गडड़ा

धनि-धनि ओ राम बेनु बाजै ॥
मधुर-मधुर धुनि अनहत गाजै ॥ रहाउ ॥
धनि-धनि मेघा रोमावली ॥
धनि-धनि किसन ओढ़ैं कांबली ॥ १ ॥
धनि-धनि तूं माता देवकी ॥
जिह गृह रमइआ कवलापती ॥ २ ॥
धनि-धनि बन खंड बिन्द्रबनां ॥
जह खेलै स्त्री नाराइना ॥ ३ ॥
बेनु बजावै गोधनू चारै ॥
नामें का सुआमी आनन्द करै ॥ ४ ॥

व्यापक राम की मधुर ध्वनि जो सब आकारों में बज रही है बिस्मयजनक है उसकी आवाज मीठी है जो बिना जबाए गूंज रही हैं । उस प्यारे की हर चीज प्यारी है । उसका कृष्ण रूप भी धन्य है और कृष्ण जी की कम्बली भी ।

कम्बली की ऊन और भेड़ जिसकी ऊन से कम्बली बनी हैं वह भी धन्य हैं । हे माता देवकी, तू भी धन्य है जिसके घर में लक्ष्मी पति परमेश्वर कृष्णा के रूप में पुत्र बनकर आया ।

धन्य वह वन है और वृन्दावन है जहाँ श्री नारायण जी खेले हैं ।

नामदेव का प्रभु आप बांसुरी बजाता है और गाए चराता है । और सारे आनंद रूपी खेल करता हैं ।

34
MALI GAURA

The following glorification of Krishan was composed after Namdev had embraced with worship:—

Happy, happy that flute which Krishan played!
A very sweet unbeaten sound issueth from it.
Happy, happy that blanket which Krishan wore!
Happy, happy that ram and his fleece *it was made from.*
Hail, hail to thee, mother Devaki,
In whose house god, the lord of Lakshmi, *was born*!
Blest, blest he forest glades of Bindraban,
Where Nama's god Narayan sported,

Played his hute, herded his cows,
And was happy.

(३५) राग-माली गउड़ा

मेरो बापु माधउ तू धन कैसो सांवलीओ बीठुलाई ले ॥ राहाउ ॥
कर धरे चक्र वैकुंठ ते आए, गज हउती के प्रान उधारीअले ॥
दुहसासन की सभा द्रोपती, अंबर लेत उबारीअले ॥ १ ॥
गौतम नारि अहिलिया तारी, पावन केतक तारीअले ॥
ऐसा अधमु अजाति नामदेउ, तउ सरनागति आइअले ॥ २ ॥

मेरे पिता माधव, केशव सावले बीठल तू धन्य है । हे मायापति हाथों में चक्र धारण किए तू ही पधारा था और गजराज के प्राण बचाए थे ।

दु:शासन की सभा में जब द्रोपदी के वस्त्र उतारे जा रहे थे तब तूने ही उसकी इज्जत बचायी है । गौतम ऋषि की पत्नी अहल्या को तार दिया और अनेकों को पवित्र करके पार किया ।

मैं नामदेव भी ऐसा ही एक ही दीन तेरी शरण में आया हूं ।

35

God my father, hail to thee, dark complexioned Vitthal with the long hair!
Holding in thy hand the discus, thou didst come from heaven and save the life of the great elephant;
Thou didst save Draupadi when her clothes were being torn off her in Duhsasan's court;
Thou didst save Ahalya the wife of Gautam;
How many hast Thou purified and saved!
Thus the lowly Namdev without caste hath entered Thy sanctuary.

God is in everything and Namdev has become absorbed in Him. The following marks a stage in Namdev's progress to divine unity.

(३६) राग-माली गउड़ा

सभै घट रामु बोलै, रामा बिना को बोलै रे ॥ रहाउ ॥
एकल माटी कुंचर चीटी, भाजन है बहु नाना रे ॥
असथावर जंगम कीट पतंगम, घटि-घटि रामु समाना रे ॥
एकल चिता राखु अनंता, अउर तजहु सम आसा रे ॥
प्रणवै नामा भए निहकामा को ठाकुरु को दासा रे ॥ २ ॥

सभी हृदयों में व्यापक राम की बोल रहा है । राम के बिना और कोई नहीं बोल सकता । हाथी, कीड़ी, आग, बर्तनों के समान एक ही मिट्टी के बने कुएँ हैं चाहे इनके रूप अलग-अलग हैं । वनस्पति, स्थिर पदार्थ तथा अस्थिर जीव जन्तु और कीट पंतग आदि सब के हृदय में वही प्रभु समाया हुआ है ।

हे जीव ! अब सारी आशाएँ छोड़ के एक ही चिंता रख के हे प्रभु ! मुझे बचाओ।

नामदेव जी कहते हैं कि मैं तो इस तरह इच्छा रहित हो गया हूं कि मालिक और दास में कोई फर्क नहीं रहा । (राम कबीरा एक भय हैं कोई ना सके पछानी ।)

36

In every heart God speaketh, God speaketh;
Doth any one speak independently of Him?
There is the same earth in the elephant and the vessels of many kinds *are made from earth.*
In mobile and immobile things, in worms and moths, and in every heart God is contained.
Think of the one God who is endless; abandon all other hope.
Nama representh; I have become free from desires; *and in this state* who is Lord and who is slave?

(३७) राग-मारू

चारि मुकति चारै सिधि मिलिकै दूलक प्रभ की सरनि परिओ ॥
मुकति भइयो चउहूं जुग जानिओ,
जसु कीरति माथै छत्र फरिओ ॥ १ ॥
राजाराम जपत को को न तरिओ ॥
गुय उपदेसि साध की संगति भगतु, भगतु ताको नामु परिओ ॥ दहाउ॥
संख चक्र माला तिलक बिराजित देखि प्रताप जमु डरियो ॥
निरभउ भए राम बल गरजित जनम-मरण संताप हिरिओ ॥ २ ॥
अम्बरीक कउ दीनो अभैपदु राजु भभीखन अधिक करिओ ॥
नउ निधि ठाकुरि दई सुदामै धू अटलू अजहूं न टरिओ ॥ ३ ॥
भगत हेति मारिओ हरनाखसु नरसिंघ रूप होइ देह धरिओ ॥
नामा कहै भगति बसि केसव अजहूं बलिके दुआर खरो ॥ ४ ॥

चारों मुक्तियां और चारों सिद्धियां उस प्रभु की दासियां हैं प्रभु की शरण प्राप्त होने पर मनुष्य मुक्त हो जाता है, उसकी चारों युगों में ख्याति हो जाती है यश मिलता है और संसार उसके माथे पर छत्र, चामर आदि रखते हैं, ऐसे राजा राम का नाम जपने से भला कौन नहीं तरसता । जो मनुष्य अपने गुरु की सीख पर चलकर साधु-संगत में आ जाने

से उसका नाम भक्त हो जाता है (राहउ) । उस शंख, चक्र, माला और तिलक धारण किए हुए का तेज देखकर धर्मराज भी डर जाता है । वह प्रभु नाम का सहारा पाकर निर्भय होकर गरजता है और उसका जन्म-मरण का दुख निवारणहो जाता है । प्रभु ने अमब्रीष भक्त को आय पढ़ दिया था और विभीक्षण को राज्य में वृद्धि का । प्रभु ने भक्त सुदामा को नौ-निधि सम्पन्न किया और ध्रुव भक्त को अटल पदवी दी जो अभी तक स्थिर है। अपने भक्त प्रह्लाद की रक्षा करने के हेतु नरसिंह रूप धारण किया और हिरण्यकश्यप् को मार डाला ।

नामदेव जी कहते हैं कि प्रभु सदा ही व्यक्ति के आधीन रहते हैं । इसी कारण वह अभी तक राजा वलि के द्वारा पर पहरा दे रहा है ।

37
MARU

God has showered His favours on Namdev as He did or other saints.

> When I entered the asylum of God the Bridgegroom, I obtained the four stages of salvation and the four supernatural powers.
> I have been saved, I have become famous through the four ages, and I have put the umbrella of praise and fame over my head.
> Who hath not been saved by repeating *the name of* the Sovereign God?
> They *who listen* to the guru's instruction and associate with holy men are called saints.
> On eholding the effulgence of *the guru*, who is conspicuous with his shell, discus, necklace, and sacrificial mark, Death becometh afraid.
> Man then becometh fearless and by the power of God thundereth forth that he hath escaped the pain of transmigration.
> God gave king Ambarik[2] the gift of salvation and aggrandized Babhikhan with sovereignty;
> The Lord gave the nine treasures to Sudama, and made Dhru immovable *in the north pole*, where he is fixed to the present day;
> God having assumed the body of Narsinh *the man-lion,* killed Harnakhas for the sake of his saint *Prahlad.*
> Nama saith, Vishnu is in the power of the saints, and is till now standing at the door of Bali.[3]

(३८) राग-भैरउ

रे जिहबा करउ सत खंड । जो मि न उचरसि स्री गोविंद ॥ १ ॥
रंगीले जिहबा हरि कै नाई । सुरंग रंगीले हरि हरि धिआइ ॥ रहाउ ॥
मिथिआ जिहबा अवरें काम । निरबाण पदु इकु हरिको नामु ॥ २ ॥
असंख कोटिअन पूजा करी । एक न पूजसि नामै हरि ॥ ३ ॥
प्रणवै नामदेउ इहु करणा । अनंत रूप तेरे नाराइणा ॥ ४ ॥

अरी जिहवा, मैं तेरे टुकड़े-टुकड़े कर दूंगा यदि तू प्रभु का नाम उच्चारण नहीं करेगी। अपनी जिहवा को प्रभु नाम के रंग-में-रंग लो उस का नाम जप कर श्रेष्ठ रंग-में-रंग लो । उनका नाम जपने के सिवाय अनरू जो जीभ में नाम है वह सब व्यर्थ और झूठे हैं।

मुक्ति पाने का साधन केवल हरि नाम स्मरण ही है । प्रभु प्राप्ति के लिये चाह हजारों ढंग से पूजा करूं । पर उन में से एक भी नाम जपने के तुल्य नहीं है । नामदेवजी कहते हैं कि मुझे तो केवल आपका नाम जपना ही प्रिय है चाहे मुक्ति प्राप्ति के अनंत प्रकार हैं ।

38
BHAIRO

Namdev enjoins his tongue under severest penalty to utter God's name.

O my tongue, if thou utter not God's name.
I will break thee into a hundred pieces.
O tongue, dye thyself with God's name;
Meditating on God's name dye thyself with a good dye;
False, O my tongue, are *all* other occupations
The dignity of Nirvan is *only obtained* through the name of God.
Wert thou to worship countless millions of other *gods*.
It would not be equal to repeating God's name alone.
Namdev representh, this do, *O my tongue, and say* 'O God, Thy forms are endless.'

A man may in other respects be perfect but he is lost if he repeat not God's name.

(३९) राग-भैरउ

परधन परदार परहरी । ताकै निकटि बसै नरहरि ॥ १ ॥
जी न भंजंते नाराइणा । तिनका मैं न कर दरसाना ॥ रहाउ ॥

जिनके भीतरी है अंतरा । जैसे पसु तैसे ओइ नरा ॥ २ ॥
प्रणावती नामदेउ नाकहि बिना । ना सोहै बत्तीसु लखना ॥ ३ ॥

जिस ने पराया धन और पराई स्त्री का त्याग किया है उसी के निकट प्रभु रहता है । जो जीव प्रभु को याद नहीं करते मैं उनका दर्शन मात्र भी करना नहीं चाहता । रहा।

जिनके अन्दर द्वेष-भाव है, वह मनुष्य होते हुए भी पशु है ।

नामदेवजी कहते हैं जैसे नाम के बिना चाहे बत्तीस गुण हों, वह जीव शोभायमान नहीं होता ।

39

God dwelleth near him
Who coveteth not another's wealth or another's wife,
I will not look at him
Who repet teth not God's name.
As a beast is that man
Whose heart is estranged from God.
Namdev representh, a man without a nose
Doth not look well even with the other thirty-two marks of beauty.[1]

(४०) राग-भैरउ

दूधु कटोरै गडवै पानी । कपल गाड नामै दुहि आनी ॥ १ ॥
दूध पीओ गोविदे राइ । दूध पीउ मेरो मनु पती आइ ॥
नाहीं त घर को बापू रिसाइ ॥ रहा ॥
सोइन कटोरी अंम्रित भरी । लै नामै हरि आगे धरि ॥ २ ॥
एकु भगतु मेरे हिरदै बसै । नामे देखि नराइनु हंसै ॥ ३ ॥
दूधु पीआइ भगतु वरि गइआ । नामे हरिका दरसनु भइया ॥ ४ ॥

नामदेव ने कपिला गऊ दुह कर दूध कटोरे में लिया और लोटे में पानी लेकर ठाकुर के समीप आकर विन्ती को कि हे गोबिंदराय यह स्वीकार कीजिये । इससे मेरा मन भी प्रसन्न होगा और पिता भी गुस्से नहीं होगा । (रहाउ) ।

सोने की कटोरी में दुग्ध डाल कर नामदेवजी ने ठाकुर के आगे रख कर प्रार्थना करके कहा कि मेरे हृदय में तो केवल आप की भक्ति ही बस रही है ।

नामदेवजी के भोलेपन को देख कर प्रभु हंसे, इस प्रकार नामदेवजी दुग्ध पिला कर घर गए तथा प्रभु-दर्शन भी पा लिया ।

40

Nama having milked his brown cow took
A cup of milk and a jug of water for the idol
Drink milk and my mind will be at ease;
Otherwise my father will be angry
A golden cup filled with milk
Nama took and placed before the idol—
The saints alone abide in my heart—
On seeing Nama the god smiled;
On giving milk *to the idol* the worshipper Nama went home,
And God appeared unto him.

(४१) राग-भैरव

मैं बउरी मेरा राम भतारु । रचि रचि ताकउ करउ सिंगारु ॥ १ ॥
भले निंदउ, भले निंदउ, भले निंदउ, लोगु । तनु मन राम पिआरे जोगु ॥ रहाउ ॥
बाद-बिबाद काहू सिउ न कीजै । रसना राम रसाइनु पीजै ॥ २ ॥
अब जीअ जानि ऐसी बनि आई । मिलउ गुपाल नीसानु बजाई ॥ ३ ॥
उसतति निंदा करै नर कोई । नामे श्री-रंगु भेटल सोई ॥ ४ ॥

मेरा पति परमात्मा है । मैं उसी के पीछे बावरी हुई हूं । उस की प्राप्ति के लिए मैं प्रेम-भक्ति के शुभ-गुणों का श्रृंगार करती हूं ।

ऐ लोगों ! तुम मेरी कितनी ही निंदा किये जाओ मैंने तो अपना तन मन प्रभु को अर्पित कर दिया है । अब किसी से वाद-विवाद करने की आवश्यकता ही है केवल अपनी जिहवा पर राम-रूपी रसायन का पान करना चाहिए । प्रभु को हृदय में बसा जान कर अब ऐसी प्रीती उपज आई है कि मन चाहता है कि नाम-रुपी नगाडे को बजाकर उस प्रभु प्रियतम में समा जाऊंगी ।

अब चाहे मेरी कोई बढ़ाई करे या निंदा करे नाम देव को तो लक्ष्मी-पति (श्री रंग) मिल ही गये हैं ।

When Namdev gave up trade, and devoted himself exclusively to the worship of God and attendance on His saints, people began to slander him. The following is his apology:—

41

I am a mad woman and God is my spouse;
It is for Him I decorate myself elaborately.
Abuse me well, abuse me well, abuse me well, O people;

My body and soul are for my beloved God.
I hold no idle discussion with any one;
I sip with my tongue the elixir of God.
Now I know in my heart that such an arrangement hath been made.
By which I shall meet God with banners and music.
Whether any one give me praise or blame;
Nama hath met God.

(४२) राग-भैरव

कबहूं खोरि खांड घीउ न भावै ॥
कबहूं घर-घर टृक मंगावै । कबहूं कूरनु चने बिनावै ॥ १ ॥
जिउ रामु राखै तिउ रहीअै रे भाई । हरिकी महिमा किछ कथनु न जाई ॥ रहाउ॥
कबहूं तूरे तुरंग नचावै । कबहू पाइ पनहीओ न पावै ॥ २ ॥
कबहूं खाट सुपेदी सुवावै । कबहूं भूमिपै आरु न पावै ॥ ३ ॥
भनति नामदेउ इकु नामु निसतारै । जिह गुरु मिलै तिह पारि उतारै ॥ ४ ॥

इस जीव को कभी तो खीर, खांड, घी, जैसे उत्तम पदार्थ भी अच्छे नहीं लगते पर कभी घर-घर टुकड़े मांगने पड़ जाते हैं और वह प्रभु उसे बिखरे हुए चने चुनने पर मजबूर कर देता है ।

ऐ भाई ! जैसे प्रभु रखे, वैसे ही निर्वाह कर लेना चाहिये, क्योंकि उसकी महिमा कही नहीं जा सकती ।

प्रभु कभी तो सुन्दर घोड़ों पर सवार करा देता है और कभी पांव में जूती तक डालने को नसीब नहीं होती वह प्रभु कमी तो सफेद बिस्तर वाले पलंग सोने को देता है, परन्तु कभी भूसी पर फटी चादर भी बिछाने को प्राप्त नहीं होती ।

नामदेव जी कहते हैं कि केवल एक नाम लेने से ही निस्तारा हो सकता है पर जिसको गुरु कहता उसी का बेड़ा पर होता हैं ।

Man ought to be satisfied with his lot, he will be saved by devotion.

42

Sometimes man is not satisfied even with milk, molasses, and clarified butter;
Sometimes he beggeth morsels from house to house;
Sometimes he picketh up pulse-sweepings.
Remain as God hath placed thee, O brother—

The greatness of God cannot be described—
Sometimes man rideth on prancing steeds;[2]
Sometimes he hath not shoes for his feet;
Sometimes he putteth himself to sleep on a couch with a clean coverlet;
Sometimes he cannot get straw to *sleep upon*—
Saith Namdev, the Name alone saveth;
He who hath found a spiritual guide shall be delivered.

(४३) राग-भैरउ

हसत खेलत तेरे हेदुरे आइआ । भगति करत नामा पकरि उठाइआ ॥ १ ॥
हीनडी जात मेरी जादम राइआ । छीपके जनमि काहे कउ आइआ ॥ रहाउ ॥
लै कमली चलिओ पलटाइ । देहुरे पाछै बैठा जाई ॥ २ ॥
जिउ जिउ नामा हरि गुण उचरै । भगत जना कउ देहुरा फिरै ॥ ३ ॥

मैं बड़े चाव से तेरे मंदिर में आया था पर पुजारियों ने मुझे वहां से भक्ति करते हुए को उठा दिया ।

ऐ यादव राया ! क्या मेरी जातिहीन अथवा छोटी है । यदि ऐसा है तो मुझे शिल्पी घराने में क्यों पैदा करना था । मैंने अपनी कमब्ली उठाई और चल पड़ा मैं मंदिर में पिछवाडे में जा बैठा (पर ईश्वर की अद्भुत लीला देखी) कि मैं नामदेव जैसे-जैसे नाम रटने की मस्ती में गुणगान करता गया, तैसे ही देहरें का मुख्य द्वार भी उसकी और फिरता गया ।

43

I went, O Lord, with laughter and gladness to Thy temple, But while Nama was worshipping, *the Breahmans* forced him away.
A lowly caste is mine, O King of the Yadav, why was I born a calico-printer?
I took up by blanket, went back,
And sat behind the temple.
As Nama repeated the praises of God
The temple turned towards His saint.

Namdev returned to the subject in the following hymn in the Bhairo measure:—

Forget me not, forget me not,
Forget me not, O God!
Those misled Brahmans of the temple were all furious with me;
Calling me a Sudar they beat me and turned me out; what shall I do, Father Vitthal?

If Thou give me salvation when I am dead, nobody will be aware of it; save me now.
If these pandits call me low, then, O God, Thine honour will be in the background.
Thou who art called the compassionate and the merciful, altogether unrivalled is Thine arm—
God turned round the front of the temple towards Nama, and its back towards the pandits.

(४४) राग-भैरव

जैसी भूखे अनाज । त्रिखावंत जल से ती काजू ॥
जैसी मूढ़ कुटंव पराइण । ऐसी नामे प्रीति नाराइण ॥ १ ॥
नामे प्रीति नाराइण लागी । सहज सुभाइ भइयो बैरागी ॥ रहाउ ॥
जैसी पर-पुरुखा रत नारी । लोभी नरु धनका हितकारी ॥
कामी पुरखु कामनी पिआरी । ऐसो नामें प्रीति मुरारी ॥ २ ॥
साई प्रीति जि आपे लाइ । गुर परसादी दुविधा जाइ ॥
कबहूं त तुटसि रहिआ समाइ नामे चितु लाइआ सचि नाई ॥ ३ ॥
जैसी प्रीति बारिक अरु माता । ऐसा हरि से तो मनु राता ।
प्रणवै नामदेउ लागी प्रीति । गोबिंदु बसै हमारै चीति ॥ ४ ॥

जैसे भूखे को अनाज में प्रीति है, जैसे प्यासे को जल की चाहत है, या जैसे अनजाने मनुष्य कुटम्ब पालने की फिक्र रहती है, ऐसे ही नाम देव को प्रभु से प्रीत हैं :–

नामदेव की परमात्मा से प्रीत लग गई हैं अब वह स्वतः ही वैरागी हो गया है । जैसे व्यभिचारणी स्त्री पराए पुरुष से प्रीत करती है लोभी आदमी को धन से प्रीत होती है, और विषयी पुरुष को स्त्री संग प्यारा है वैसे ही नामदेव को प्रभु प्यार हैं

असली प्रीत वही है जो प्रभु आप लगाता है । गुरु की कृपा से फिर भेदभाव मिट जाता है । नामदेव ने सच्चे नाम से ऐसा चित लगा लिया है कि उसकी प्रीत कभी नहीं टूटती और प्रभु में तल्लीन या समाया रहता हैं । जैसे बच्चे और माता की आपसी प्रीत होती है वैसे ही मेरा मन प्रभु के रंग में रंगा हुआ है । नामदेव जी कहते है कि मेरी प्रीत लग गई है और मेरे हृदय में परमात्मा बसता हैं ।

Namdev describes by familiar examples how dear God is to him.

44

As food is dear to the hungry,
As the thirsty need water,

As the fool is attached to his family,
So God is dear to Nama.
Nama's love is devoted to God,
And he hath easily severed himself from the world.
As a woman is smitten with a strange man,
As a greedy man loveth wealth,
As woman is dear to the lustful,
Such is Nama's love for God.
That is real love by which God attached man to Him,
And by which through the guru's favour duality depareteth.
Love for Him who filleth *my heart* shall never be sundered;
Nama hath applied his heart to the true Name.
As the love between a child and its mother,
So is my soul imbued with God.
Namdev representh, I love God;
He dwelleth in my hearty.

Man should rather seek the guru's protection than devote himself to sinful pleasures.

(४५) राग-भैरउ

घर की नारि तिआगै अंधा । पर नारी तिउ घालै धंधा ॥
जैसे सिंबलु देखि सुआ बिगसाना । अंत की बार मूआ लपटाना ॥ १॥
पापीका घरु अगने माहि । जलत रहै मिटावे कब नाहीं ॥ रहाउ ॥
हरि की भगति न देखे जाइ । अंम्रित डारि लादि बिखु खाइ ॥ २ ॥
मूलहु भूल आवै जाए । अंर्मित डारि लादि बिखु खाइ ॥ ३ ॥
जिउ वेरवा के परै अखारा । कापरु पहिरि करहि सींगारा ॥
पूरे ताल निहाले सास । वाके गले जमका है फास ॥ ४ ॥
जाके मसतकि लिखिओ करमा । सो भजि परि है गुरकी सरना ॥
कहत नामदे इहुवीचारू । इन बिधि संतहु उतरहु पारु ॥ ५ ॥

अज्ञानी पुरुष अपने घर की स्त्री से परे रहना चाहता है और पराई नारी से अयोग्य संबंध जोड़ता हैं । परन्तु जैसे सिम्बल के वृक्ष को देख कर तोता खुश होता है और अन्त में उससे ही चिपक कर मर जाता है वैसे ही इसका हाल होता है । पापी जीव का मन सदैव ही अग्नि में निवास करता हैं । जो हमेशा जलती रहती है और कभी तृप्त नहीं होती।

ऐसा पुरुष प्रभु की भक्ति करने वालों का संग नहीं करता । सत्संग और भक्ति के श्रेष्ठ रास्ते को छोड़कर कुसंगति के खोटे रस्ते पर जा पड़ता हैं । अपनी वास्तविकता परमात्मा से भूल कर जीवित होता है और मरता है । नाम रुपी अमृत को छोड़ कर विषय

वासनाओं को बोझ लादकर मानो विष (जहर) का पान करता है । जैसे वैश्या के घर लोगों का अखाड़ा लगता और दिखावे के पकड़े पहन कर श्रृंगार करती है वो ताल पर नाचती है और तरह-तरह के इशारे करती है पर उसके और देखने वालों के गले में फांसा पड़ती हैं । जिसके मस्तिक पर श्रेष्ठ कर्मों का लेख लिखा हुआ है वो दौड़ कर गुरु की शरण जा पड़ता है ।

ऐसा विचार कर नामदेव जी कहते कि कि हे संतजनों इस विधि से संसार समुद्र को पार कर लो ।

45

As a fool leaveth the wife of his home,
Hath intercourse with a strange woman, *and is ruined.*
As the parrot is pleased on seeing the simmal,
But at last dieth clinging to it,
So the home of the sinner shall be in hell-fire;
He shall continue to burn and never have respite.
He never goeth to see where God is worshipped,
He leveth the right path and goeth the wrong one,
He orgetteth God and suffereth transmigration,
He rejecteth ambrosia and eateth a load of poison.
When a dancing-girl arriveth on the dancing floor,
She putteth on rich dresses, adorneth herself,
Danneth to measure, and modulateth her voice,
While Death's noose is on her neck,
He on whose forehead such destiny hath been written,
Quickly entereth the protection of the guru.
Saith Namdev, this is my decision—
O Saints, thus shall you obtain salvation.

(४६) राग-भैरउ

सडा मरका जाइ पुकारे । पढ़े नहीं हमारी पचिहारै ॥
राम कहै करताल बजावै । चटीआ सभै बिगारै ॥ १ ॥
रामा नामा जपिबो करै । हिरदै हरिजीको सिमरनु.धरै ॥ रहाउ ॥
वसुधा बसि कीनी सभ राजे । बिनती करै पटरानी ॥
पूतु प्रहिलादु कहिआ नहीं मानै । निनि तउ अउरै ठानी ॥ २ ॥
दुसट सभा मिलि मंतर उपाइआ । करसह अउख धनेरी ॥
गिरि तर जल जुआला भै राखिओ । राजारामि माइआ फेरी ॥ ३ ॥
काढि खडगु कालु भै कोपिओ । मोहि बताउ जु तुहि राखै ॥
पीत पोतांबर त्रिभवण । थंम माहि हरि भाखै ॥ ४ ॥

हरनाखसु जिनि नखह बिंदारिओ । सुरनर कीए सनाथा ॥
कहि नामदे हम नरहरि धिआवहि । रामु अभैपद दाता ॥ ५ ॥

प्रह्लाद के अध्यापक संडा और मकी ने राजा हरिण्यकश्यप् के पास फरियाद की, हम तो तंग और निराश हो गए है क्योंकि प्रह्लाद पढ़ता नहीं । हाथों से ताल बजा कर राम राम जपता है और पाठशाला के सारे विद्यार्थी बिगाड़ डाले है । राम नाम ही सदा जपता रहता है और हृदय में प्रभु की याद रखता हैं । प्रह्लाद की माता बड़ी रानी प्रह्लाद को कहती है कि तेरे पिता राजा ने सारी धरती अपने बस में की हुई है पर पुत्र प्रह्लाद उसका कहा नहीं मानता और मन में कुछ और ही धारण किए हुए हैं । दुष्टों के टोले से मिलकर हरिण्यकश्यप् ने मार डालने की सलाह बनाली । परमात्मा ने अपनी माया के तत्वों का स्वभाव ऐसा बदला कि प्रह्लाद को पहाड़, पानी, अग्नि आदि से बचा लिया।

फिर राजा ने तलवार निकाल कर काल रूपी गुस्से के साथ ललकारा, कि बता अब तुझे कौन बचा सकता है ।

प्रह्लाद ने कहा कि पीताम्बर धारण किए प्रभु जो तीन लोकों का स्वामी जो खम्बे में भी है उस परमात्मा ने हरिण्यकश्यप् को नाखूनों से चीर दिया और देवताओं एवं मनुष्यों को मालिक सिद्ध किया ।

नामदेव जी कहते है कि उसी प्रभु को ध्यान करो वो राम ही पदवी देने वाला हैं।

The fate of Harnakhas who objected to his son Prahlad's devotion.

46

Sanda and Marka went and complained *to Harnaakhas*—
Thy son Prahlad will not study and we are tired of *teaching him*;
He singeth God's praises, beateth time with his hands, and corrupeth all the other pupils;
He repeateth the name of God;
In his heart the remembereth God.
The queen represented to her son—The king hath reduced the whole earth to suibjection;
My son Prahlad thou doest not his bidding; he hath some design on thee.
A council of his enemies met and passed a raesolution. We will lengthen his life.
They terrified him by throwing him from a height, by putting him into water and fire, but God changed for him *the properties* of matter.

Harnakhas enraged drew his sword, and threatened him with death, *saying,* Show me who will save thee.
Prahlad replied, God who weareth yellow clothes, the Lord of the three worlds, is in the pillar.
Upon this God tore Harnakhas with his nails, and rendered demigods and men happy.
Saith Namdev, Immediate on that God who bestoweth salvation.

(४७) राग-भैरउ

सुलतानु पुछ सुनु बे नामा । देखउ राम तुमारे कामा ॥ १ ॥
नामा सुलताने बांथिला । देखउ तेरा हरि बीठुला ॥ रहाउ ॥
बिसीमुल गऊ देहु जीवाइ । ना तरू गरदनि मारउ ठाइ ॥ २ ॥
बादिसाह ऐसी किड होइ । बिसमिलि कीआ न जीवै कोइ ॥ ३ ॥
मेरा कीया कछ न होइ । करि है रामु होइ है सोइ ॥ ४ ॥
बादिसाहु चड़िओ अंहकारि । गज-हसती दीनो चमकारी ॥ ५ ॥
रूदनु करै नामे की माई । छोड़ि राम की न भजहि खुदाह ॥ ६ ॥
न हउ तेरा पूंगडा ना तू मेरी माइ । पिंडु पड़ै तउ हरि गुन गाइ ॥ ७ ॥
करै गजिंदु सुंड की चोट । नामा उबरै हरि की ओट ॥ ८ ॥
काजी मंलां करहि सलामु । इनि हिंदू में राम लिया मानु ॥ ९ ॥
बादिसाह बेनतो सुनेहु । नामे सरभरि सोना लेहु ॥ १० ॥
माउ लेउ तउ दोजकि परउ । दीनु छोड़ि दुनीआ कउ भरउ ॥ ११ ।
पावहु बेड़ी हाथहु ताल । नामा गावै गुन गोपाल ॥ १२ ॥
गंगा जमुन जउ उलटी वहै । तउ नामा हरि करता रहै ॥ १३ ॥
सात घड़ी जब बीती सुणी । अजहु न आइओ त्रिभवण धणी ॥ १४॥
पाखंतण बाज बजाइला । गरूड़ चढ़ै गोविंद आइला ॥ १५ ॥
अपने भगत परि की प्रतिपाल । गरूड़ चढ़े आए गोपाल ॥ १६ ॥
कहहित धरणि इकोडि करउ । कहहि त लेकरि उपरि धरूं ॥ १७ ॥
कहहि त मुई गऊ देरू जीआइ । सभु कोई देखे पती आई ॥ १८ ॥
नामा प्रणवै सेलमसेली । गउ दुहाइ बछरा मेलि ॥ १९ ॥
दुधहि दुहि जब मटुकी भरी । ले बादिसाह के आगे धरी ॥ २० ॥
बादिसाहु महलमहि जाइ । अउघट की घटलागी आइ ॥ २१ ॥
काजी मुला बिनती फुरमाइ । वखसी हिंदु मैं तेरी गाइ ॥ २२ ॥
नामा कहै सुनहु बादिसाह । इहु किछ पतीआ मुझै दिखाइ ॥ २३ ॥
इस पतीआका इहै परबानु । साचि सील चालहु सुलितानु ॥ २४ ॥
नामदेउ सभ एहिआ सताइ । मिलि हिंदू सम नामे पहि जाहि ॥ २५ ॥
जऊ अबकी बार न जीवै गाइ । त नामदेव का पतीआ जाइ ॥ २६ ॥

नामे की कीरति रही संसारि । भगत जना ले ऊधरिआ पारी ॥ २७ ॥
सगल कलेस निंदक भइआ खेदु । नामे नाराइन नाही भेदु ॥ २८ ॥

बादशह मुहम्मद बिन तुगलक के नामदेव को कहा, कि मैं तुम्हारे राम की शक्ति देखना चाहता हूं । बादशाह ने नामदेव को बंध्वा दिया । और कहा कि तेरा राम भी देख लेता हूं । या तो यह मृत गऊं को जिन्दा कर दो नहीं तो तुम्हारी गर्दन काट दूगा ।

हे बादशाह यह कैसे हो सकता है ? मरा हुआ कभी जिन्दा नहीं हो सकता है मेरा किया तो कुछ नहीं हो सकता जो प्रभु करता है, वही कुछ होता है । बादशाह अहंकार में आ गया और एक मस्त हाथी को छोड़ दिया । नामदेव की माता विलाप करने लगी और कहने लगी कि तू राम की बजाय खुद क्यों नहीं भजता । नामदेव ने कहा कि ना मैं तेरा पुत्र हूं और ना तू मेरी मां है, यदि मेरा शरीर भी नाश हो जाय, तो भी मैं हरि के गुण गाऊंगा । मस्त हाथी अपने सूड से चोट करता है पर नामदेव प्रभु की आस करके बच जाते हैं । बादशाह ने मन में कहा—मुझे काजी और मुल्ला लोग सभी सलाम करते हैं पर इस हिन्दु ने मेरा मान गवा दिया है लोगों ने प्रार्थना की बादशाह हमारी बिनती सुनिए। नामदेव जी के वजन के बराबर सोना लेना मंजूर करलो और इसे छोड़ दो ।

बादशाह कहता है यदि मैं बेईमानी का धन लूँगा तो मैं नरक में जाऊंगा और दीन को छोड़कर इस दुनिया को प्राप्त करने वाली बात होगी ।

नामदेव के पैरों में बेड़िया पड़ी है पर वो फिर भी हाथों से तालिया बजा कर प्रभु के गुण गा रहा है । यदि गंगा और जमना नदियाँ उल्टी बहने लगे तो भी नामदेव राम नाम ही लेता रहेगा । जब घंटे की आवाज से सातवीं घड़ी गूँजते सुनी और तीन भवनों का मालिक प्रकट नहीं हुआ तो उसी समय पक्षी के उड़ने की आवाज सुनाई दी और देखा कि गरूड़ पर सवार भगवान आ गए है ।

अपने भक्त की रक्षा की ओर जगत पालक गरूड़ पर आ गए । भगवान ने कहा कि नामदेव कहो तो धरती को उल्टा कर दूँ ।

यदि तु कहे तो इसे अपने हाथ पर धारण करलुँ। यदि कहे तो गउ को जिन्दा कर दूँ। ताकि सारे देख लें कि भगवान का भरोसा कितना होता है। नामदेवजी ने विनती की, कि गऊ को जीवित कर दो इतना कहते ही बछडे को छोड़कर (बाँध कर) और गऊ का दूध दोह कर जब मटकी भर गई तो बादशा के आगे रख दी । बादशाह उसके पश्चात् महल में जाता है वहाँ उसको कठिन दु:ख की घड़ी आ घेर लेती है । काजी और मुल्लाह द्वारो में विनती करके कहता है कि हे हिन्दु मैं तेरी गऊ हूँ । भाव तेरी दया का पात्र हूँ, मुझे क्षमा कर दो ।

नामदेव जी कहते हैं ए बादशाह मेरी बात सुन और मुझे भी कुछ भरोसा दिखा। जिस भरोसे का माप ये है कि आगे से सच और शीलवंत होकर चलो।

नामदेव का यश सब जगह फैल गया और सारे हिन्दु नामदेव के पास गए और कहा कि यदि गऊ जिन्दा न होती तो संसार में नामदेव पर बना भरोसा चला जाता। अब संसार में उसका यश कायम है। और वो और भक्तों को लेकर संसार सारग से पार हो गया है। यह यश सुनकर निन्दकों को बड़ा कलेश और दु:ख हुआ पर नामदेव और प्रभु में भेद नहीं रहा।

47

The two saints set out from Pandharpur for Hastinapur, the name by which Dihli was then known. The Emperor Muhammad bin Tughlak hearing of Namdev's influence with the people and suspecting that it would lead to an insurrection, resolved to arrest his career. The following hymn in the Bhairo measure gives the result:—

The emperor said, Ho, you Nama.
Let me see the deeds of your God,
The emperor had Nama arrested—
Let me see your God Vitthal;
Restore to life this slaughtered cow,
Otherwise I will strike off thy head on the spot.
Your majesty, how can that be?
No man can reanimate what is slaughtered.
All I could do would be of no avail;
What God doeth taketh place.
The emperor fell into a passion,
And set a huge elephant at Nama.
Nama's mother began to cry—
Why dost thou not abandon the God of the Hindus and worship the God of the Musalmans;
Namdev: I am not thy son, nor art thou my mother;
Even though I perish, I will sing God's praises.
The elephant struck him with his trunk.
But Nama was saved by the protection of God.
The king said, 'The Qazis and the Mullas salute me,
But the Hindu tampleth on mine honour.'
The Hindus said, 'O king, hear our prayer;
Take Nama's weight in gold.'
'If I take a bribe I shall go to hell;

Shall I amass wealth by abandoning my faith?
While Nama's feet were being chained
He sang the praises of God and beat time with his hands.
The Ganges and the Jamna may flow backwards,
But Nama will repeat God's name.
When seven gharis were heard to strike,
The Lord of the three worlds had not yet arrived.
God afterwards came mounted on His garur,
Which beat the air with its wings.
He took compassion on His saint.
And came mounted on His garur,
Say but the word and I will turn the earth on its side;
Say but the word and I will upturn it altogether.
Say but the word and I will restore the dead cow to life,
So that every one may behold and be convinced.
Nama said, Spancel the cow.
They put the calf to her and milked her.
When the pitcher was filled with the milk the cow gave, Nama took and placed it before the emperor,
And the time of trouble came on him.
He implored Namdev through the Qazis and the Mullas—
Pardon me, O Hindu, I am thy cow.
Nama said, Hear, O monarch,
Hath this credential been exhibited by me?
The object of this miracle is
That thou, O emperor, shouldst walk in the paths of truth and humility—
Namdev, *God* is contained in everything.
The Hindus went in procession to Nama.
And said, If the cow had not been restored to life,
People would have lost faith in thee.
The fame of Namdev remained in the world;
He took saints with him to salvation.
All trouble and sorrow befell the revilers—
Between Nama and God there is no difference.

(४८) राग-भैरउ

जउ गुरदेउ त मिलै मुरारी । ज गुरदेउ त अतरं पारि ॥
जउ गुरदेउ त बैकुन्ठ तरै । जउ गुरदउ त जीवत मरै ॥ १ ॥
साति साति सति सति सति गुरदेउ । झूटू झूटू झूटू झूटू आन सभ सेव ॥ रहाउ॥
जउ गुरदेउ त नाम द्रिडावै । जउ गुरदेव न दह दिस धावै ॥
जउ गुरदेउ त पंचते दूरि । जउ गुरदेउ न मरिबो झूरि ॥ २ ॥
जउ गुरदेउ त अंम्रित बानी । जउ गुरदेउ त अकय कहानी ॥
जउ गुदेउ त अंम्रित देही । जउ गुरदेउ नामु जषि लेही ॥ ३ ॥
जउ गुरदेउ भवन त्रै सूझै । जउ गुउदेउउच पद बूझै ॥
जउ गुरदेउ त सीस अकासि । ज गुरदे सदा साबासि ॥ ४ ॥
जउ गुरदेउ सदा बैरागी । जउ गुरदे परनिंदा तियागी ॥
जउ गुरदेउ बुरा भला एक । जउ गुरेउ लिलाटहि लेख ॥ ५ ॥
जउ गुरदेउ कंध नहीं हिरै । जउ गुरदेउ देहुरा फिरै ॥
जउ गुरदेउ त छापरि छाइ । जउ गुरदेउ सिहज निकसाइ ॥ ६ ॥
जउ गुरदेउ त अठाठि नाइया । जउ गुरदेउ तीन चक्र लगाइआ ।
जउ गुरदेउ त दुआदस सेवा । जउ गुरदेउ सभ बिखु मेवा ॥ ७ ॥
जउ गुरदेउ त संसा टूटै । जउ गुरदेउ त जमते न छटै ॥
जउ गुरदेउ त भबजल तरै । जउ गुरदेउ त जनमि न मरै ॥ ८ ॥
जउ गुरदेउ अठदश बिउहार । जउ गुरदेउ अठारह भार ॥
बिनु गुरदेउ अवार नहीं जाई । नामदेउ गुरकी सरणाई ॥ ९ ॥

इस शब्द को बाबा पूर्णादास जी ने नामदेव जी की जीवनी का बीज मन्त्र बताया है इस में जहाँ गुरु महिमा का वर्णन किया है कि वह क्या कुछ कर सकते हैं वहाँ गुरु की कृपा से उन्हें स्वयं क्या प्राप्त हुआ, इस का भी उल्लेख किया है:–

गुरु की कृपा से ईश्वर की प्राप्ति हो सकती है अथवा मुझे स्वयं हुई है गुरु की कृपा से संसार समुन्द्र से तरना हो जाता है और बैकुन्ठ से भी परे परमात्मा का साक्षात्कार होता है । इसकी कृपा से मनुष्य जीवन मुक्त हो जाता है । इसलिए गुरुदेव की सेवा ही सत्य है और सत्य है और दूसरे किसी का सेवन करना व्यर्थ है । गुरु कृपा से मन की चंचलता का नाश हो जाता है और पांचों मनोविकार मिट जाते हैं । गुरु के सद्उपेदश से मनुष्य भटकता नहीं गुरु प्रसाद से शिष्य की वाणी अमृतमयी हो जाती है । गुरु कृपा से बहुत उत्तम प्रभु भक्ति की कथायें सुनने में आती है और तीनों लोकों को ज्ञान प्राप्त होता है, ऊंची पदवी पर बैठता है, शिष्य की दिव्य दृष्टि हो जाती है । स्वाभिमान जागृत होता है सन्यासी पुरुषों द्वारा धन्यवाद का पात्र बन जाता है, गुरु की कृपा का पूर्ण वैराग्य

मिलता तथा परनिन्दा आदि के दोषों से रहित हो जाता है बल्कि स्तुति निन्दा होने से ऊपर उठ जाता है । गुरु की भक्ति से मस्तक का भाग्य उदय होने लगता है ।

यदि गुरु प्रसन्न हो तो ना हिलने वाली दीवार तो क्या साारा भवन ही घूम जाता है । गुरु की कृपा से ही छप्पर छाये गये मन्दिर फिर गया । गुरु की कृपा से ही 68 तीर्थों (आभयन्तर और बाहरी) में स्नान किया बारह ज्योति लिंग के दर्शन किये अथवा वैष्णवों के बारह तिलक धारण किये । गुरु कृपा से विष भी अमृत हो जाती है । मेरे सार सशंय मिट गये है यमो का भय अब मुझे नहीं रहा जन्म से रहित होकर अमर पद पाया है । गुरु की कृपा से सब जगत व्यवहार का परित्याग हो गया है । गुरु के बिना मेरा कोई ठौर-ठिकाना नहीं नामदेव जी कहते हैं कि मैं सब प्रकार से अपने गुरु की शरण में ही उपस्थित रहता हूं ।

The advantages of a guru.

48

When one hath a guru, he meeteth God;
When one hath a guru, he is saved;
When one hath a guru, he goeth to heaven;
When one hath a guru, while he liveth he is dead—
True, true, true, true, true is the guru;
False, false, false, false is all other service *than his*—
When one hath a guru, he inculeateth the Name;
When one hath a guru, he runneth not in the ten directions;
When one hath a guru, he is far removed from the live evil passions;
When one hath a guru, he dieth not of grief;
When one hath a guru, he obtaineth the ambrosial Word;
When one hath a guru, he heareth the story of the Ineffable;
When one hath a guru, his body *bccometh* immortal;
When one hath a guru, he uttereth the Name;
When one hath a guru, he seeth the three worlds;
When one hath a guru, he knoweth *how to reach* the exalted position;
When one hath a guru, his head toucheth heaven;
When one hath a guru, he is ever congratulated;
When one hath a guru, he is ever estranged from the world;
When one hath a guru, he abandoneth slander;
When one hath a guru, he deemeth evil and good the same;
When one hath a guru, good destiny is written on his forehead;
When one hath a guru, *evil passious* seduce not his body;
When one hath a guru, the temple turneth *towards him*;
When one hath a guru, his hut is rebuilt for him;

When one hath a guru, his bed cometh forth *from the river;*
When one hath a guru, he batheth in the sixty-eight places of pilgrimage;
When one hath a guru, the quoit of Vishnu is impressed on his body;
When one hath a guru, he performeth the twelve adorations;
When one hath a guru, all poisons become wholesome;
When one hath a guru, doubts are dispelled;
When one hath a guru, he escapeth from Death;
When one hath a guru, he crosseth over the terrible ocean;
When one hath a guru, he suffereth not transmigration;
When one hath a guru, he obtaineth the advantages of the eighteen *Purans;*
When one hath a guru, he obtaineth the eighteen loads of *vegetables;*
Without the guru, there is no *resting*-place—
Namdev hath entered the guru's protection.

Namdev once fell into a trance, and thought he was playing cymbals in God's honour. God is said to have appeared before him as a Qalandar, and taker his cymbals from him. Namdev on awaking composed the following in God's praise:—

(४९) राग-भैरउ

आउ कलंदर केसवा । करि अबदाली भेसवा ॥ रहाउ ॥
जिनि आकस कुलह सिर कीनी, पउसै सपत पयाला ॥
चमर पोस का मंदरु तेरा, इह विधि बने गुपाला ॥ १ ॥
छपन कोटिका पेहनु तेरा, सोलह सहस इजारा ॥
भार अठारह मुदगरु तेरा, सहनक सभ संसारा ॥ २ ॥
देही महजिदि मनु मउलाना, सहल निवास गुजारै
बीबी कउला सउ काहनु, तेरा निरंकार आकरै ॥ ३ ॥
भगति करत मेरे ताल छिनाए किह पहि करउ पुकारा ॥
नामेका सुआमी अंतर जामो, फिरै सगल बेदेसारा ॥ ४ ॥

आओ ! कलन्दर रुप में, केशव जी आओ आप ने अबदाती फकीरों का वेष बनाया हुआ है । और सिर पर आकाश रूपी कुन्ठां धारण किया हुआ है और पैरों में सात पाताल रुपी खड़ावें हैं सारा संसार मानो तेरी चमड़े की देह है, ऐ धरती के रक्षक ! तू इस तरह का बना हुआ है छप्पन करोड़ बादल (मेघमाला) का तेरा चोला है और सोलह (16) हजार आलम तेरा पायजामा है । गोपियें (सारी बनस्पति) तेरा मुगदर है । और सारा संसार

तेरी कुनांली है। सभी जीवों की देही तुम्हारी मस्जिद है उस का मौलाना मन है और ज्ञान का रूपी नमाज पढ़ते हैं। बीबी कमला (भाषा) से आप का निकाह हुआ है जो निरंकार को आकार में बदल देती है। (है कलंदर थूभू) भक्ति करने हुए मेरे ताल तूने ही छिनाए थे। और अब किस के आगे पुकार करू, नामदेव का स्वामी हर एक हृदय की जानता है वह सर्वव्यापी होने से सब देश अर्थात् में बसा हुआ है।

49

Come God, the Qalandar
Wearing the dress of an Abdali.
The firmament is the hat on Thy head, the seven nether regions Thy slippers;
All animals with skins are Thy temples; thus art Thou decked out, O God!
The fifty-six millions of *clouds* are Thy robes and the sixteen thousands *queens of Krishan* Thy waistbands;
The eighteen loads of vegetables are Thy clubs, the whole world is Thy slaver;
Nama's body is Thy mosque, his heart Thy priest who tranquilly prayeth.
O Thou with and without form. Thou who art wedded to lady Lakshmi.
While I was worshipping Thou hadst my cymbals taken from me: to whom shall I complain?
Nama's Lord is the Searcher of all hearts, and wandereth in every land.

(५०) राग-बसंत

साहिबु संकट व रेवकु भजै। चिरकाल न जीवै दोऊ कुल लजै ॥ १ ॥
तेरि भगति न छोड़उ भावै लोगु हसै। चरण कमल तेरे हीअरे वसै ॥ रहाउ॥
जैसे अपनी धनहि प्रानी मरनु कांडै। तैरे संतजना राम नामु न छाडै ॥ २ ॥
गंगा गइआ गोदावरी संसार के कामा। नारायाणा सुप्रसंत होइ त सेवकु नामा॥३॥

यदि परमात्मा कुछ संकट डाल दे तो सेवक को कष्ट से डर कर भागना नहीं चाहिए। सदा तो जीवित रह नहीं सकता संकट में त्याग देना अपने माता-पिता के कुलों को लज्जित कर देता है। हे प्रभु लोग चाहे मुझ पर हंसे पर मैं तेरी भक्ति नहीं छोड़ुगा। तेरे कमल रूपी चरण मेरे हृदय में बसे हैं। जिस प्रकार जीव अपने धन हेतु मरने के लिए भी तैयार हो जाता है वैसे ही संत जन प्रभु का नाम नहीं छोड़ते।

गंगा, गया और गोदावरी आदि का तीर्थ करना दुनियादारी के काम हैं। पर हे नामदेव सेवक वही है जिस पर प्रभु कृपालु हैं।

50
BASANT

Man ought not to abandon God's service even though it be irksome.

If a servant run away when his master is in trouble,
The servant shall not be long-lived, he *shall bring* shame on his father and mother's family.
I will not abandon Thy service, *O Lord,* even though men scoff at me;
Thy lotus feet dwell in my heart.
As man accepteth death to secure wealth,
So the saints relinquish not God's name.
Pilgrimages to the Ganges, Gaya, and Godavari are worldly acts;
If God be pleased, Nama shall be His worshipper.

Namdev's prayer when in danger of drowning in the stormy ocean of worldly love.

(५१) राग-सारंग

लोभ लहरि अति नीझर बाजै । काइआ डूबै केसवा ॥ १ ॥
संसार समुंदे तारि गोबिंदे । तारिलै बाप बीठुला ॥ रहाउ ॥
अनिल बेडा हउ खेवि न साकउ तेरा पारू न पाइआ बीठुला ॥ २ ॥
होइ दइआलु सतिगुरु मेलि तूँ मोकउ पारि उतारे केंसवा ॥ ३ ॥
नामा कहै हउ तरि भी न जानउ मोकउ वाह देहि बाह देहि बीठुला ॥ ४॥

इस संसार समुन्द्र में लोभ की लहरें एक रस ठाठें मार रही हैं ।

हे केशव । इस में मेरा शरीर डूब रहा है । संसार समुन्द्र की भांति है, हे प्रकाश रूपी परमात्मा, तू मुझे तार ले ।

हे पिता बीठल, मुझे तार ले । रहाऊ । वासना-रूपी पवन चल रही है, अथवा शरीर रूपी बेड़े को आप की ओर ठेल नहीं सकता ।

और हे प्रभु ! आप का किनारा भी नजर नहीं पड़ता ।

हे केशव ! मुझ पर दया कर मुझे सतगुरु से मिला दे । नामदेव कहते है कि मैं तो तैरना भी नहीं जानता, मुझे अपनी आसरा रूपी बांह पकडा दे ।

Namdev prayer when in danger of drowning in the stormy ocean of worldly love

51

> The waves of covetousness sound like a cataract, my body is drowning therein, O God.
> Float me over the ocean the world, O God, float me over, Father Vitthal.
> In *this* gale I cannot steer my boat, I cannot reach Thine opposite shore, O God.
> Be compassionate and cause me to meet a true guru; take me across, O God.
> Nama saith, I do not even know how to swim; give me Thine arm, give me Thine arm, O God.

Man slowly grows up. He then becomes thesport of the world and commits sin, but his soul can be washed pure by the guru.

(५२) राग-सारंग

सहज अवधि धूड़ि मणी गाड़ी चालती । पीछै तिनका लैकरि हाकती ॥ १ ॥
जैसे पनकत थरु टिटि हांकती । सरि धोवन चाली लाडुली ॥ रहाउ ॥
धोबी धोबै बिरह बिधाता । हरि चरनन मेरा मनु राता ॥ २ ॥
भणति नामदेउ रमि रहिआ । आपने भगत पर करि दइआ ॥ ३ ॥

पहले पापों-रूपी धूल से लदी शरीर-रूपी गाड़ी (सतसंग रूपी सरोवर की ओर आहिस्ता-2 चलती है ।

फिर जीव-स्त्री को (मन रूपी बैल) को प्रेम की उत्साह रूपी डंडी (चाबुक) से हांकना पड़ता है । जैसे कीचड़ से गाड़ी को थिलिट कह कर निकालते है वैसे ही बुद्धि ज्ञान द्वार मल कीचड़ आदि को धोने सदगुरु रूपी तालाब की ओर ले जाती है ।

अथवा जैसे प्रेम-भरी जीव-भरी सतसंग सरोवर पर मैलेमन को मानो जबरदस्ती धोने के लिए ले जाती है ।

प्यार में रंगा हुआ गुरु रूपी धोबी, इन के मन को पवित्र करता है ।

इसीलिये मेरा मन भी प्रभु के चरणों में लगा हुआ है । नामदेव जी कहते हैं कि हे सर्वव्यापक प्रभु अपने भक्तों पर इसी प्रकार दया कीजिये ।

52

As an ant draggeth along a bit of cow-dung,
So thiscart fashioned from dust and seed
At first moveth slowly;
But afterwards *the world* driveth it with a rod.
My darling soul goeth to the wash-tank.
The washerman dyed with love washeth it *with the water of God's name;*
My heart is fascinated with God's feet.
Saith Nama, Thou, O God, who art everywhere diffused,
Have compassion on Thy worshipper!

(५३) राग-सारंग

काए रे मन बिखिआ बन जाइ । भूलो रे ठगमूरी खाइ ॥ रहाउ ॥
जैसे मौनु पानीमहि रहै । काल जाल की सुधि नहीं लहै ॥
जिहबा सुआदी लीलित लोह । ऐसे कनिक कामनी बांधिओ मोह ॥ १ ॥
जिठ मधु मारू संचै आपार । मधु लीनो मुखि दीना छारु ॥
गउ बाछ कउ संचै खीरु । गला बांधि दुहि लेह अहीरु ॥ २ ॥
माइआ कारन त्रमु अति करै । सो माइआ लै गाडै धरै ॥
अति संचै समझै नहीं मूड । धनु धरती तनु हाइ गइअी धूडि ॥ ३ ॥
काम क्रोध त्रियना अति जरै । साध संगति कबहूं नहीं करै ॥
कहत नामदेउ वाची आण । निरभै होइ भजीए भगवान ॥ ४ ॥

हे मन ! तू विषय रूपी जंगल में क्यों जाता है । ऐ भाई ! तू भूल कर धोखा देने वाली बुटी क्यों खा रही है जिस प्रकार मछली पानी में रहती है ।

पर काल-रूपी जाल की खबर नहीं रहती और जीभ के स्वाद के कारण लोहे की कुंडी को निगल जाती है ।

इसी प्रकार तुझे सोने और सुन्दरी के मोह ने बाँधा हुआ हैं । शहद की मक्खियां यत्न से शहद जुटाती हैं, पर जैसे मनुष्य सारा शहद निकाल लेता हैं, और मधु-मक्खी के मुंह में राख और धुआं ही पड़ता है, गऊ अपने बछड़े के लिए (थनों में) दुग्ध इकटा करती है परन्तु गजाला गले में रसी बांध कर दुग्ध ले लेता है ।

वैसे ही मनुष्य माया की प्राप्ति के लिए अति मेहनत करता है और माया प्राप्त कर के धरती में गाड़ देता है । माया बहुत सी इक्कठा करता है, पर समझता नहीं । कि यह धन, शरीर के नाश होने पर दबा ही रह जायेगा, मूर्ख मनुष्य काम, क्रोध तथा तृषणा की

अग्नि में जलता रहता है । पर साधू संगत में कभी नहीं ठहरता नामदेव जी कहते है कि प्रभु की शरन में आकर बिना डर के उस का भजन करो ।

53
SARANG

Man is intoxicated with worldly love but what he amasses will not go with him, wherefore he ought to prepare for hereafter.

O man, why hast thou gone into a forest of evil passions?
Thou hast partaken of the thieves' plant and gone astray.
A fish abideth in water,
And taketh no notice of thedeadly net;
It swalloweth the bait to gratify its palate,
So man is bound by the love of gold and woman.
When the bees hoard up a great store of honey.
Man taketh the honey and throweth dirt on the bees
The cow storeth up milk for her calf,
But the milkman tieth the calf up by the neck and milketh the cow.
For wealth man maketh great endeavours;
That wealth he taketh and burieth in the ground.
He amasseth a great deal, but the fool understandeth not
That his riches shall remain on the earth and his body become dust.
He burneth with great lust, wrath, and avarice;
He never joineth the company of holy men.
Saith Namdev, seek God's protection;
Become fearless and worship God.

(५४) राग-सारंग

बदहु की न होय माथउ मोसिउ ॥
ठाकुर ते जनु ते ठाकुर खेलु परिओ है तीसिउ ॥ रहाउ ॥
आपन देउ दैहुरा आपन आप लगावै पूजा ॥
जल ते तरंग, तरंग ते है जलु कहन सुनन कह दूजा ॥ २ ॥
आपहि गावै आपहि नाचै आप बजावै तूरा ॥
कहत नामदेउ तूं मेरो ठाकुरू जनु उरा तूं पूरा ॥ ३ ॥

हे माया-पति परमात्मा ! तू मेरे साथ शर्त लगाले (कि मेरा कहना ठीक है ।)

स्वामी के लिए सेवक, पर सेवक होने ही से स्वामी जाना जाता है। और इस प्रकार ही यह जगत का तमाशा तुम्हारे और हमारे बीच चल रहा हैं।

तू स्वयं: मंदिर और देवता है और आप ही लोगों को पूजा में लगाता है। पानी से लहरें उठती हैं ओर फिर पानी बन जाती हैं केवल कहने सुनने में ही भेद पड़ता है।

तू आप ही गायक है, आप ही नाचता है और आप ही बजाने वाला है। नामदेव जी कहते है कि इस खेल में फिर भी तू मेरा स्वामी है और मैं तेरा सेवक हूं मैं अल्पज्ञ तथा तू ही एक सर्वज्ञ हैं, मुझ में न्यूनतायें है और आप पूर्ण हैं।

God is contained in everything.

54

Why layest Thou not a wager with me, O God, *that there is nothing but Thee*?
The servant is known from his master, and the master from his servant; this is my game with Thee.
Thou art God and Thine own temple. Thou worshippest Thyself.
From water proceed waves, from waves water, though both have different names in conversation.
Thou art the Singer, Thou art the Dancer, Thou art the Trumpet-player—
Saith Namdev, Thou art my Lord; Thy servant is imperfect; Thou art perfect,

(५५) राग-सारंग

दास अनिंन मेरो निजरूप ॥
दरसन निमख तापत्रई मोचन परसत मुकति करत ग्रिह कूप ॥ रहाउ॥
मेरी बांधी भगतु छुड़ावै, बांधे भगतु न छूटै मोहि ॥
एक समै मोकउ गहि बांधै तउ फुनी मोपै जवाब न होइ ॥ १ ॥
मैं गुन बंध सगल की जीवनि, मेरी जीवनि मेरे दास ॥
नामदेव जाके जीअ जैसी, तैसो ताकै प्रेम प्रगास ॥ २ ॥

हे नामदेव ! जो दास मेरे सिवाय किसी और से प्यार नहीं करता, वह मेरा अपना ही स्वरूप है।

ऐसे दास का तनिक दर्शन मात्र करने से आधि, व्याधि और उपाधि (तीनों ताप) नाश हो जाते हैं। रहाउ उस के चरणों के लगने से गृहस्थ रूपी कुएँ से मुक्त हो जाता है।

मेरी बोधी (मोह की गांठ) को भक्त खोल लेता है पर जब भक्त मेरे से प्रेम-गांठ बांधता है । वह मुझ से नहीं खुलती ।

यदि मेरा भक्त किसी समय मुझ पकड़ कर बांध ले तो में उसे कुछ भी कह नहीं सकता उसके वश हो जाता हूं मैं शुभ-गुणों द्वारा बाधा जाता हूं और सब का जीवन-आधार हूँ । और मेरा जीवन का आधार मेरे दास हैं । नामदेव जी कहते हैं कि जिस के मन में यह बात जितनी अधिक बैठ जाती है उस के अन्दर उतना ही प्रेम का प्रकाश हो जाता है ।

In the following God is supposed to address Namdev:—

55

The man who worshippeth none but Me is in Mine own image;
The sight of him even for a moment removeth man's three fevers, and his touch extricateth man from the pit of family life.
A saint can release one bound by me, but I cannot release one bound by a saint.
If a saint seize and bind Me at any time, I can say naught to him.
I am bound *by men's* merits: I am the life of all things, but My slave is My life.
O Namdev, My love shall shine over him whose heart hath such *faith.*

(५६) राग-मलार

सेवीले गोपाल राइ अकुल निरंजन ॥
भगति दानु दीजैं जाचहि संत जन ॥ रहाउ ॥
जांचै घरी दिग दिसै सराइचा ॥
बैकुठं भवन चित्रसाला सपत लोक सामानि पूरी अले ॥
जांच घरी लछिमी कुआरी । चंदु सुरजु दीवड़े ॥
कउ तकु काल बपुडा कोटवालु सुकरा सिरी ॥
सु ऐसा राजा श्री नरहरी ॥ १ ॥
जांच घरी कुलालु ब्रह्मा चतुर मुख डांवडा ॥
जिनि बिस्व संसार राचिले । जौके घरि ईसरू ॥
बावला जगतगुरु तनसारिखा गिआनु भाखिसे ॥
पापु पुनु जांचै डांगीआ हुआरै चितर गुपतु लेखीआ ॥
धरमराइ परूली प्रतिहारू । सो ऐसा राजा श्रीगोपालु ॥ २ ॥
जांचै घरी गण गंधरब रिखी बपुडे ढाढीआ गावंत आछै ॥

सरब सासत्र बहुरूपीआ, अन्न गरूआ आखाडा ॥
मंडलीक बोल बोलहि काछे । चउर ढूल जांचै है पवनु ॥
चेरी सकति जितिलै भवण । अंड टूक जांचै भसमती ॥
सो एसा राजा त्रिभवणा पती ॥ ३ ॥
जांचै घरी कूरमा पालु सहस्त्र फनी बासुक सेज वालुआ ॥
अठारह भार बनासपती मालणी छिनवै करोडी मेघमाला
पाणी हारीआ । नख प्रसेव जाचै सुरसरी ॥ सपत समुदं
जांचै घडथली । एते जीअ जांचै वरतणी ॥
सो ऐसा राजा त्रिभुवणा धणी ॥ ४ ॥
जांचै घरी निकट बरती अरजनु, धू प्रह्लादु अंबरीकु
नारदु ने जै सिथ बुध गण गंधरव बानवै हेला ॥ एते जीअ
जांचे हहि घरी । सरब बिआपक अंतर हरी ॥ प्रणावै नामदेउ
तांची आणि । सगल भगत जांचै निसाणि ॥ ५ ॥

सृष्टि के रक्षक, परमात्मा जो कुल-रहित और माया रहित है, सिमरण करने योग्य है । संत महात्मा उसी की भक्ति का दान मांगते है । रहाऊ वह ऐसा राजा है जिस के घर की दसों दिशा रामायण है, बैकुठं भवन चित्रित मंदिर है और सातों लोकों में वह समान रूप से व्यापक है । जिस के महल में सदा लक्ष्मी रहती है । जहां चांद और सूरज दीये की तरह है और बेचारे काल जो लोगों के सिर पर कर वसूल करने वाला मानों कोतवाल हैं, एक खेल समान ही है, वो परमात्मा ऐसा राजा है । जिस घर में कुम्हार ब्रह्मा चार मुख वाला एक बालक ही है उसने, सारी सृष्टि रची है ।

जिस के घर में शिव जी एक भोला भाला है, जो जगत का गुरु ही है क्योंकि वह मरने का डर देकर यथार्थ का ज्ञान देता है ।

जिसके दरवाजे पर पाप और पुण्य दोनों चोबदार है और चित्रगुप्त लिखारी है । प्रलय के करने वाला धर्मराज जिसका दरबान है । वो सृष्टि का रक्षक ऐसा परमात्मा है। जिसके घर में देवताओं के सेवक ऋषि मुनि गन्धर्व स्वर्ग लोक में गाते हैं । सारे शास्त्र मानो बहु-रुपिये है । इन शास्त्रों के छोटे-छोटे अखाड़े है जिसमें साधूजन अपनी-अपनी बोली बोलते हैं । जिसके घर पर पवन देवता चवर करता है जिसकी दासी माया ने अपनी शक्ति से चौदह भवन जीत लिये हैं । ब्राहमंड का टुकड़ा जिसका चूल्हा है ।

वह तीनों भवन का मालिक हैं और ऐसा राजा है जिस के घर विष्णु का कुछ अवतार मानो पलंग है । हजार फनो वाला शेषनाग जिसकी सेज है । जगत की सारी वनस्पति मालकिन है । छियान्वे करोड़ बादलों की कतारें पानी भरने वाली कहारनें हैं जिसके दर

पर गंगा मानों नाखून का पसीना मात्र हैं आज सातों समुद्र जिसकी घड़ौचिया है और जगत के सारे जीव जिस के घर की सामग्री है ।

वह तीनों भवनों का मालिक परमात्मा ऐसा राजा है जिसके घर में अर्जुन, धुव, प्रह्लाद, राजा अम्बरीष, नारद मुनि, नेजा, परपक योगी, ज्ञानवान पुरुष, देवताओं के सेवक, स्वर्ग के गर्विये और बानवीर निकटवर्ती हैं । जिसके घर में इतने जीव जन्तु हैं, और उन सब के अन्दर प्रभु व्याप रहा है । नामदेव जी फरमाते हैं कि हे ! जीव तु उस परमात्मा की शरण ग्रहण कर । सारे भक्त जिस का चिन्ह-रूपी निशार न है ।

56
MALAR

The extent and greatness of God's palace, in which the demigods and all created things are servants.

Serve God who is unknowable and stainless.
Give me, O God, the gift of service *for which* saints beg.
God's palace hath pavilions on every side; in heaven is His gorgoeous dwelling and mansion;
He filleth equally the seven regions of the world.
In His palace dwelleth the ever youthful Lakshmi;
The moon and sun are His lamps, the wretched mountebank Death, who levieth a tax on all, is His judge—
Such a Monarch is God.
In His mansion Brahma with the four faces who created the whole world is the fashioning potter;
In His mansion enthusiast Shiv, the world's teacher, preacheth pure divine knowledge;
As His gate are the mace-bearers Evil and Good, and the accountants Chitr and Gupt;
Dharmraj the destroyer is His porter—
Such a Monarch is God.
In His mansion are the heralds, the heavenly dancers, the rikhis, and the poor ministrels who melodiously sing;
All the Shastars are His actors; His theatre is stupendous; kings sweetly sing His praises;
The winds are His waving chauris;
His handmaiden is Maya who hath vanquished the world;
His fire-palace is the blind pit of *hell fire,*
Such a Monarch is the Lord of the three worlds.
In His mansion the tortoise is a bed; Vasuki with its thousand hoods the cords to bind it;

His flower-girl is the eighteen loads of vegetables; His water-carrier the ninety-six millions of clouds:
The Ganges is the perspiration of His feet,
The seven seas His water-stands.
All living things His vessels—
Such a Monarch is the Lord of the three worlds—
At His mansion wait Arjan, Dhru, Prahlad, Ambarik, Narad, Nejai, the Sidhs, the Budhas, the heralds, and the heavenly dancers who extol Him and play *before Him*.
In God's mansion are so many living beings
Within all of whom He is diffused.
Namdev representh, seek God's protection.
Whose standard all His saints *bear*.

(५७) राग-मलार

मोकउ तू न बिसारि तू न बिसारि तू न बिसारि रामईआ ॥ रहाउ ॥
आलबंती इहु भ्रमु जो है मुझ उपर सभ कोपिला ॥
सुदु सुदु करि मारि उठाइओ कहा करउ बाप बीठला ॥ १ ॥
मूए हुए जउ मुकति देहुगे, मुकति न जानै कोइला ॥
ए पंडिआ मोकऊ ढेढ कहत तेरी पैज पिछंउडी होइला ॥ २ ॥
तू जु दइआलु किपालु कहिअतु है अतिभुज भइओ अपारला ॥
फेरि दीआ देहुरा नामे कउ पंडीअन कउ पिछवारला ॥ ३ ॥

हे सर्वत्र व्यापक परमात्मा ! मुझे तू न भुला ! तू न विसार ! मुझे तू न भुला ! रहाऊ मन्दिर वालों को यह भ्रम है कि देव पूजन का मुझे अधिकार नहीं, जिस कारण वह सब मुझ से कुद्ध हैं ।

क्षुद्र-क्षुद्र कह के और मार पीट करके मुझे उठा देते हैं, हे पिता परमेश्वर बता अब मैं क्या करूं ! मेरी मृत्यु के बाद यदि मुक्ति देनी है तो उसका किसी को क्या पता होगा ।

वह पंडित लोग मुझे नीचा कहते हैं इससे आपकी अपनी आभा ही बिगड़ती है ।

हे ! परमात्मा तू दयालु और कृपालु है और तू बे अन्त भुजान्बल वाला है (यह सुनते ही) देहरे का द्वार नामदेव की ओर कर दिया और पिछला भाग पेड़ों की ओर घूम गया ।

57

Forget me not, forget me not,
Forget me not, O Lord!
Those misled Brahmans of the temple were all furious with me;
Calling me a shudra they beat me and turned me out; what shall I do, Father Vitthal? If Thou give me salvation when I am dead nobody will be aware of it; save me now.
If these pandits call me low, than O God, Thine honour will be in the background.
Thou who art called the compassionate and the merciful, altogether unrivalled is Thine arm God turned round the front of the temple towards Nama, and its back towards the pandits.

(५८) राग-कानड़ा

ऐसी रामराइ अंतरजमी । जैसे दरपन माहि बदन परवानी ॥ रहाउ ॥
बसै घटाघट लीप न छीपै । बंधन मुकता जातु न दीसै ॥ १ ॥
पानीमाहि देखु मुखु जैसा । नामेको सुआमी बीठलु ऐसा ॥ २ ॥

परमात्मा जो प्रत्येक हृदय की बात जानने वाला है, प्रकाश रूप होकर व्यापक है। जैसे शीशे में मुँह का प्रतिबिम्ब प्रमाणित रूप में व्यापक है ।

वह प्रभु चाहे सर्व व्यापी है, परन्तु उसे माया की कोई लेश नहीं । वह जाति और माया के बन्धनों से मुक्त है ।

जैसे पानी में अपना मुँह दिखाई देता है, वैसे ही सबके हृदय में नामदेव का स्वामी बिराजमान हैं ।

58

KANRA

God compared to reflection in a mirror.

God the Searcher of hearts,
Like a body reflected in a mirror.
Dwelleth in every heart; *nothing* produceth an effect or impression on Him.
He is free from all entanglements and devoid of caste.
When one looketh at one's own face in the water, *the water can produce no impression on it.*
So *nothing can produce all impression on* Vitthal, Nama's Lord.

(५९) राग-प्रभातो

मन की विरथा मनु ही जानै, के बूझल आनै कहीऐ ॥
अंतरजामी रामु खाई, मैं डरू कैसे चहीऐ ॥ १ ॥
बेधीअले गोपाल गोसाई, मेरा प्रभु रविआ सरबे ठाई ॥ रहाउ ॥
मानै हाटु मानै पाटु मानै है पासारी ॥
मानै बासु नाना भेदी भरमतु है संसारी ॥ २ ॥
गुरके सबदि एहु मनु राता दुविधा सहजि समाणी ॥
सभी हुकमु है आपे निरभउ समतु बीचारी
जो जन जानि भजहि पुरखोत्तमु ताची अबिगतु बाणी
नामा कहै जग जीवनु पाइआ हिरदै अलख बिडाणी ॥ ३ ॥

मन के दुख को मन ही जानता हैं या (अन्तर्यामी पूछने वाले को कोई क्या बतावे। प्रभु सब स्थानों में रमा हुआ हैं उसके होते मुझे किसका डर है । मेरा मन गोपाल गोसाई से बिंधा पड़ा है, मेरा प्रभु हर जगह रम रहा है मेरा मन में हाट (दुकान), मन में हो शहर हैं और मन में ही सारा पसारा है अनेक प्रकार के भेदों में विचरने वाला, मन में ही बसता है । पर संसारी लोग उसे बाहर ढूढ़ते हैं ।

जब गुरु के उपदेश द्वारा यह मन नाम में रंग जाता है तो द्वेष भाव स्वत: ही मिट जाता है सभी जगह उसका हुक्म चलता है और हुक्म रूप वह स्वयं ही है । मैंने अभय प्रभु को ही सर्वत्र देखा है जो जीव उत्तम पुरुष परमात्मा को इस प्रकार जानकर भजते हैं, उनकी वाणी अटल होती है । नामदेव जी कहते हैं कि मैं जगत के जीवन आधार अलख प्रभु को, अपने हृदय में ही पा लिया है ।

59
PRABHATI

Everything is unreal; God alone is real.

Only the heart knoweth its own state; *either keep thy secret to thyself,* or tell it to a man of understanding.
Since I repeat the name of God, the Searcher of hearts, why should I be afraid?
God, the Lord of the earth, hath penetrated me.
My God is diffused in every place.
Shops are only phantoms, shopkeepers are only phantoms, cities are only phantoms.
The different grades of men who inhabit the *earth* are phantoms, and the world wandereth *in error.*

When the heart is imbued with the guru's instruction, duality is easily effaced.
All things are subject to the Commander's order; He is fearless and regardeth all alike.
He who knoweth and worshippeth the Supreme Being, *uttereth* words of divine knowledge.
Nama saith, I have obtained the Life of the world in my heart; He is invisible and wonderful.

God communicates to man the perfume of holiness and changes him to gold.

(६०) राग-प्रभाती

आदि जगादि जुगादि जुगो जुगु ताका अंतु न जानिआ ॥
सरब निरंतरि रामु रहिआ, रवि ऐसा रूपु बखानिआ ॥ १ ॥
गोविंदु गाजै सबदु बाजै । आनन्द रूपी मेरो रामईआ ॥ रहाउ ॥
बावन बीखू बानै बासु, ते भुख लागिला ॥
सरबे आदि परमलादि कासट चंदनु भैइला ॥ २ ॥
तुमचे पारस हमचे लोहा संगे कंचनु भंइला ॥
तू दइआलु रतनु लालु नामा साचि समाइला ॥ ३ ॥

परमात्मा जो सब का आदि है ओर युगों के आदि से अगादि स्वरूप हर युग में है उसका किसी ने अन्त नहीं पाया ।

राम सर्वत्र व्यापक है, यह सभी कहते हैं । नाम रूपी अनाहद शब्द बसता हैं जिससे गोबिन्द जी प्रंकट होते हैं । मेरा प्रभु सर्व-व्यापक आनन्द रूप है ।

जंगल में जैसे चन्दन का वृक्ष होता हैं, जिससे सब को सुख मिलता हैं । (भाव सभी सुगन्धित हो जाते हैं) ऐसे ही सब का आदि प्रभु, सब गुण-रूपी सुगान्धियों का भी मूल है । उस के संग से लकड़ी रूप जीव चन्दन रूप सुगान्धियों का भी मूल है । उस के संग से लकड़ी रूप जीव चन्दन रूप हो जाता है ।

हे राम ! आप पारस रूप हैं और हम लोह रूप हैं । पर आपके संग रहने से हम सोना रूप (भाव गुणवान) हो गये हैं । तू रत्न और लाल हैं और नामा आपके अवनाशी रूप में समा गया हैं ।

60

God was in the beginning before the ages and in every age: His end is not known.

God is contained in everything uninterruptedly; thus is His form described.
The *unbeaten* strain resoundeth for him who repeateth God's name—
Happy is my God—
The sandal-tree by its perfume is pleasant *to the other trees* of the forest;
Through God who was before all things and who perfumeth like sandal, common wood becometh sandal.
Thou, *O God,* art as the philosopher's stone; I am as the iron; in Thine association I have become gold.
Thou art compassionate, Thou art the jewel and the ruby,
Nama hath been absorbed in the True One.

Man cannot hope to obtain bliss until he has learnt to know God who is within him.

(६१) राग-प्रभाती

अकुल पुरख इकु चलितु उपाइया । घटि घटि अंतरि ब्रहमु लुकाइआ ॥ १ ॥
जीअ की जोति द जानै कोई । तै मै कीआ सु मालूमु होई ॥ रहाउ ॥
जिउ प्रगासिआ माटी कुंभेउ । आप ही करता बीठुल देउ ॥ २ ॥
जीअका बंधनु करभु बिंआपै । जो किछ कीआ सु आपै आप ॥ ३ ॥
प्रणवति नामदेउ इहुं जीउ चितवै सु लहै । अमरु होई सद आकुल रहै ॥ ४ ॥

राग प्रभाती

कुल-रेहत, सर्व परमात्मा ने एक खेल रचाया हैं, जीव, जंतु पैदा करके उन सबके हृदय में स्वयं आप बैठ गया है । जीवों को प्रकाश देने वाले को कोई नहीं जानता । पर जो कुछ आप और हम करते हैं, उसे सब मालूम होता है । जैसे मिट्टी से घड़ा बनता है । वैसे ही परमात्मा से सारी सृष्टि का निर्माण हुआ है और घड़े की मिट्टी के भाँति सब में विद्यमान हैं । जीव के बंधन पूर्वले करमों से ही व्याप्त होते हैं । परन्तु जो कुछ भी किया है, प्रभु ने आप ही किया हैं–नामदेव भी फरमाते हैं कि जीव को चिन्तन करता हैं, वहीं उसे मिल जाता हैं और जो अमर हो जाते हैं वह सदैंव ईश्वर में समाए रहते हैं।

61

The inscrutable Being invented a play—
God is concealed in every heart,
No one knoweth the nature of the soul's light;
What we ourselves have done Thou knowest.
As an earthen vessel is produced from clay,

So Vitthal created the world.
The soul's entanglements depend on its acts;
It is itself *responsible* for what it hath done.
Namdev representh, the soul obtaineth the result of its thoughts;
The soul which always remaineth fixed on the Inscrutable One, becometh immortal.

Index

S

T

U

V

❑❑❑